ALL THOSE
TOMORROWS

ALL THOSE TOMORROWS

Mai Zetterling

JONATHAN CAPE
THIRTY-TWO BEDFORD SQUARE LONDON

First published 1985
Copyright © 1985 by Mai Zetterling Ltd

Jonathan Cape Ltd, 32 Bedford Square, London WC1B 3EL

British Library Cataloguing in Publication Data
Zetterling, Mai
All those tomorrows.
1. Zetterling, Mai   2. Moving-picture actors and
actresses—Sweden—Biography
I. Title
791.43'028'0924   PN2287.Z4

ISBN 0-224-01841-8

Phototypeset by Falcon Graphic Art Ltd
Wallington, Surrey
Printed in Great Britain by The Anchor Press Ltd
and bound by Wm Brendon & Son Ltd
both of Tiptree, Essex

For

Mother, who gave me my life

David: 'Oh I have loved him too much to feel no hate for
him'
Racine, *Andromaque*

Glen, who said: 'You talk too much about yourself, why
don't you write a book instead?'

Barbro and Brother Earl, who moved into the shadows

Sheila: 'A good friend is my nearest relation'
Thomas Fuller

Contents

Illustrations

Illustrations

Acknowledgments

The author would like to thank Robson Books for permission to reproduce extracts from *My Drama School* and Jonathan Cape Ltd for extracts from *Shadow of the Sun* and *Bird of Passage*. Grateful thanks are also due to Faith Evans, who pulled the typescript into shape, and Glen, without whom this book would not have been written.

The author and publishers wish to thank the following for their kind permission to reproduce photographs and film stills: British Film Archive, London, 10 (copyright © AB Svensk Filmindustri, Stockholm, Sweden); HandMade Films Ltd, 36; Interstate/Zellstro Films, 15; the Rank Organisation Plc, 12 (still from *Portrait from Life*, a Gainsborough Picture directed by Terry Fisher at Shepherds Bush Studios: photo by Bert Chapman), 13 (still from *The Lost People*, a Gainsborough Picture directed by Bernard Knowles at Gainsborough Studios: photo by Lawrence Turner), 14 (still from *Desperate Moment*, directed by Compton Bennett: photo by Cornel Lucas); Sandrews, 26, 27 (photo by David Hughes), 34; John Stokes, 31; Thorn EMI Screen Entertainments Ltd, 11 (still from *Frieda*, a Michael Balcon Production directed by Basil Dearden at Ealing Studios), 16, 19; Twentieth-Century Fox, 28, 29, 30; Margreth Weivers-Norström, 6, 7. All other pictures are from the author's private archives.

We are grateful to David Hughes for allowing us to reproduce the letter on p. 198 and his article headed 'Forged in Fire' on pp. 162-4, which also appears by kind permission of *Woman's Realm* (1950s).

Curtain-Raiser

Never to talk about oneself
is a very refined form of hypocrisy.

Nietzsche

Two years ago I happened to be in the city of Manchester directing a documentary film about lady policemen. I had been travelling a great deal and had worn out the zips of my suitcases, so needed them repaired. After a long search I found a forlorn little shop in a back street, filled to bursting point with dusty old suitcases and umbrellas. Eventually a character straight out of Dickens appeared from behind a grey curtain. He blended in perfectly with the surroundings. Not only did he look ancient, he behaved as if he was at the end of his tether, peering at me over old-fashioned glasses. He was hunched up, with a feeble voice, a shaking hand: all the sad attributes of old age. Yes, he could have the suitcases ready in three weeks. As he wrote down my name with those shaking hands, I began to feel sorry that I had disturbed him and to doubt that I would ever see my suitcases again.

'Are you by any chance a relative of Mai Zetterling?'

I was embarrassed, as I always am by the mention of my name. I muttered vaguely: 'Yes, yes.'

He didn't look at me; as a matter of fact he was not the slightest bit interested in me. 'I remember her,' he said with a little chuckle. 'That dates me, doesn't it?'

I walked out of the shop sideways, like a Walt Disney cartoon.

1

On Not Being a Man

I thank thee Lord that Thou hast not created me a woman.

Orthodox Jewish prayer for men

I have been a child, a girl, a party doll, a mistress, a wife, a mother, a professional woman, a virgin, a grandmother. I have been a woman for more than fifty years and yet I have never been able to discover precisely what it is I am, how real I am. I ask myself – perhaps my femaleness is just a human disease?

At a party in London, a flushed drunken male shouted at me as I entered the room: 'You can never be equal, you have the wrong-shaped brain.' I was disturbed and embarrassed by his greeting. I had not come there to destroy the party mood. This damned equality business seems still one of the most important and sticky things between the sexes; although it is not as dire as in Napoleon's time, when the irritable emperor shouted at the top of his voice: 'What a bad idea, to demand equality for women; women are nothing but machines for providing children.'

As an actress, singer, dancer, showing my legs and my cleavage, I had been no threat at all: men could fantasise about me. Actresses are never taken that seriously; we are supposed to have even fewer brains than the rest of our sex. But now that I have managed to take that decisive step and become a director of films, I am considered unusual: I am not the same any more in the eyes of men.

I can sense the withdrawal symptoms: the coolness, even sometimes the hostility, which of course makes me want to withdraw in turn. I had been used to men trying to flatter, charm me, win me over. Men still think there must be something basically wrong with a woman who wants to be in the position of boss, who wants to be successful in a male profession. An unnatural woman then . . . I seem to belong to that race.

When the reviews of my first full-length feature movie came out, I was horrified to read that 'Mai Zetterling directs like a man.' What did that mean? Because I succeeded in a male profession, did that make me masculine? How could I have changed that quickly? From having been gossiped about as a Swedish sexpot, I was now suddenly being treated and discussed as a tough film director. I didn't understand what had happened. Inside, I felt the same. I looked at myself in the mirror; was it true what they were saying, that I had begun to change even physically because of my new responsibilities? I felt that as a woman I was still imprisoned in a man's world which I didn't quite belong to and whose language I didn't really speak.

But then, what was it that I wanted, as a woman? Not to be a man, for a start. It is not that I think that a woman is better than a man; we are as good or as bad as one another. I don't want to be an imitation, but something unique, *myself*. I want to dare to discover my own energies and be a person sufficient to myself. I don't want to have to count on male protection. I want to be able to change the love relationship, which too often becomes desperate and clinging, into something much freer and stronger and more positive. I would like to find a common aim, a friendship with men as well as women. To be strong without feeling guilty. Yet I don't want to lose my femininity. When men look for the old 'dream of woman' in me, I see their anger and frustration and fear, and it disturbs me. For years I walked around with troubled heart and mind, thinking that there was something wrong with me, until I realised that the change I had made was positive and, in the end, the only way.

Who was I? Who was the real me? I searched in others for

3

answers. I read women novelists, their autobiographies, diaries, books on women's psychology. I read Freud and Jung. I read astrology books, about relating to one another in this Aquarian age. To my delight, I found that Jung, as a learned and intellectual as well as an intelligent man, did not spurn the signs of the zodiac.

Let's take my sign, then. I was born under Gemini, the twins. According to Linda Goodman, 'A Gemini can be a producer, a singer, a lawyer, an actor, a salesman and the chairman of a few boards of directors all at once – and express himself *ad infinitum*. But a woman can't swing all that, or she would be considered freakish.' Well, I have certainly been called a freak many a time, because of my varied life. Singing in low dives, working in a buttonhole factory, becoming a star overnight at the Royal Theatre in Stockholm. Washing, ironing, sweeping my house, flying to Hollywood the next day. Eating raw seal-liver with Eskimos on the ice cap in Greenland, learning the Tarot cards from Russian gipsies in the Camargue, driving a reindeer herd in the Arctic Circle, directing movies in several languages, writing books without being able to spell, being a regular *chef de cuisine*, being considered a witch-doctor by the village in which I live because of my interest in herbalism and healing ... Making compost at full moon, growing plants in Sweden, England and France, passionately digging, weeding, my face in the flowers, my arse towards the sun – that's how my children remember me from a certain period.

Then there is the guilt, that has its roots in my bowels. The beds of sleep and play, all those crumpled sheets, the clothes, my gipsy robes that are all dead and gone. The books that I have marked and loved and hoarded: the collection of aphorisms, epigrams, proverbs, which are as important to me as friends. And the music which I will never forget and which makes me feel less lonely in lonely moments ...

And there is time. Like all Geminis, I'm time-ridden, time-obsessed, time-infatuated. I pay great respect to time. At my age, I should be mature, wise: a serene lady. But still the battle goes on. I'm as demanding and as impossible and as young in spirit and body, if not in years, as I ever was. If I don't get what I want and need, I feel cheated. I can't take a sedate little life; I want passion and all that goes with it, even the bad bits.

A friend of mine once said to me, 'You think too much about sensuality.' Reconciling oneself to getting old when you don't *feel* old is hard. I have been a fool most of my life and still am. I didn't grow up properly: the childhood neuroses still linger. All those years, those days, minutes, seconds, where did they go? When I think of those short-lived minutes, not to mention those shifty seconds, they seem to have passed like greased lightning. I lived in a grey, misty landscape of my own, killed time without being aware of it, with not the slightest thought that time was killing me. I behaved like a robot, as if time was there for ever. Perhaps it is true what they say, that a person who contemplates time and complains how quickly it goes makes bad use of it.

As you will have gathered by now, you meet a rather large company of women when you meet me. This makes, you might say, for fickleness, unsteadiness. Yes, perhaps. There always seem to be surprises around the corner; that's why I don't mind living with myself and being in my own company. Does that sound conceited? Anyway, I'm always fascinated to see which one of my personalities is going to come up next. As for all the travelling I do, that's absolutely normal because the Gemini sign is an air sign and must always be on the move. If I could I would be in two places at once.

Gemini people mix reality and fantasy and sometimes it seems that we are telling lies when in fact we have just splashed a little bit of extra pepper on to the story we are telling. Oh, we can irritate people a lot.

A Gemini, then, is a somewhat split personality. And to be a Gemini *and* a woman – that's no joke.

Who is this woman then, who yesterday was all loving and gentle, shy and thoughtful? Today she's somewhat ironical, even cynical ... and as for tomorrow, she'll be boring and pompous but perhaps also full of new ideas, many of them totally impossible. It is certainly very puzzling for people but it is most confusing for the poor woman

herself, as I suppose I will never find out what I really am –
and perhaps it is better that way. I have a strong feeling that
if I knew all about myself, I'd run away.

As for marriage, I have a sneaking suspicion that it wasn't
the Church that invented marriage, but a woman. Was it fear
of loneliness, the need to share things, that made me do it
twice? I had been so confident in the past towards my
attitude about marriage, arrogant almost, making bitter
remarks such as: 'Ten seconds bliss, ten years of hell. It is a
method which keeps society going,' and 'I was so bloody
depressed that I almost succumbed to marriage.' I have been
ruled by love most of my life and I know that marriage is not
the answer.

An old Eskimo friend had something to say about this
land of women:

> I have grown old
> I have lived much
> Many things I understand
> But four riddles I cannot solve
>
> The sun's origin
> The moon's nature
> The minds of *WOMEN*
> And why people have so many lice

On Not Being a Child
... Being a Child

How could Jimmy criticise me? I'm his mama.

President Carter's mother

I am not here to criticise my mama, a hostile planet or the environment that I was born in. When things went wrong, I could only blame myself.

It is normal that we begin by loving our parents; it is equally normal that when we get to our teens we start judging them and decide not to become like them. It seems that parents are more patient and loving to us than we are to them. If they feel disappointed in us, they try to hide it. I'm sure my mother must have felt many qualms about me. Pictures show a plump and dogged-looking girl and, however hard I search for redeeming features in my character, I just can't find any. My childish pranks weren't charming but complex and I think, on the whole, rather nasty. I also seemed to have inherited a certain Swedish gloom. I was an old person dressed up in baby clothes. It was only later, much later, when I was not a child, that I became childish and playful. I have done it all in reverse. That childhood of mine is a sort of enigma and it is most disagreeable to take that backward glance, though writing about it in a foreign language does help a little, puts it more at a distance.

'Begin at the beginning,' the King said gravely, 'and go on till you come to the end; then stop.'

Lewis Carroll

7

Many full moons ago, then, Mai Elisabeth was born. The town was Vasteras, the country Sweden. The town was known for its gherkins. A month before her birth, a very curious object had landed in a field not far away. A ball had fallen from the sky, burst and left all kinds of fragments, like fossils and shells. It had been quite spectacular and was written up by the press. In contrast, Mai's birth had been so discreet that there was not even the usual announcement in the local paper. Before she knew it, she had been whisked out of the country.

My father, Joel, was not really my father at all – I had been the result of a summer romance. Joel had taken a job as deck hand all the way to Australia, while mother and I went by regular ship, the trip having been paid by my real father, who had been Joel's best friend . . . By trade Joel was a top-hat maker. He soon discovered that, on the whole, Australians prefer not to wear top hats, particularly in the middle of a slump. The land of limitless opportunities turned out to be strictly limited. My mother responded badly to the climate, fell ill and spent some months in hospital. I was farmed out and had to discover independence of a sort. My chief memory from that period is of a gnawing, longing pain. I was restless and self-willed and full of day-dreams. I seemed to spend most of my time in the little front garden which was stuffed with sweet-smelling lilies and hedged in by blue grapes I don't remember eating.

Once, I bit a man quite hard in the arm because day after day I had seen him bite his girlfriend on the beach and never seem to get enough of it. But he was not at all pleased when I did it to him, which rather surprised me. I had a small white dog whom I so smothered with love that he finally ran away and I was inconsolable. I cut my fringe into a jagged mass and, while at work with my scissors, I cut off the tail of a mouse in a trap. I made a tent of old mats in the garden and sat there in the heat of the day, mostly in vague day-dreams, sometimes with two little black twin brothers. We sat there for hours, feeling each other. We were never disturbed, so we quietly pursued our explorations and must have enjoyed them.

We had an old wind-up gramophone and two records, both Sousa marches, and I used to play them non-stop, dancing to the music. Standing in a window, draping myself in the curtains, I showed off to the boys and girls coming back from school. I wanted them to take notice of me; they hardly ever did. But I continued swinging the curtains and dancing on the chair I had drawn up to the window. I danced and danced. At least the donkey bread-man liked it: he used to stop for a long time and look at me.

The donkey wore a big paper hat against the sun and the man always gave me a bun and patted me on the bottom and said how well I could dance. Mother used to tell me I had the dancing sickness, whatever that means. But that I could never be quite still except under that hot-house tent was plain fact.

I spoke fine broad Australian and, despite going to the kindergarten, had no friends apart from the black twins, who loved to push their hands under my well-rounded bottom. But there was an old uncle of theirs who also wanted to do such things to me, which I found less of a compensation for my loneliness, so I stopped going to their house. The storms rattled over our tin roof and I was terrified of the thunder because mother was. We both hid, she in the closet, I under the bed. It grew cold and sometimes I cried in fear.

In the rainy season, the road outside became a pond where lots of ducks gathered. There were long hours of doing nothing but watching things not happening from the window with the rain falling in sheets. I desperately wanted something to happen. I remember staring up at those sullen heavy skies, begging the fairies to make a miracle, because I had always hoped that the fairies might one day appear just for me. 'Let it rain yellow mice and stones or snakes,' I once asked – anything to liven up the boredom that I felt, the sadness. I sat for hours staring out of the window, hoping, looking until my eyes ached, perhaps until I fell asleep. At school the next day, I told everyone that I had seen yellow mice falling from the sky; the whole street had been full of them and birds too, hundreds of birds, all different, but they had all been dead, so I had been sad. This scene is very

9

strong in my memory because I was laughed at and ridiculed a great deal afterwards and called a liar. But I insisted I had seen it all. And now, so many years afterwards, I have found to my great astonishment that in that very year somewhere in the States it really did rain mice, sort of yellowish in colour – and, what's more, snakes too, and hundreds of different types of birds had fallen in the street during a rainstorm . . .

We were supposed to send grandfather a picture of me for Christmas, so we trooped off to a photographer. I had been scrubbed clean and was allowed to wear my best dress. In my excitement – I hadn't understood at all – I had picked far too many flowers, which I was going to present to my grandfather. This had made my mother cross. When at the studio I had found he wasn't there, at first I stubbornly refused to have my picture taken and had to be cajoled into sitting between my parents. I showed a very sour and disappointed face. I looked a horrible little girl.

Nobody understood why I was unhappy and neither did I. I had to have things my own way. I was obstinate. I didn't communicate much with anyone. I had already started to create an imaginary world which I found more interesting than the real one.

As soon as enough money had been scraped together and after many family disasters, my mother and I went back to Sweden; I was about seven. Joel stayed on in Australia for another year, and during this time we lived with my grandparents in a boring industrial town called Ekilstuna. It was a real killer; most of the people seemed as grey as the buildings.

My grandfather's name was Hjalmar – I loved him very much as soon as I saw him. I remember him being very tall and he had the bluest eyes I think I have ever seen, and the kindest. We had a sort of spiritual attachment; I can't explain it any other way; there were uncanny, totally inexplicable events at the time of his death.

It was harder than ever to communicate as I spoke only English, so when I found myself unable to ask in Swedish for what my mother wanted from the corner shop, I was thrilled

10

to find that I could communicate in verse and song. In English I scored great hits with things like 'Little Jack Horner'.

Perhaps that was my first lesson in the magic powers of art. Even stiff Swedes unbent and smiled. I learnt that exhibitionism of this sort was something that people expected to pay for. I came away stuffed with chocolates and success, having completely forgotten what my mother had sent me to get.

One of the many houses in which we lived had a smelly, junky backyard full of dirt but also of mysteries; I thought it huge. There was a large metal factory behind the wall forever churning and forging, and at the very bottom of the yard was this heap which grew curiously every day. The strange thing was that I never saw anyone put anything on it; it just grew. There were long metal rods curling and twisting into one another, shining hard shapes, odd objects with sharp edges, rusty sheets that rattled almost like thunder when you shook them – which the boys did to frighten me.

They had decided to gang up on me from the start. When not showing their teeny pricks or telling me dirty words to add to my scanty vocabulary, they were displaying how far their streams of piss would reach. There were a few variations on these games and they happened almost every day, always in the vicinity of the heap. It seemed appropriate to me even at that time.

The heap was sheltered by some very old and spreading lilac bushes which never seemed to bloom. The suckers running across the ground took all the strength from the mother tree. Then there was a row of crumbling wooden outhouses which stood like so many sentry boxes on the alert, a barrier between the courtyard and the street outside. The boys would lure me on some silly pretext close to the toilets and then, if I didn't do as they said, they would knock me about, soft and hard at the same time, pushing me up against a wall; pressing themselves against me as if for protection, practising forbidden words on me. There seemed no way of escape, there were so many against me and I was the only girl. And it usually ended up with me crying and

11

them running away. Later, I would always avoid going to that toilet, preferring to crouch in the bushes.

The badly built outhouses looked as though they would collapse in the next storm, so loosely were they put together, and I hated the musty smell and the mound of excreta that grew monstrously and was never taken away. I had fantasies of falling into one of the holes and never being able to climb out, and I loathed the buzz of the big fat flies and the rustling of the newspapers down below – I had been told of snakes living among them. Then there was my fear of the boys who always seemed to hang around the place, tapping on the slats, trying to peep through holes. I detested them with a small cold fear in the pit of my stomach. Even today, the smell of the factory is vivid in my memory – a rusty, penetrating, acrid smell that lingered in my clothes.

I had short, almost albino-blonde hair with a fringe that touched my eyelashes. I had freckles and hairy arms and I was chubby. Grandfather had given me a tame crow which he had found one morning on the heap and this bird used to spend a lot of its time sitting on my head picking imaginary lice. There were no toys that I can remember but I made shops with leaves and grasses, or built farms, the cows being constructed of cones and matches.

I used to be allowed to lie between grandfather and grandmother in the early morning. The wooden bed, which creaked and was uncomfortably hard, was converted into an upright sofa during the day. It stood in the kitchen and was painted pale blue. I was fascinated by my grandparents' body smells, which were slightly sweet, reminding me of rotting apples. When grandmother, whom I didn't much like, got up to make the coffee, I would snuggle closer to grandfather to discover some of the secrets which I knew he was hiding underneath the nightshirt of soft wool he always wore. He was loving and gentle and liked having me there. I enjoyed his early-morning beard of stubbly white growth and used to rub my cheeks against it until they became rosy pink and a bit sore. It felt good, even exciting, in a way I didn't quite understand. I would try to put my hand underneath his shirt for warmth and to get closer and lick his arm like a puppy. Then I would try my own dumpy arms in comparison. They were so different.

Sometimes I caught glimpses on washing night that frightened and at the same time fascinated me. On Saturday, the kitchen was full of pots and pans and steaming kettles, bowls for the foot baths and a slightly larger vessel in which you stood to rub yourself down. I never liked looking at my grandmother when she washed; I remember thinking how ugly she was, with her sagging breasts and skinny, dried-up-looking body, and she had a face which I avoided looking at – unfriendly, I thought, and not a bit nice. I liked looking at grandfather though. He must have been handsome for his age. Pictures of him as a young, newly-married man showed remarkable features of a very un-Swedish kind: dark curly hair and a rather aristocratic nose. There was talk of an intricate bastard affair in the family from rather grand quarters and he really did look royal in a way, out of key with his surroundings. He was still a pleasing figure, with a mane of white hair, only the slightest of bellies and as tall as ever.

While I was hanging about the kitchen trying to catch sight of things that were always so carefully hidden, as if there were something shameful in them, granny scolded me and finally chased me out, saying I was too nosy and rude, that people ought to be alone when they washed.

Later, grandfather and I took little walks together, round the church, to the pond with the swans, sat down on a bench, while he either did his football coupons, or looked for four-leafed clovers. But four leaves were not enough for him: he was forever going in for competitions of all kinds, and he was trying to find a clover with as many as six or even seven leaves. In the end he actually found one with ten and he was sure he would win but he never did.

While there was a deep connection between grandfather and myself, between mother and me there was a void. We were strangers to one another and I mistrusted her; perhaps I felt she was cheating on herself, wasn't living the life she had planned, married the wrong man. Who influenced me then, apart from grandfather? Of my immediate family, it was the

13

aunts who made the strongest impression on me. One of them fascinated me long before I had ever met her. She was said to be raving mad and lived in an institution. She came to visit us from time to time and would stay overnight. Sometimes she seemed a bit incoherent. She had an odd way of expressing herself: she talked about ghosts and spirits in the same way that mother talked about the milkman, and she treated me like a grown-up. Or was it that she was a child at heart?

She whispered stories about how she could make herself invisible, about how she had a fly living in her ear that would set off at night to places where the souls lived, then come back and tell stories of how the world really had been invented, how everything we see is alive, even stones and metals, of how the sky was filled with spiders' webs so that we should not be able to see God and the angels, because if we did we would be blinded. My mother thought I had gone a little mad, too, when I told her about the two crows that would come and have long conversations with me. So Aunt Good, which is what I called her, was barred from the house. 'Bad influence,' they said. What I didn't know, or rather couldn't know at the time, was that my poor besotted aunt was steeped in Nordic myths and sagas, picked up by her subconscious. I was both thrilled and a little frightened by her strange tales of the supernatural. Perhaps my deep-rooted interest in this subject stems from her.

The clothes and furniture which she had made for my doll's house all had a very strong scent. At first I had thought that the hospital of which she was an inmate must smell like that. Then I realised that she wore this musty, tangy perfume like an aura; when she opened her bag, it would fill the room like incense. Aunt Good's bag was no ordinary handbag. It was a strange world of its own that I loved to rummage in. Old paper bags with all kinds of dried herbs that had spilled out gave, I suppose, that wild, heady smell; everything was steeped in it, all the little tassels, bits of string, embroidery. Then there were the small metal cigar boxes that she collected, worn and buckled as if they had been through a small earthquake, housing objects of the greatest value to her. She would show me the little black stones with white crosses or strange markings that she had collected over the years, the bark from her favourite trees, some textured plaster from a wall, the brittle bones of mice and birds, all polished, and the legs and arms of dolls and teddies. Then, at the bottom of that large bag, lay the object that she called her 'main business' – the crystal ball, wrapped up in a piece of old red velvet, and some bits of candle that she would light in front of it when she was in the mood; but only when we were alone. The others would not understand.

She told me strange things: about the flight of the soul, about transformations, about dreams; for her, reality was nothing but a chimera. She told me that one day I would live in a haunted castle; she told me that people had a different colour around them. Certainly Aunt Good had. I told her she shone like melted butter. 'I know, I know,' she laughed, 'but not always fresh butter, sometimes on the rancid side.' And she would laugh again, her special little bird laugh. 'I'm afraid your mother looks a bit dappled in my crystal ball. Black and grey with many heavy shadows.'

'What about me? What colour do I have?' I wanted to know.

'Nothing yet; you will have to work hard to find your colour.'

Aunt Good vanished from our lives and I never dared to ask what had happened to her. I don't think I wanted to know the sad facts about her miserable lonely life in an institution that finally killed her.

Then there was the aunt whose hands and feet were knobbled with arthritis and who drummed into me how bad everything and everybody was. It was not only children who were bad; grown-ups were worse. According to her everyone was wicked, nasty, malicious. 'You can't trust anybody, they always have it in for you, like to see you go under,' she would tell me knowingly.

Her bitterness was engraved in the hard lines of her face. She never looked you in the eyes, just casting sideways glances to see the effect of what she had just said. I did my best not to listen to her gloomy view of life, yet I felt tainted

15

by her blackness. She warned me against men:

> When they kiss you, they mean to destroy you; they just want to do this dirty thing. A man is full of bad habits, smelly. They are less house-trained than a dog and just as sex-mad, spying with binoculars through the windows for naked women. They are all the same. I know what I am talking about; so does your mother, only she is too delicate to talk about such things. Men never know what women feel, they never even bother to find out, but secretly they are frightened of us because we can see through them, and that makes them feel guilty.

Poor Aunt Bad, with her tall, silent, brutal-looking boy-friend who came to visit her every week-end for as long as I can remember. They would spend their holidays in damp tents, travelling on an old motor-bike with a dangling side-car, which cannot have done her arthritis any good. She put up with his bullying and crude manners and even started to adopt them herself. Sometimes mother and I would visit them in Aunt Bad's one-roomed flat. They wouldn't have much to say to one another or to us but would burp and blow farts that almost lifted the roof. Mother pretended not to notice but it wasn't an easy thing to ignore.

Their ugliness fascinated me. When I had my first success in the theatre, Aunt Bad sent me the only rotten notice I received, just to make sure I should not imagine I was someone important. Her gift to me was my resolve never to become like her.

There was yet another aunt who was big and haughty, somewhat vulgar but friendly enough. She was married to the uncle I liked best, Uncle Manne, who used to sing in a raucous manner while stuffing stinking socks into the cold stove:

> Hi ho Barcelona,
> my feet are still dirty
> and I've got last week's dirty socks on
> hi ho Barcelona

This aunt and I discussed forbidden topics; all the things I could not talk to mother about. I believe my aunt was a little flattered and pleased because she didn't like my mother, thinking her snobbish for not taking a job in order to help my stepfather, who never earned much. We were in league against mother, and would stop talking when she entered the room; all a bit nasty and childish. Aunt Sexy, as I called her, had inherited a small wooden summer-house which seemed to me the height of luxury. I remember a hammock between the pine trees. All the relations envied her the windfall. She was rich, they said, and stuck up. To me she seemed friendly and always jolly.

Then there was Cousin Friendly, who lived in the country on a small farm. Mother was always deeply shocked by the smell of dirt, the fly-papers which dangled everywhere, covered with dead and dying flies. She was even more disgusted when I let the flies crawl over my bare arms; I liked the attention they paid me and the feel of their little feet, which tickled me pleasurably.

It was in this fly-ridden place that I had my first sexual experience. Cousin Friendly and I used to roll over one another down a small grassy hill, again and again. Sometimes we locked ourselves in the smelly outdoor loo. We would look at each other's 'instruments', as we used to call them, and press our bodies to one another. I felt pleasure but also guilt. We looked at the small 'thing' of another, younger cousin under a blanket and giggled; it seemed so odd and frightening, like a small grass-snake. For some reason I always got asthma when I went to my cousin's and I could not wait to get home. Perhaps I was influenced by mother's disapproval of the place but once back in town I would remember the cherry tree, the strawberries, the funny inexplicable games, and I would long to return.

Grandmother came from peasant stock and outlived grandfather by years. Tough and wiry, with not the slightest trace of humour, she had a hard time communicating, not just with me. There seemed to be no kindness in her, yet there must have been some good characteristics that grandfather once upon a time had fallen in love with. But later on

17

he suffered, and we suffered too; loving him, hating her. Granny Horrid, which is what I called her in my mind, had one great talent that does not fit into my picture at all. She had an exceptional gift for growing things. Pot plants dominated her little house and there were always lilies or cactuses in bloom. She was hard-working, never laughing while she cut sugar from a solid sugar pyramid, or scrubbed the wooden floors with a sweet-smelling green soap made from olive oil – the same that I use myself today. (She also used an ancient coffee-grinder, held tightly between her knees, of the type which I use every day, so I often think about her.) She was an enigma to me and will always remain so. 'A small wolf-person,' Aunt Good called her. Do I myself belong to this kind of wolf-mother tribe? Am I making as many mistakes as her, always giving orders and correcting people, never giving any understanding? I suppose I am making my own mistakes. To my children, I may appear just as incomprehensible as my mother or my grandmother did to me.

Next to the small house my grandparents rented was an outdoor café, and I longed to be in it. There was a small orchestra always scraping away behind our hedge of lilac. It made me dream and soften within. Then there was the constant natter of the diners' knives and forks – what delicious things could they be eating? How I envied them. But I never envied the tight-mouthed, skinny women with hair done in tight knots who assembled on the other side of the street, waiting to enter the nonconformist church. They would sing and pray for hours on end. Several of us used to creep to the frosted windows, trying to peep down into the swaying screaming mass of bodies shouting for their god. And did I or did I not see odd events taking place there which excited me? Certainly there were terrible rumours which we discussed endlessly.

As for the furniture at my grandparents' place – I only really remember one thing that fascinated me: a rather bad oil painting of the volcano Etna, below which was a lake with a boat and fishermen. I used to stare at it for hours, lose myself in it, make up stories. I loved that painting. Many

18

years later, I spent a very important period of my life just where that scene had been painted; it figured in my youth as a kind of precognitive dream.

I can't remember very much of my stepfather, Joel, during those years. He had not wanted to leave Australia, and when he eventually turned up, having to start a new life yet again, he was depressed and frustrated; there were quarrels and sulks between my parents. It was not easy, and certainly he and mother were an ill-matched couple. I have always been good at guessing people's feelings, however hard they try to hide them. I knew things were bad between them; so I was uneasy and gloomy myself.

We moved from our industrial backwater to the big city of Stockholm. I hated it. We were living in the poorest part of the town. I remember tales of woe and complaints about lack of money. There was a man who put on a record of 'O sole mio' every single night and cried . . . There was a cousin of eight or more whose fat mother still suckled him. Fears built up in me, one after the other, but what I think I dreaded most during that period was drunken men. I had had a bad experience of a drunken fellow showing his erect penis to me; he had cornered me on some steps; put it in my face and laughed at my fear. God knows what would have happened if the door hadn't opened on the floor above; it gave me just enough time to escape.

The days dragged. I can't remember any laughter, any happy moments, though surely there must have been some. Saturday nights were spent reading cheap magazines while my parents played cards with their friends. Boredom would make me fall asleep at last, to be woken up in the middle of the cold night for the walk home, disgruntled, frozen, eyes fixed on my feet. I felt that life had nothing in store for me, and a heaviness enveloped my body. We were continually on the move, into the country for a spell, then back again to different parts of the city. Holidays were bicycle trips to my grandparents' – dusty roads, endless pine forests. There was no joy in it. Once there, I would steal as much as I could from my grandmother's purse; the coinage taken was never enough to be noticed.

I had presents from my jolly Uncle Manne, who worked in a paper factory – faulty reams of paper and writing blocks. I started to write poems. My first collection was called 'My Fleeting Youth'. I was ten years old and I felt like a hundred, but without the wisdom of those years. In the morning my pillow was always wet with the tears I had shed, yet I don't really remember what I cried about. I sleep-walked; once I woke up with mother's pin cushion on my chest and hundreds of pins in my hands. Another time I found myself half-hanging out of a third-floor window, and one morning I was discovered at the back of a large black wardrobe. I had frightful nightmares which I never told anybody about.

I have long lost count of how many schools I attended between the ages of seven and thirteen. We never stayed long enough in one place for me to learn anything or make any friends, and I was always one of the girls to be avoided. At one particular school, I remember the other misfits were a fat, red-headed girl with freckles called Little Mother and a Jewish girl whom everyone said smelled. Although I was set apart as much as they were, I didn't try to become their friend but sniggered and made jokes about them. I was beastly, to say the least. My marks in school were disastrous; the teachers pulled my hair, nose, ears, but nothing helped. But there was one thing in which I excelled. I could cry on demand and was able to shed tears for hours on end. I enjoyed it, as it made me the centre of attention. Whenever a new child was brought to our class I would do my trick. I became such an expert that I could cry with one eye at a time, and also stop the flow of tears at will. It was like turning a tap on or off, and what's more it was soundless, apart from the dripping of the tears. Only once had I been in trouble when, unusually, I hadn't been able to stop. I don't know for how many hours I had kept it up. I became swollen-faced and could hardly breathe, yet I kept on crying as if my life was at stake. I was out of control. Finally the school nurse gave me something which made me stop. Who was I crying for? For myself only, or did it go deeper than that? I don't believe it was for humankind; I didn't think about such things then. I was too caught up in myself and in my own hopelessness.

However hard I tried, I could not pull myself out of my self-imposed inertia. I was living in a kind of zombie land where people were just shadows, and nothing seemed real, least of all myself.

I hoarded stolen goods in paper parcels which I hid in the cellar. I had no sign of any breasts but I had pinched a bra from the fat red-head. It was rather ugly and dirty, yet I folded it carefully and put it with my other bits; like the long cigarette-holder, the powder-puff, the imitation pearl comb with several teeth missing. I would go and look at these things at least once a week without feeling any remorse; they were not important except that I needed them; then I forgot about them completely.

I was a problem, not only to myself but to my parents, my teachers. Nobody knew what to do with me; so in the end most people gave up. I wasn't even charming or pretty, just sullenly keeping my face hidden. I sneaked into parties I wasn't invited to. I listened behind doors. My despair was so intense that I even tried to hide from myself what I had heard. I didn't want to exist, and I made a very good job of trying not to.

Once I carried the coffin with five other girls at a Brownie funeral, tears streaming although we had been given strict orders not to cry. She, the girl in the coffin, had been my first ever friend, though I had only known her for a couple of months. There had been a number of strange coincidences in the week before her death; everyone talked about it later. Everything she owned had broken – her ring, her doll, her skis, even one of her teeth. Another strange little thing happened which only I and a few other girls knew about. One evening we had gone to the Philadelphia Church service to have a good laugh. They had been beckoning people to come forward to tell their sins so that they could be saved. We girls were giggling at the back of the congregation and then, all of a sudden, *she* had stepped forward and knelt at the altar. We didn't understand it one bit. Her death took everybody by surprise, as she seemed to be a healthy, normal girl. There was a party after the funeral and when the cake was cut – white with a black chocolate cross – I was sick

and wept again, but more in horror than grief, not understanding.

I left the Brownies soon afterwards and learnt English
songs like 'Night and Day' from a record; I sang them at
get-togethers – with little success, as they always seemed to
play the piano in the wrong key on purpose. They told me it
was my fault: I had copied the words out wrong. I heard the
tittering and cried in the vestibule among the clothes. But,
keeping pretences up all the time, I walked around with a
book of psalms and boasted that I sang at serious concerts. I
was a brilliant liar. Once, I completely fooled a group of
schoolmates into believing I had gone blind. I kept it up for
an hour, then laughed; they never forgave me. Even when I
found a sympathetic teacher in one of my many schools and
was suddenly, for one term, no longer bottom of the class, I
continued to steal, borrow, copy and cheat, since I dared not
trust myself. At the exam was hung a painting which I had
done during that glorious term, of a princess locked in the
tower of a castle, a dragon circling its foundations and
spitting fire. It's the perfect image of me, locked within
myself, my own worst enemy, at once the princess and the
dragon.

I remember a few girls from the housing estate in Lundagatan, one of the many places we lived, boring girls who
were forever painting their toenails, doing their hair, sitting
in the windows ogling boys. There was one girl who helped
me with my homework; I don't think I could have gone
through the next class without her help. Her father, she told
me, liked her too much but he didn't like me, so I was barred
from her home. He was later to go to prison for being a spy;
it was quite a scandal. Another girl told me how her father
would put a French letter round his waist to show her how
strong it was. There was quite a lot of incest going on
according to the girls but I didn't really understand what it
meant . . . Otherwise I aped the others, painted myself with
cheap make-up, went to the hairdressing school, where they
experimented on us and made us look even worse and
certainly a lot older. At night, we would walk the ugly main
street in high heels that we had borrowed. One of the girls

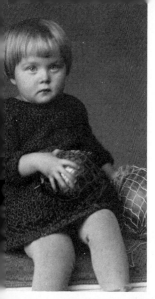

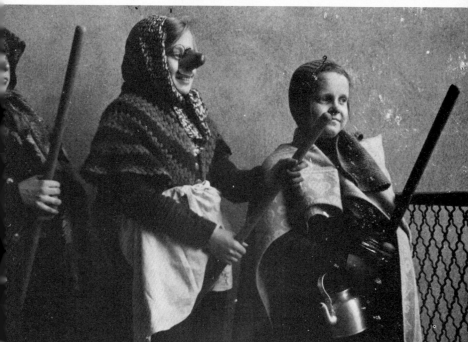

1 *Above left*, me aged two

2 *Above right*, with my mother in Ceylon, on our way home from Australia

3 *Above*, Easter play at Lundagatan. I'm the one in the middle with the false nose.

4 *Above*, me acting the part of a witch in the children's theatre in Stockholm

5 *Below*, with Lars Hanson in *Shadow and Substance* by the playwright Paul Vincent Carroll

TILL OPERETT

6 *Above left*, Calle Flygare, my first mentor

7 *Above right*, Calle's mother, Ebba Flygare

8 *Below left*, with Boj, my co-star in the Bluebird club act

9 *Below right*, Tutte and I in front of the town hall where we were married in April 1944

10 *Above*, in *Frenzy*, my first film role, directed by Alf Sjöberg, with screen-play by Ingmar Bergman

11 *Below*, with David Farrar in *Frieda*, directed by Basil Dearden

used to flirt with the men by the hot-dog stand; she would disappear into a doorway and come back after several minutes, tousled and giggling, with a few coins that we spent on hot dogs.

We used to walk in a notorious park where the police patrolled with dogs, and there the same girl would disappear into the bushes, sometimes coming back with enough money for us to go to a café and eat cream cakes. I remember being frightened of the whole business. I was always the one who was on the look-out for the police while she was busy. I didn't really want to think about what she was doing, and we didn't talk about it. I was very innocent at that time. I remember her as a rather ugly girl with a silly laugh which I tried to imitate, as it sounded tough. I was already a good mimic, but my mother was horrified when she heard me laugh like that.

Everyone was cheating – it was taken for granted: a great many things seemed to have fallen off lorries. Owners of factories, shops, businesses, were often out of pocket due to their employees' fiddling and I myself came to believe in giving the rich bastards one on the nose. There was so much hatred behind the petty thefts, so strong a sense that we would never be able to crawl out from under our stones and sit in the sun like the lucky ones. We would never even win prizes in the tombola. Only the rich did that. So we gave them all the dirt we could and revelled in our ignorance.

I was slothful, inert, untrustworthy, joyless, insecure, vacant, indifferent, dishonest, aloof, suspicious, apathetic, unhopeful. Sometimes I felt like a little old woman walking empty-eyed and crippled; the days seemed permanently overcast. I lost so many precious years in this sloth, so many seconds. I felt comfortless because I knew there was no one there to give me any comfort even if I had asked for it. It seemed that no one cared for anyone.

A nasty little affair occurred once at a girl guides' summer camp I went to for a week. A titled girl had her birthday there and her mum turned up, fat and bejewelled from another world, with cream and strawberries for us all. The daughter, herself quite dumpy, always over-ate, but that day she could not finish her strawberries for the excitement. I never liked her, she talked and behaved differently from the rest of us. That night I was in the washing-up team and initiated the polishing off of the left-over strawberries. As we divided them up, we giggled and thought nothing of the consequences.

Next morning, everyone owned up except me. I denied that I had eaten any and blamed it on the others, who were listening outside the door when the leader interrogated me. They said I was bad. In my heart I agreed with them; I neither liked nor respected myself.

I was in a state of pitiable ignorance about all matters, including sex. Things like periods were never mentioned and I was deeply scared when mine first came, not daring to tell anyone for days. I was given a sanitary towel crocheted by hand. I hated it and felt ashamed.

It was on a seedy camp-site just outside Stockholm that I lost my virginity, a place infested with ticks and mosquitoes. There was a stone pit with the juiciest of raspberries but it also housed vipers which I had seen coupling in the midday sun: there seemed to be hundreds of them coiling and hissing, reminding me of the activity in the camp. In all those blue, green, red, impermanent little canvas dwellings, similar things were happening.

The police often turned up. There was always trouble of some kind – brawls, drunks, stolen goods, wrecked tents, whining girls – a squalid place that held one like a magnet. Bluebottles and wasps hovered round the overfilled waste-bins, and sweet-papers stuck to your feet. There was the usual kiosk with the usual bitter-faced lady who had seen all, yet nothing.

It is difficult to eradicate that smell of half-rotten fruit from my mind, the chocolate melting, the bad ice-cream. The showers were always full of hair and grit – you caught foot-rot there – and used rubbers floated in the dirty water of the lake. On the shore, a drunk had fallen asleep in the noon heat and his brain had melted; a young boy had dived from a rock and split his skull; a young couple had committed suicide badly and their screams agonised the memory for weeks afterwards. These were everyday happenings. The place should have been marked on the map as an evil spot; instead we all flocked there, bored teenagers in search of excitement.

It was never really hot or cold that summer but it was clammy; the mind became sticky and fatigued. People who played cards in the bushes ended up quarrelling. Clothes were strewn about, towels hung sour and wet between the tents. There was so much paraphernalia: pots and pans, half-eaten potatoes, enamel wash-basins with a ring of dirt and grey water at the bottom, a soggy piece of soap floating in a plate, boxes and papers, bottles and flies everywhere.

Saturday nights were especially frightening because of the number of drunks moving in the shadows ready to pounce. I kept bad company, put on make-up crudely, behaved noisily, ogled boys. I wanted to know their secrets. I wanted to be loved. In love. To be totally immersed in love. All my longings, my ambitions, my needs, were centred on love, perhaps because of the loveless world I saw all around me. Those boys I picked up, those crude empty-faced creatures so full of themselves, could not possibly have been anybody's darlings.

The boy, who was but a year or two older than me, was dull but tough, a bad sketch drawn by the Almighty, but hard in body as the sun struck the green canvas. The heat inside was intense. Outside, the boys were quiet, not wanting to miss anything. But everyone missed the penetration. There was great disappointment. Through the laced-up tent, eyes were peering, bright as lizards but with drooping lids – 'She's bleeding!' But there were only a few sickly drops. Bicycling home, rigid with loneliness, I nearly had an accident on the tram-line. Got caught on the curve, a tram coming fast downhill, wildly clanging bell. I wanted that accident. Why not? But my brain snapped back at the very last moment. I worked ferociously to get out of the oncoming tram's path, and did.

It was at that time I started to create my own reign of terror. When, how and why it first happened I had no idea. I was terrified whenever alone – which was often – but it wasn't simply fear of the dark. I even scared myself by mistrusting the blinding daylight.

At night, when my mother and father would go out, I sat down at the far end of the room, back pressed against the wall, waiting for things to happen. What sort of terror was I waiting for? I had no answer to my question. I suppose I was frightened of answers; for it seemed that a dreadful truth was in store for me around some corner and I could not face it. I became scared of what lay behind walls or lurked on the other side of doors; the dark was filled with monsters of every description and even the sun had its shadows that could never be trusted. It was different when people were around and using all the well-known objects. The walls and the furniture seemed to have no secrets then. But how very different when alone. The papers in the waste-paper basket would suddenly crackle as if alive. The sofa gathered a long, unreal shadow that lay flat on the carpet as if dead. As for the mirror, which during the day threw back predictable images, it too changed personality, with all kinds of lights hitting it from all angles, making the surface ripple.

It gave me an uneasy feeling that there was more in the room than met the eye – ghostly, yes, but I could not deny the possibility of intruders with wicked intentions, thieves, murderers. In constant panic, I kept my ears pricked for footsteps that would reach the door, the key that would rattle in the lock, while at the same time I kept a check on my body, counting, for instance, in cold sweaty terror, my uneven heartbeats.

It was destructive, it was a waste of energy, it was narcissistic. Why this instinct for self-preservation when I really believed there was nothing to preserve? I just sat in my corner, surrounded by walls, and laid out my strategy of self-defence, waiting for the unexpected.

Why was I so desperately frightened? Mother seemed to be frightened of a lot of things too and I always hated the fact that, in spite of myself, I had caught some of those despised little fears, like the fear of snakes, spiders, mice, thunderstorms and then of course those long, seemingly endless nights when I lived deep down in my stomach.

On Not Being a Child . . . Being a Child

What really worried me was that I seemed to be different from other people and I didn't want to be. What's more, other people didn't seem frightened – or were they just hiding it? I looked at them carefully in the hope of seeing the slightest glimpse of fear, something I would recognise, but I never did. When I looked into my own eyes, there was a fright in them that I could not detect in anyone else's. In other respects I appeared to be the same – and surely I *was* the same, I said again and again to myself for comfort.

The same as anyone else, surely? The same – please make me the same as anyone else. I studied myself in the mirror, I even formed the bad habit of talking to others with my eyes, looking past them wide-eyed into the mirror so that I could watch my every change of facial expression; which one day, I hoped, would give me a clue to myself. My family mistrusted my elusiveness and found my introspection unbearable; for want of a better word, they called me selfish. They said that I was always frowning and asked why I had such sad eyes. 'Keep smiling,' they said, and I wanted to burst into tears. 'You've got your whole life in front of you.' They didn't understand that I was scared to death of life, that I wanted the whole frightening experience behind me.

When I looked at myself in the long gilt mirror, as the sun slid across the floor in the late afternoon and the dust was dancing in the beams, I seemed more like a ghost than flesh and bones. But I used to lose myself in contemplation for hours, making my mirrored image come into close-up, medium shot, long shot, trying to come to grips with what kind of person I was or wasn't; I used to scare myself in the close-ups by getting lost in my own eyes, finding another person there. Finally, I didn't dare to look at myself in mirrors at all, as I couldn't bear to meet my questioning eyes.

I walked in circles round my real self, which appeared not yet to be awake. And I still only remember loneliness and the sense of not being there but somewhere else, in limbo. I continually looked out of windows. I scribbled bad poetry on every available scrap of paper and typed it out with one finger on an old typewriter which my stepfather had found on a scrap-heap.

Every single word I uttered was a lie. It was quite unnecessary but I persisted, down to the smallest detail. It's strange, but now I can't tell lies at all. I fabricated the most stupid nonsense, thus creating quite a problem for myself in keeping the fantasies sorted out. I refused to be confirmed, though it would have meant a long dress and possibly a wrist-watch (I didn't bother to learn to read the time until I was sixteen). I played truant from school and never listened to any of the teachers and I certainly had no intention of learning my psalms off by heart. Was it simply that I was bone lazy, or suffered from inertia, or that I was a slow developer? Whatever the reason, I had fine-sounding excuses for my refusal of that confirmation. The fact that the other girls thought I was mad bothered me not at all; I considered them so many ninnies with nothing in their thoughts but clothes, jewellery and the party they were going to be given on the great day. I thought it immoral to rattle off the catechism without caring about the words.

Instead, I started to attend church regularly with a view to discovering more about it, but in the end I resisted the Lutheran harshness, the near-empty cold buildings, the ugliness of the people, the declamatory style of the preachers and the dull sermons. I stopped going. I have never gone since.

Brave in some ways, I was a frightened mouse in so many others. I seemed always to be followed in the streets by dirty old men; every park I entered had its exhibitionists. I always felt pursued, scared, to the point of nightmares, still walking and talking in my sleep, wetting my bed well into my eleventh year. My only reading matter was cheap magazines, which was all there was around. I knew nothing of what was going on in the world. I remember vague talk of war and seeing the worried faces, but nothing changed in our lives except for the rationing of butter and confectionery, and as we had little enough of those things in normal circumstances, who cared?

I was interested in nothing, but hated many things, most of all school. I became highly skilled at feigning illness. Once, I managed to produce spots before an exam in maths; I was whisked off in an ambulance to the isolation hospital while they fumigated the school.

In my lonely wanderings around the city, I had come upon a very posh school called the French Lycée. I kept going back to it, and timed it so that I would arrive when the children came out after their last class. I used to sit on a park bench opposite the big gates waiting for them to pour out, spellbound. I was not one bit interested in the boys but I watched the girls and made comparisons between myself and my schoolfriends. I soon discovered that these girls were totally different. Their legs for a start. There was a distinct difference between working-class legs and upper-class legs. Theirs one could only admire, stare and whistle at, as they seemed perfect, long and slim. In my school we were inclined to be short-legged and plumpish. I myself had a pair of sturdy legs, not a bit stylish, and my bottom was far too close to the ground. As for the bodies of the Lycée girls, they seemed almost emaciated, perfect model material. Their faces had dignity, aloofness, their cheeks were hardly ever pink. The girls would often come out arm-in-arm and part with a handshake, like old ladies. Their hair was well-groomed, shining with care, the 'hundred strokes of the hairbrush every night before bed' treatment, I was sure, by a loving mother. I could never imagine in my wildest dreams that they would catch lice in that hair; I could never see one of those girls bent over a paper while her mother combed the beastly creatures out. I also studied their clothes carefully. Their winter coats always had fur collars and some of the girls had muffs; they certainly all wore smart leather gloves. As I sat outside the Lycée nobody took the slightest notice of me; I was so insignificant that I effectively disappeared. Sometimes, I would follow one or two girls to where they lived. The houses were heavy, ornate, so very different from the ramshackle buildings in which we always seemed to end up.

I was neither pretty nor ugly, too small for my age, always looking, to my annoyance, a lot younger than I was. I wanted so badly to grow up fast; my life was so dull, and I was beginning to realise with fury that all the things I wanted to do – to become a sailor and travel, climb mountains, go exploring – were forbidden me because of my sex. I felt bitterly that life had cheated me out of all the possibilities.

I used to wonder about all these things as I sat on the top floor in some dingy house in a seedy part of Stockholm. I would sit for hours, trying to get time to pass instead of going to school, doing nothing at all, only moving down another flight of steps if I heard somebody coming.

Then lies again the next day at school, as I had no note from my mother. My father had been taken ill – my mother had gone to hospital – nearly been killed by a car, I'd had to go to the police station and wait for hours. Sometimes, of course, I did have notes from my mother, when I convinced her that I was ill. But when I invented the impossible story that as I was walking to school a man had claimed me as his long-lost daughter, had taken me home and made me stay for two days, I was found out. I had gone too far. I was a fraud: everybody despised me, the teachers and children alike. I could not be trusted.

For a time, we lived above an old cinema; the neon lights were just below our kitchen window. As this wasn't exactly the most respectable part of town, the cinema was a fine old flea-pit which I came to know well, finding my way into it through an underground labyrinth. I never remember paying, but I do remember that I loved, adored, venerated Shirley Temple. Smack opposite the cinema was the abominated school which looked and felt like a prison. I used to sit in the window over the neon signs, dreaming about Shirley and identifying with her world.

If I could never be that adventurous person I longed to become, why at least not base my life on that dummy-faced little doll of a girl? I too had dimples in my cheeks, though that was about as far as our likeness stretched. My hair could scarcely have been straighter, I was disappointed every time I looked in the mirror. But so star-struck was I, so hooked on that famous little rich girl, that after much wheedling I persuaded my mother to give me the money for a Shirley Temple perm. I thought it was going to change my life. I practised saluting and tap-dancing in private, sweating for hours in front of a full-length mirror. The hair would clinch it, I decided. I would become a famous film star myself.

The hairdresser, who was a friend of mother's, tried unsuccessfully to talk me out of the perm. After it was done, mother was horrified – and so, finally, was I. I stayed in bed for a week and refused to look at myself. That hair, which had at least had a shine and silkiness to it before, was now as crinkled as wire wool. It hit me then, as I lay there in my gloom and despondency, that the rich uncle who would turn me into a princess would never come. I was forever to be disappointed with my life, never to be pretty, never to own those wardrobes that covered whole walls and were stuffed with frilly dresses. Now I began to hate the dumpy doll who had given me the idea of possessions and who had made me so envious. And somehow I knew that my mother shared that very kind of bitterness about life that I had begun to feel.

From that moment, I realised that I would never get anything easily. I would have to work for it, to change in some miraculous way – but how? It would be a long time before I knew.

Wild Child

When you are poor you grow up fast.

Billie Holliday

I kept following the evil star. Nothing could shift me to another course. I was virtually unemployable when I left school at fourteen. Teachers were relieved to see me go. I couldn't even work as a shop assistant because my maths were almost non-existent. The humdrum was so surely mapped out for me that I was quite prepared to accept the lowest-paid and most deadening job.

But I wasn't even taken by the shoe factory, as I didn't dare to show my school report which they had demanded. However, I managed to get a job in a textile factory. This prison opened its arms to me and I served a sentence – but for what offence? I obeyed orders, sat on a wooden bench from eight to five with seven other girls as downtrodden as I was, removing the tacking from men's suits. We knew we were mediocre, we had been driven into a corner, and we gave grudging service, clockworking our way in and out of the factory, having to ask the foreman permission to go to the lavatory. He placed his beady eyes on our legs and we pushed our skirts up higher so that he could see our knickers and plump thighs. Agonise the bastard was our motto.

Supervision was strict and no talking was allowed, but as soon as the fellow had turned his back there was no stopping us, even if the range of topics was limited. I sang everything

I knew, from nursery ditties, hymns and school songs to those with filthy words, especially when the self-made Führer was on his way down with the whip between the clanging looms.

They tried to make robots of us and with some they succeeded. The two fat women on the machine in front of us had been well and truly brain-washed. The only thing they hated as much as us was this little swine of a watchdog. One of them had given in to him once. He had taken out his wretched little prick and commanded her to suck it until he came in her mouth. She had been unable to eat anything for days afterwards. As the story went round the factory, everyone compared notes on how filthy men were.

I hated that feminine stale smell of armpits and curses. There were always bloody sanitary towels stuffed in corners in the toilet; we would smoke half a fag while looking out of the high prison windows with empty eyes. In the cellar, for our lunch-hour, we gossiped sex over our tin boxes of cold fry-ups.

In the evening I was off to the seedy dance place which lay in a rotten part of the town, furious whenever I was asked to dance by proper nice boys. I wanted the really tough ones. You could see how bad they were, how rottenly they would treat you, and this was what I wanted; it fitted my life. But they never came my way. They saw a shy, undersized girl sitting alone, and never even bothered with a second glance. But the nice boys played their tricks too. The circumstances were always sordid, at beer parties, on someone's filthy mattress, in some dark, pissy entrance; stockings laddered, face drawn, black rings under eyes. I would traipse back next morning to the factory, trying to be a puppet again, the tool of my trade in my hand, a sharp blade ripping away those stitches and a blunted pen ticking off how many coats I had unpicked – until one day in despair, hysteria, boredom, something happened in that feeble brain of mine: I threw the precious instrument away and walked out of the damned prison, never to see it again.

An old-fashioned haberdashery on the other side of town took me on to dust the boxes of buttons and ribbons and to run errands. The fat old lady who owned it was certainly not kind and there was a smell of stale urine about her, so it was a relief to get out of the shop. The parcels were always small and the grand ladies living in large Strindbergian mansions in the smarter streets sometimes gave me a tip. Although I would usually spend it on a hot dog or ice-cream, I never liked this money that was handed to me so easily and always with an expression of guilt.

Once a man in pyjamas opened his door and asked me to come in and wait. Then, in a doorway, he beckoned to me, taking out his thing which grew in his hands until somebody came and pushed him out of sight and there was much shouting behind doors. I left with the largest tip I had ever had.

Then there was the fat brother of the shop lady. Sitting down together in the little room behind the shop they almost filled the available space, he with his belly on the table beside the coffee cups. They were gluttons. I was always running off to the confectioner to fetch boxes of creamy cakes for them. The brother's hobby was photography, and one day I was asked to deliver a parcel to his flat. I don't know why I felt uneasy; perhaps because of his wet eyes when he looked at me and his handshake on both meeting and parting, a perspiring, soft as dough, overlong handshake. I stood outside the door for a long time and heard him walking about inside emitting loud burps.

He took his time opening the door. Again he shook my hand, this time enclosing it in both of his, and his eyes were exceedingly moist. Wouldn't I join him in a cup of coffee as I had such a long walk back and it was raining? It was all set up. A carnation with a feathery bit of greenery stood in a vase; cigarettes lay on a silver plate. The coffee stood on an ornamental Turkish table and he looked extraordinarily silly perching next to it on a small chair. I dared not smile. With the second cup he started to tell me how pretty I was and how he really wanted to take my picture. I was embarrassed; he offered money; I gave no answer. He offered more. Could I come after I finished work? He would have all the lamps set up, I ought to get into films, he had connections. Well, why

34

not? I had once waited outside a film company's grand gates in the hope of being an extra and had finally been admitted to fill in a form and present a polyphoto, though nothing had ever come of it. So I said yes. He tipped me with a note when we shook hands, not looking at me. Once I had agreed, he seemed to want to get rid of me.

I hated going back and paced the street for an age before ringing the bell. There was a glass of punch inside me almost at once and he was playing a rather scratchy record. I saw no photographic equipment. He said he had a present for me: a large box of chocolates and a pair of silk stockings. He poured another glass; I was hot and uncomfortable. I felt just silly. He was breathing more heavily now and I was suddenly and without warning moved from my chair into a corner where there was a divan. He was on top of me before I knew it, crushing me. I screamed as he plunged for my knickers. More and more agitated he became, then abruptly limp, so I crawled from beneath that mountain of flesh, my knees shaking. Taking my coat, I didn't dare look round. The noises were dreadful. Perhaps he was dying . . .

I had forgotten my purse. It was raining. I had to walk all the way home, a good hour.

I told his sister next morning and of course she didn't believe me. I must leave at once without pay. When she phoned him I could hear the dreadful grunts at the other end. We closed the shop for the day. I was asked to wait while she saw her brother, and a taxi was called. I stayed there alone that long grey afternoon and I was frightened. On her return, avoiding my eye, she gave me my purse and his presents, put into my hand more money than I had ever seen and sent me away, with a last harsh word that she would call the police if I ever came back. That was easy. I never wanted to see either of them again.

My next job was in a pawnshop in a basement: not exactly the kind of job I had day-dreamed of. But once a week, a young man used to bring in valuable trinkets. He would park his smart sports car outside, run into the shop looking somewhat anxious, and throw snuff-boxes, silver spoons, old coins on to the counter. As if scorning the money he received in exchange, he would stuff it loosely into his pockets, looking no one in the eye, and tear off again. He never reclaimed his property but brought new objects each time, always small things that he could hide easily in his clothes.

One day, along with the delicate salt-cellars, he flung down a visiting card on the counter. He had an impressive title. The insolent eyes looked at me briefly; the arrogance of birth and money. Had I seen his picture in the paper at the hunt ball? It was good publicity for him, he said: he was going to be an actor.

He invited me to a party at his parents' home – they were away. As we drove there, he talked big. Every overtaking was a risk, but what was the point of a sports car if you didn't travel fast? The tyres screeched.

The house seemed to have class-consciousness built into its very walls. It was solemn, stuffy and elegant. Everyone showed contempt for it by vomiting over the velvet chairs and Persian carpets after pouring down vast quantities of drink. The girls, who had turned up their noses and laughed when I was brought in, went on behaving like window-dressing until they got sozzled; you could see their well-bred manners diminish with each empty glass. Shamelessly they went for the boys' trousers as though they were animals pouncing, opening their mouths without discrimination. It was soon bedlam; I crept into a corner, mouse-like, sober and intimidated. I was horrified by the speed and ugliness of the turn of events.

I was expected to join in. I shook my head and cringed further into my corner until finally I couldn't speak at all. My host then took me up to the parental bedroom. He had thought me a virgin but, on learning the truth, he feebly shouted – these working-class whores start early. He was bored and in any case couldn't make it. He took a revolver from a drawer and aimed at the window. The glass shattered. Others turned up to see what was going on and uniforms from a former war were hauled out of boxes. Rusty medals hung from the moth-eaten cloth. The gun-room was ransacked for muskets and rifles, sporting guns, fencing equipment.

African spears were unhooked from the walls. The place had been turned into a battleground.

I stood unarmed, trying desperately to make myself small, but it was no use. I was the one who had to be caught and destroyed for not playing their game, for not being one of them. With heart pounding, I was chased up and down stairs and along endless corridors. I was afraid there would be bullets in the guns they kept triggering away behind me. The girls laughed wildly as I raced for the third or fourth time through the big room where they lay in their own vomit, egging on the boys who cornered me and flicked at me with their fencing swords. They had found the perfect scapegoat.

They started chasing me up and down the house. Out of the corner of my eye I had glimpsed a balcony, and I dashed frantically towards it. But there was no way of locking the door from outside, no time to think, and no alternative but to jump to whatever lay below, with their voices storming behind me.

Screams of anger followed the fall. A sharp pain stiffened my body and I could hear the clicking of guns above me. There was a pause. Then, in the stillness of the clear blue night, the shot I had been expecting rang out at uncomfortably close range. I held my breath; not a branch or leaf moved. Questions flashed through my mind: why had I been dealt such a rotten hand?

A commotion on the balcony brought me back to reality. A fight seemed to have broken out. Another shot split the air and a long, surprised scream widened the split. I belly-crawled out through the damp bushes. The earth had a rotten smell; there was smoke in the air. I did not dare to cry and my throat was dry and aching. Gorse clung to me and I fought against it with my hands in pain. Limping along the road towards some street lights I heard my pursuers gaining on me. I hid in a ditch. A police car flashed past and I could hear my persecutors running away. The villa quarter was sound asleep, secure behind its locks and bolts, its burglar alarms; nothing woke to the cruel noise of the sirens, not even a dog. I had no idea where I was but managed to get a lift in a newspaper van. I was crying at last, and continued to cry silently all the way into town.

It was high summer. Mother, who had good reason to be worried about me, found us both a job fruit-picking for a month outside town. We stayed in a small wooden house where everything could be heard through the walls. The son of the proprietor lived above us and a farm girl slept with him every night – endless thumps and creaking bedsprings – not to mention the groans from next door, where two middle-aged pickers were up to something that always seemed to continue until I fell asleep.

The white heat outside went on day after day. Among the raspberry canes we were stung by angry wasps; they were as restless as we were. And I had a toothache that lasted over a week. We drank hot cow's milk with the hair still floating in it. It was a month when all food rotted within a day or two and I dragged my feet among the strawberries, back aching, fingers stung; I wanted to forget everything and go back home and sleep. Then the storm came. It was so violent that a whole family was burnt to death when their one-room house was struck by lightning.

It seemed to storm for days. Birds screamed under forbidding clouds, cows were restlessly noisy. We were all frightened as we sat round our coffee cups and playing-cards. Nor did the storm clear the air; it was just as sultry afterwards. And there was the funeral to attend, with burnt corpses lying in their coffins.

The old man who owned the place and was suffering from cancer went out with his rifle day and night and shot at imaginary apple thieves. He was mean and lonely and never spoke as he paid your salary from his safe, where the notes were piled high. He was surrounded by weapons, as he was by enemies. He didn't even get on with his son; you could hear them shouting curses at each other across the grounds. At the goodbye party at the end of the month, the lady pickers opened tins of evil-smelling rotten fish that were supposed to be a delicacy. The aquavit bottles, which had been lying in cold water, were soon consumed. Nobody had much to say. The two next-door ladies became really violent and swore at each other, when not being sick in the bushes. Amid the stink from the fish one of the ladies fondled me and mother grew angry.

Somehow I fell asleep among the debris, angry words and smells. Later, when I opened my eyes, I saw the ladies kissing in full view of everyone; nobody cared; what did it matter? And I still had my toothache, which by now was affecting my whole head. I was taking aspirins all day and I was exhausted. Back in town I dragged my feet along hot paving stones, looking for work, visiting the dentist.

I only got my next job because the owner was taken into hospital. I often wonder how she dared to leave me in charge. I was just fifteen and I had been there for a bare week when the ambulance came for her. It was the tiniest shop imaginable with a cubby-hole at the back where even I, small as I was, could only just about turn round. But there was a gas ring, running water, a chair and a small table, and a curtain one could pull for privacy. There was no toilet so one had to climb on the chair, squat over the sink and hope no customer would arrive. I heated up my tin box of sausages and mash for lunch and drank endless cups of sweet, creamy coffee. It was dreary, the clientele meagre and poor.

And it was a drug-store, so when the dirty-minded discovered that the formidable lady had been replaced by a girl who hardly reached up to the counter the trouble began again. At first it was telephone calls, nasty words, suggestions, abuses. And then they came personally for their jock-straps and rubbers and I blushed my way through the sales. Sometimes they would go so far as to play with themselves in full view of me, and I was too weak and frightened to say anything; I only hoped they would finish quickly and leave.

Then gangs of boys from the park opposite gathered in front of the shop. Sometimes they came in and I lied to them, saying we didn't stock such things. But most of all I hated those coarse whispers on the telephone. I ordered things from the factories, kept the cash in my bag and embezzled, curiously enough, very little – after all, I was in charge. And once, in the middle of the night, I woke with a start, remembering that I hadn't locked the door. I was in luck: nobody had noticed the open shop.

But to be persecuted by all the frustrated sex maniacs in that part of the city, to be on the verge of tears all the time, that was a nightmare; that was a life of fantasy filled with horror. So as soon as the owner returned, I left in favour of a big store, once more in a part of the city populated by drunks, layabouts, grey middle-of-the-road people; and where did they put me but in the men's underwear department. I cried when I was alone behind the counter, sitting on a box of, needless to say, jock-straps. In a place like that a customer would only whisper suggestions under his breath – though I was eventually fired because, tears rolling down my cheeks, I had been unable to contain my laughter when asked – or so I thought – for a pair of 'moonbeam trousers'. Such a relief, it was. And again I ended up in an odd corner, a mail-order business owned by an old gentleman whose office was at home. One wall was lined with dull grey boxes. Opened up, they revealed exotic pure silk négligés, mostly black, and expensive knickers inlaid with lace. I had never seen such things before and, though I took some, I never dared wear them and wondered who could – though I looked at them every night and had my fantasies about them, as perhaps he did too. There was almost no work, apart from writing one letter a day and dusting the boxes, for the old man preferred to pack the clothes himself; but I always had to be present as, taking his time, he stroked out every little wrinkle. I was supposed to be learning how to do it.

Though worried by the strange way he looked at me, I stayed because he had a library and I started to read for the first time in my life: Tolstoy, Chekhov, Gorky, Maupassant, Zola. The only thing he asked of me as I read, was that I perch in a special chair without my shoes and stockings, skirt up above my knees, while he sat behind a desk fiddling with papers. I would totally forget about him because of the potency of the words I was reading, so we were both happy. To my surprise I even got a rise in salary. Although I was quite aware of his business behind the desk, I took no notice of it. I felt by now that it was my lot to be pursued by lecherous men, and as long as they didn't spring at me, and left me alone, it was just as well to accept it, especially with a comparative gentleman like this.

Somewhere at the back of my mind, I kept a hope, a day-dream of becoming a film star. I cut out pictures of Hollywood idols from glossy magazines. Tyrone Power was my hero in those days. I had a whole scrapbook filled with pictures of him and his wife, Annabella. They seemed such a happy and romantic couple – anyway, that's what the press said, and I of course believed every word. When grandfather had asked me what I wanted to be when I grew up, I had promptly answered 'Sailor'. His only reply was to smile benevolently. He himself had been in the Swedish Navy in his young days, as second best to becoming a film star. Later I was teased mercilessly by the rest of the family, who began to call me 'the diva'. Anyway, it was an outlandish idea; I didn't have the looks, for a start. Why this nagging hope, then? Well, in the girl guides' summer camp where I had been so unhappy, there had been one positive incident. We had given a concert party for the local children. I had played only a small part, a duet with another girl, but I stole the show, as the saying goes. Instinctively, I had known exactly what to do, surprising everyone, myself included. The applause went to my head. I had been delirious with joy. That special moment had stuck in my mind and I had thought that perhaps one day . . . I had told mother about this momentous happening but how could she possibly have understood? Instead, she warned me about the insecurities of that kind of life: she voiced all the usual prejudices about the world of actors . . . drink, drugs, sexual debauchery. I listened with one ear when she told me that I had to find myself a job that would give me some stability.

Though the idea horrified me, I went back to school again for half a year in an attempt to qualify as a shop assistant, but I wrote poems down the margins of the textbooks that told me the customer was always right. I made no friends in that school either; I went my own way. I was not liked because

41

they thought I was stupid. Only once did I mean something in their eyes and that was when I was invited out for an evening by one of the pretty boys whom all the girls fancied. I was astonished, almost speechless. But the evening turned out to be a disaster. At this time I was full of hang-ups, one of which was not being able to go to the toilet if anybody was in the same room, for fear that they should hear the slightest noise. Perhaps it had all started at that first and last summer camp: I don't remember it worrying me before. There the lavatory had indeed been very communal, a large space with open cubicles and wash-basins opposite. The other girls never seemed to bother about it. They would sit and hold conversations from the seats as if they were sitting on ordinary chairs, never worrying the slightest bit about the pongs they made or the noise; in fact if anyone released a loud fart the laughter would ring out and someone would try to do one better.

I was horrified by their vulgarity. I could hardly bring myself to use the lavatory at all, but if I had to, I tried to save it up for times when no one else would be there, with the result that I became constipated. I was given laxatives which I took, though panic-stricken. After that I tried to hold out until night-time, but then, if I succeeded, the relief was so great that I passed out like a light afterwards and wet my bed. To say that I was ashamed is to put it mildly; and then, a further humiliation, I would be made to wash the sheets in front of all the others, who would giggle and snigger. It happened again and again with agonising regularity.

Even when I was older, I was still desperately reluctant to admit to my body and its basic functions. When using a lavatory anywhere I always flushed even before sitting down so as to hide the noise. And if there was a basin, even better – I would turn the taps full on to disguise the fact that I was human. So it was on the evening with the pretty boy from school. We had travelled by train to his parents' place just outside the city, been to a little dance in the park, necked a bit, but not very seriously. I discovered that he was as shy as I was when we were alone together, and it had been difficult to converse. Finally he insisted on taking me home. Having trained myself from an early age, I did have a remarkable capacity for holding myself in, but I hadn't been to the loo all evening, and there had been a few soft drinks which I had tried to resist, but couldn't altogether; that would have been rude. So by the time we got on the train back to Stockholm I was in poor shape. I sat numb and stiff, trying to hold back the rumbling of my stomach. I was deeply embarrassed. He wanted to accompany me home by tram when we arrived in Stockholm. I tried to find all kinds of excuses; all I wanted was to be alone, so that I could sneak behind some building or into a park, anything. I was in agony but I could not explain. When I saw the Number Ten tram speed towards us I could not hold it any longer. My bladder burst. He ran away in horror, and I stood there like a stupid animal with pee running down my legs, a great pool under me. I could not go back to school after that; I made myself ill with shame.

After that trauma life didn't seem worth living for a very long time. I went back to all kinds of strange jobs – washing dishes, waiting in a snack-bar. I still went to the dancing place, stayed out late, was sullen at home. I didn't care for sex, it didn't mean a thing to me. What I was in search of was love, so I just put up with the physical bit. I have never forgotten the boy who, standing in a doorway somewhere, said: 'One day you will shake with desire for it.' I was horrified by the idea and answered: 'Oh no, never, never.'

I had begun to look very common; I thought it was tough. I was spending my hard-earned money on silly things, tottering around on far too high heels, and smearing myself with heavy make-up. I started to walk the streets with the idea of selling myself, like my friend with her earnings she'd used to buy hot dogs. Why not? But I was lucky because the first man who picked me up was more or less an idiot. I got frightened and was pursued. The man had a knife; he ripped my coat and I got a few cuts, but nothing serious. I arrived home in a terrible state only to find my parents up and waiting, having finally had enough of my behaviour, not understanding what was happening in my life. I was told in no uncertain terms by my stepfather, who had kept himself to himself most of his life, that I was not his child anyway, so why should he care? Mother was horrified by what he had blurted out in anger; I was stunned. That I had not expected. Perhaps, like all children in unhappy moments, I thought I didn't fit into my family, that I wasn't really their child.

For the first and last time in my life, I wanted to commit suicide. I walked the cold unfriendly streets for hours, contemplating how I would do it. I blamed it all on myself. I hated myself at that moment, and when you hate yourself what is there to live for? Finally I went home, when everybody had gone to work, and cried myself to sleep. But at least I had been shocked into realising I could not continue like this, and gave up the tarty behaviour and all that went with it.

I still only functioned. I was that many kilos of flesh, had eyes made of stones that didn't see, ears that were deaf to stars and dew and all that was myself, and I lay buried in something very black.

This was the time when there was a lot of talk about children having been brought up by wild beasts: bears, monkeys, wolves . . . Perhaps I was one of these children? I identified with them like mad because I thought that such a child, taken out of its wild surroundings, would find it as hard as I did to be reconciled to human ways, to fit in.

Things began to look up when I joined a children's theatre club on the housing estate where I lived. In the first production I had only a walk-on part, but I was hooked on the theatre from the very start. In the play were two girls from the Opera ballet whom I was greatly in awe of. I watched them dance until I knew every turn and pirouette. In the corridor leading to the dressing-rooms I tried to imitate their movements, standing on points in my gym-shoes. I became so absorbed that I didn't notice them watching me in amazement. When the show was over they gave me their old ballet shoes and, at home in front of the mirror, I practised like a fanatic, until my toes were a bleeding mess. In the next production I got a part as a fairy and danced on points, with bended knees, in my own choreography to the accompaniment of the 'Blue Danube', played on a wind-up gramophone in the wings. It must have been quite horrendous to watch, but I struggled through it. My first big success was as a witch in a children's amateur production. I got my first review: 'Quite a remarkable feat, a sixteen-year-old girl looking and acting like a hundred.' Then one day in the tram I overheard someone saying that a young girl was wanted for a part in a play written by the Nobel prize-winner, Pär Lagerkvist, whose poems at that time were my favourite reading matter.

I was one of fifteen girls auditioning for the part and it was the very first time that I had been in a real theatre. I was awed but, strangely enough, not scared. I am amazed even now at my courage in turning up for the audition because at that time I was still so full of a sense of inferiority that I never spoke until spoken to. I had thought the part would be small, but in fact it was the female lead. And I got it! Nobody would believe me when I said I had got a big part opposite one of the leading actors in Sweden in a play by Pär Lagerkvist. My parents by now were so used to my lies and exaggerations that I could only convince them when I showed them the contract saying that I would earn twenty-five pounds a month. I thought it was a fortune.

Aunt Bad sent me flowers; some grey home-knitted woollen socks and that single bad review: 'She is pigeon-toed, lisps and is inclined to baby-talk, but she has some talent.'

Pär Lagerkvist made a great impression on me, mainly, I think, because he looked the epitome of the romantic poet, with a white silky mane of hair, strong piercing eyes and a nose like an eagle's beak. He seemed tremendously shy: I can't remember him saying a word to me but he looked me up and down searchingly at the audition. Not only did I play the leading part but I also helped the stage manager, putting on music, cleaning up after the performance: I would have stayed at the theatre all night if he had asked. During the run I also met the man who was to become my first real teacher. He attended the performance and came backstage to talk to me.

I consider my meeting with Calle one of the most important of my life. Calle Flygare was his full name. The second name means 'flyer' in Swedish and he really was a sort of flyer: impossible, selfish, but also enthusiastic, generous and a true eccentric. He didn't try to be one, he just was.

'My dear girl,' he said, 'you've got talent, but you must learn something about acting. Come to my school and I'll teach you.' But how could I? There was no money for such things. As if reading my mind, he said, 'Come to my school three evenings a week. Tuition will be free.' I acted, I danced, I cried, I laughed for a whole year under Calle's guidance. And how I changed!

Actually he had adopted four of us, 'Little Orphans', as he used to call us. We were supposed to be exceptionally talented. Though we hardly grasped this point, we did eagerly grasp the affection and security which he gave us. If you were a cynic, you might say that Calle, whom we now called 'uncle', liked little girls, but all he did about that was to eye us quietly from time to time with his hands stuck firmly down his pockets, which made us laugh – we didn't take it seriously and we certainly weren't frightened. We decided to accept and forget about that aspect. His four orphan children became friends, we stuck together. We were poor, not only financially but also in spirit and background, and we needed him.

One day, we four girls were sitting around in someone's flat, talking of nothing in particular. Picture a very ordinary room with its four solid walls, a shabby Christmas tree in a corner, all fairly humble. The only reason for being together was that we were all pupils in a dramatic school run by this character called Calle.

The street noises were shut off because the flat was on the third floor and turned inwards towards a bleak grey stone wall. The light was dimmish, the candles in the tree were flickering. We were all fairly buried people with not many thoughts in our heads and I was perhaps the most buried, living in a world of shadows where everything seemed blacker than black.

And suddenly there was light.

My sky could not have been more overcast; you would not think that the smallest ray of sunshine could filter through that blanket which I had spun so carelessly over my head.

But then came this light, this overwhelming light, which flooded everything, swamping the room and hitting me with the suddenness of an electric shock. It filled me with radiant energy. It was like looking into the sun without being blinded. My whole being was, as it were, transported to another world that seemed to me infinitely more real than the one I had been living in. Physically, I stopped being aware of my body, although my mind was registering all the changes. The white light was shimmering with energy and had limitless depth. Although I knew I was sitting in a room in Stockholm, that room no longer existed, nor did sounds or smells. The world had halted for me and I was filled with awe, a deeply religious feeling that took over my whole being. I could see my past with the utmost clarity, into my half-animal being, the chaos, the lostness, the web of ignorance that enshrouded me, into all of which I had seemed to be rushing, hellbent on destroying myself. All those years I had looked outwards for consolation; now I realised that I must look inwards to find myself.

Apparently the light had been reflected on my bewildered face. And if the others had not actually shared the experience, they could see how it had luminously painted me. When I found myself back in the room again, I was still radiant within and felt totally at a loss to explain what had happened.

I don't know how to make this inexplicable event explicable, even to myself. I couldn't then, I cannot now. I only know that these short and intense moments can never ever be forgotten, that their power has always remained and worked within me. I knew that I had been touched, but by what? Is that how conversions are made? Perhaps. Or just great changes. Because suddenly there was meaning to my life; I felt innocent in spite of my murky past. I felt as though I were a child at last, as though I had been pulled out of a black hole by my hair just in time. It was as if my brain cells had been given a good shake-up and all that had been lying dormant in me had come alive. It was the death of the old self and the birth of the new. The extraordinary thing about the whole happening was that I was absolutely certain that the light field that I had found myself in was reality. What I glimpsed, whether it was truth, God, love or a combination of all three, was the best and most real thing that had ever happened to me. I was open to everything at last.

This is how another of Calle's 'orphans' and my best friend at the time, the actress Inga Landgré, describes what happened that day:

The beginning of February 1943 we were all in my place. My mother worked in the restaurant until well after midnight. We all sat on the big divan. The Christmas tree was still there, it was lit. I remember the tree because it made a background to Mai. I can see her sitting there. Her back is slightly bent, she has her hands on her knees, she is relaxed. Her whole body seems to rest, her face a bit tilted upwards, her eyes looking beyond me. The expression in her young face is still something I remember after thirty-seven years. There was an openness, a kind of listening, looking at something that we others couldn't see or hear. Her face was so soft, the feeling suddenly so condensed, so unusual and also so fragile, that I felt I wanted to hold my breath. Jane's sudden cry, 'Mai, who are you really?', I didn't like. It is the only thing I remember anybody saying that night. Therefore, I was very happy when I found this from my diary:

February 6th, 1943
Dear diary, Something has happened tonight, or perhaps nothing has happened. I just don't know. Margreth, Jane and Mai have been here. I can't explain anything. It was as Mai herself said: 'The bad thing has left me.' Margreth stood up suddenly, disturbed. 'What were you doing, Mai?' It was as if something very bad came out of Mai and then disappeared. Margreth was shaking in her whole body and began to cry. After a while she dared to look up, but she gave out a scream as if she had seen something and carried on crying. But that was not the main thing. When the bad thing had, as it were, flown out of Mai, she just sat there and looked ahead and still past me. She had tears in her eyes and suddenly her whole expression changed; she

48

had a mild and good look in her eyes. One could not believe that she was real, she looked exalted – no, I can't describe it. Then finally she said: 'It's too big, far too big for me.' Something had happened. Mai's marvellous face, so strong, like I had never seen it before. I hope I can keep it all my life.

Jane was staring at Mai and she shouted out: 'Mai, who are you really?'; and then she fell over and cried out with fear. I didn't cry. I only looked at Mai. I felt proud to be there at this obviously important moment. We sat, I think, at least half an hour. Between quarter to twelve and a quarter after. I know that something very beautiful happened, something I will probably never see again.

It's difficult to be precise about Calle's qualities as a teacher. He used to say: 'I want to *un*-teach' – and that is perhaps the best way to describe his method. He suggested things rather than saying how they should be done. When he mimed a scene for us – with great vigour and in a way that could only be called ham-acting – he would always say afterwards, 'But you do it your own way, of course.' The less inventive among us would try to imitate him, which was not altogether good. Calle certainly didn't like it; he would tell them to do the scene over again, but in a different way. For instance, if it was a dramatic scene, he would demand that they turn it into a farce, or he would change the roles around so that sometimes Ophelia would play Hamlet, and vice versa, to the great amusement of all of us watching. But it was more than just fun because afterwards, dissecting the scene with Calle, we would clearly see the pitfalls for an actor in that particular scene, as well as the possible sources of irony. Together, we learnt new ways of coming to grips with it. He was a great admirer of Stanislavsky, so we got big doses of his teaching as well, which was, in my opinion, invaluable.

Calle had a funny habit of unconsciously miming every scene he happened to be watching, with all the appropriate expressions of sorrow, anger, irony. He had a strong sense of leadership, but was never intimidating. He was one of us, and just as childish. His laughter was infectious and though he was a mine of information, what he told us took on the quality of a fairy-tale. There was nothing professional about him and to be with him was always an exhilarating experience. He gave me my childhood, made me live it out by acting.

Everything that was good in me he brought out, and all the bad bits we threw away together. I began to acquire confidence. For the first time in my life, I dared to look at the world and myself and feel I had a place in it. There were these four under-privileged girls who had all quit school at about fourteen, whom Calle was helping by giving free lessons. When we came to him, we didn't expect much from the world, if anything at all; we had already been very hurt by it. Calle changed all that. He made us believe we could fit, but first we had to change ourselves, change our life-patterns, and be part of a changing world; we had to learn to believe in life.

Calle lived with his mother in a sombre, narrow street in the heart of the city which has now been torn down to make way for modern office blocks and five-storey car parks. Their apartment was on the first floor of a solid-looking building where everything smelled clean, proper and very Swedish; that is, it had no smell at all. But once inside the apartment, you entered another world and were met by other smells.

Calle's mother would always open the door to us. Her appearance was not exactly typical of the mother of a drama teacher in Stockholm. She would be wearing Calle's long underwear pinned to his grey socks, a pair of well-worn plimsolls, and a three-quarter-length dress in some kind of black print, which reminds me now of the material worn by little old ladies in Provence, even by myself at times. She obviously cared about the neckline, because she pinned to the dress a little lace frill, which she would change every so often. The only other coquettish streak manifested itself in her hair. Every morning she would light a small spirit-lamp and heat curling-irons on it, and do her own hairdressing job. Over the years she had singed quite badly the little curls around her forehead, so that they were slightly yellow in comparison with her otherwise silver-grey hair. The finishing touch was the big fat cigar that dangled out of the corner of her mouth. I never saw her without it, lit or unlit. It was just there – like an extension of herself. She could be friendly, she could be tough, she could be bad-tempered if anyone dared to annoy Calle. Then she would sit down at the little upright piano and bang out some Wagner very loudly, so that no one should hear his fit of temper.

She loved him more than her own life, and, in his fashion, he loved her just as much. They were inseparable. They teased and laughed at each other, and had long arguments about ballet, music, and the arts in general. Calle was an inspired talker and his mother was not bad either, but she could also be malicious and tell killing stories about some of his paying students. But hers was a very special brand of humour and the glint in her eye was basically kind.

To reach Calle, you had to go down a long passage whose walls were covered with old stage portraits, big dog-eared posters and theatre programmes, all yellowed with age and cigar-smoke. You would pass the door of the kitchen that no one, not even Calle, was allowed to enter; it was his mother's domain. Finally, you'd come to the place where Calle resided – a rather large but gloomy room, enveloped in a constant cloud of cigar-smoke, whose walls were just as cluttered as those in the passage, and rich in memories of Calle's efforts as an actor in his early days, which hadn't been too success-ful. And there he would be, larger than life, puffing, grunt-ing, holding forth, dancing to his mother's music, showing some ballet steps – which didn't vary much. He would be dressed in a brownish suit with a herring-bone pattern, which had turned a funny mouldy colour in places, and a stiff white collar, which he would throw off (to his mother's annoyance) when he got over-excited. Finally, he too had the inevitable cigar always in his mouth. He would hardly ever sit down or be still unless we had a very serious scene to play, when he would cry into his hanky.

Sometimes he would wear a curious large chequered dressing-gown, whose colour I couldn't describe for the life of me, and an old red fez with a dangling tassel – a strange outfit for a rather over-sized man. I suppose Calle and his mother could be called dirty and messy, but for us it was a welcome contrast to the sterile and clinical approach to life that we were used to.

These two people were so utterly different from everything we had ever known. They were loving, a little crazy, and they gave all they had. Not only was our tuition free, but we were constantly being taken out for little meals. It is the first memory I have of going to a restaurant, and I was very impressed. On the whole it was Calle who talked. We were grateful, we took in all his ideas on world government, on optimism, on poetry, and his enthusiasm for life itself. The four children, as he used to call us, were spoilt by both of them, but we, I'm glad to say, lapped it up, as we had never experienced this kind of overflowing love before.

We never quite knew how to show our gratitude, but once, I remember, we gave Calle's mother a present. Her handbag was falling apart, only held together by a rubber band, so we had decided that it was about time she had a new one. It was fire-engine red, in shining plastic. She was very proud of it, although it didn't fit in with the rest of her image. We felt perhaps we had made a mistake when we handed it to her, but, 'Oh no,' she said, 'it is positive.' But one day we really had an opportunity to do something for her. We had been shocked to find her in tears when we arrived. They had to leave the flat, she told us, because the building was to be demolished. 'It's impossible,' she kept on crying. 'Why?' we asked, not understanding. 'Oh, all the boxes,' she said. We had never seen any boxes. 'What boxes?' we asked. She just pointed at the kitchen door, and started to cry even more.

After much persuasion, we got her to accept our offer to go into the kitchen and help clean it out. We didn't know what we had let ourselves in for. Certainly, it was an experience not to have missed. Amongst the debris it contained, we encountered the remains of no less than four birthday parties. Over the past year, we had always been lavishly treated to cream cakes and chocolate and whipped cream on our birthdays. Well, here were the leftovers, now rotting in cartons. In the sink, the cups were floating in a mouldy layer of cream and chocolate that had turned a very weird colour indeed and everywhere there were cigar-butts. We felt a bit queasy at the first sight of it all but we went to work. In the middle of the room we discovered a filthy old armchair and some blankets – on which we were to learn that mother slept – surrounded by hundreds of stiff dirty collars and socks, and boxes, filled with all kinds of odds and ends, totally useless. I think we kept at it for almost a week before it was eventually cleared out. And every day we had a party – mother insisted that we be paid in cream cakes and chocolate. It was difficult to get it down amongst the socks and the grime. Not once did we see Calle in the kitchen. I think he pretended it didn't exist, since he never mentioned our helping mother to pack, only showing mild surprise at seeing us at unaccustomed hours.

From time to time, mother would become worried about Calle's sex life. One evening she went down the street and picked up a pretty girl for him and left him alone for more than an hour. She crept back and, hearing Calle's voice, decided she would go in. There he was, declaiming a fairy-tale by Hans Christian Andersen, whom he loved. The girl sat at his feet, her face flooded with tears. Later on, she became quite a successful pupil.

The following summer, I worked with Calle and a little group from his school at the Tivoli, a fun-fair outside Stockholm. We did a children's matinée performance on the big open stage, slotted in between acts by jugglers and trapeze artistes. We were ecstatic. We sang and danced scenes from *The Wizard of Oz* and Calle told a fairy-tale. We worked for next to nothing and a card that gave us free rides on the roller-coaster, the big wheel, all the attractions, even the rifle range and the china-breaking booth. We really got to know the ins and outs of the fairground and made friends with the giant lady with the beard. Our great heroine was the beautiful Indian snake-charmer. I don't know how many of her performances I watched – I was spellbound.

At the end of that summer, the theatre seemed tame in comparison with the life that we had had a brief taste of. I dreamed about circus life, of perhaps becoming a clown. After a few talks with one, however, I grew very downhearted: I was told that there was no tradition of female clowns. I had heard that sentence before. So I carried on with Calle. I took up singing with him and found I had a strong voice; at least there was a tradition for women singers. With Calle conducting and humming and mother banging out the tunes on the upright, I sang Gluck, I sang Schubert, I sang *Carmen*. It was my first contact with real music and I was floating on a cloud.

That autumn, I and Bojan, another girl from our select group, got an engagement in a low dive called The Bluebird, smack opposite the National Theatre. We were billed as 'Mai and Boj, Two Swedish Nightingales in Rosita Serrano Style' (at that time the Portuguese singer was a favourite with Swedes). We were dressed in some kind of Austrian outfit – Heaven knows why – in flowered skirts and dainty little aprons; a pair of Lolitas, we had trouble almost from the start. So Calle and his mother decided to sit through each of the performances at night, as both a protection and an inspiration.

What was it that Calle offered us that was so unique and so different from what I was to encounter when I joined the National Theatre? First, a great sense of adventure and an acute awareness of ourselves; then love and affection, and a home. Last, but certainly not least, he believed in us utterly.

One day, another girl in the group told me she was going to try to get into the National Theatre school which had a three-year course and a great reputation. Both Garbo and the two great Bergmans, Ingrid and Ingmar, were connected with it. It was the ultimate for an actor in Sweden, the holiest of holies; the thought of it scared me, made me feel insecure again, yet I said I too would try my luck. Why shouldn't I? I took with me three scenes that I had done with Calle: from *Easter* by Strindberg, *Children in Uniform* by Christa Winslow and *The Innocent* by Lillian Hellman. I didn't dare tell Calle about it, and felt as though I were betraying him when I filled in the form. How could I do this to him? That great institution, that monument to the arts, that temple of stone – it was against everything he believed in. However well-meaning, it was cold and sterile. It could never be a home.

12 *Above*, taken from *The Lost People*, with Richard Attenborough, directed by Bernard Knowles

13 *Below,* in *Portrait from Life,* directed by Terry Fisher

14 *Above*, with Dirk Bogarde in *Desperate Moment*, directed by Compton Bennett

15 *Below left*, Herbert Lom and myself in *Hell is Sold Out*

16 *Below right*, *Only Two Can Play*, co-starring with Peter Sellers .

17 With Tyrone Power, while he was shooting *The Sun Also Rises* in Mexico

18 *Right*, from my dangle-dolly days in England

19 *Below,* on the set of *Only Two Can Play* (photograph by Peter Sellers)

Such an institution can't compare with a great personality who needs freedom to survive, who has a tremendous vision, and who lives and eats and sleeps his passion.

I entered that mausoleum with fear in my heart. After a second audition, however, I was still among those selected for the third and last test. There were only twenty of us left out of a hundred. And I made it, and so did the other girl. It was unbelievable.

My first instinct was to rush to tell Calle. Characteristically, he was overjoyed and took us out for a celebration dinner, telling everybody about us, like a proud father. I still had a week of my contract to do at The Bluebird and one night, to my great horror, I saw all the front tables were taken by the directors of the National Theatre and the principal herself, on an outing to inspect their new pupil, who had intrigued them with her working-class accent. The party was led by Alf Sjöberg, who was to become my next teacher in the theatre.

I got a stipend and started the three-year course. I had indeed entered a grand institution, with its sacred green room. I slunk around, eyes downcast. The only place I dared to sit was on the bench with the galoshes and boots, half hidden among the fur coats and the black woollen cape of Lars Hanson, the great actor whom we all worshipped and who scared the life out of us. A lone wolf, he would stalk the corridors, and in the green room, where the actors read the daily papers and gossiped, or listened to the radio in between their entrances, he remained unapproachable, totally aloof. I would watch him with awe, seeing the concentration around him like a sacred circle. I think I learned more from just watching him offstage than I learned in the school itself.

At seventeen, I was the youngest in the school. I became silent and withdrawn – the mouse once again. My classmates were well read and academic: one of them had even been at the French Lycée. I had no manners, no culture, and what little I did know had been self-taught. Feeling inferior, I became more stupid than I really was and could never answer any of the questions in the classes on the history of the theatre. We had lessons in dance, deportment, voice technique; at none of these was I any good.

The only way I managed to communicate was on the stage, and after one year of study I got my big chance: the lead in a large public performance of Maxwell Anderson's play *The Eve of St Mark*. After that, I hardly attended any classes at the school, but played big parts in plays by Shakespeare, Sartre, Lorca and Strindberg.

Alf Sjöberg became in some ways my mentor at the National Theatre. He cast me against type in both comedy and tragedy, in the modern repertoire as well as the classics. Sjöberg was not what I would call a typical Swede: he was exuberant, large of gesture and wildly enthusiastic. It was his electric and dynamic personality that finally brought me out of my shell. He was demanding, an absolute ruler on that stage, but he was not a tyrant; at least I didn't think so, although I had heard to the contrary. But he was an innovator and a disciplinarian and he didn't believe in the word 'compromise'. At first he had wanted to be an architect or a painter (which helped him later when he did his own sketches for décor and costumes). He was always trying to find new ways of interpreting a play. He made real use of the proscenium, created lighting effects, and united mime, dance and shadow-play to create an exciting new kind of living theatre.

As for the work with the actors, he made us feel that we were the most important of all the ingredients on that stage. To give courage and inspiration and to bring out our spontaneity were his main wishes. He loved his work passionately and he himself said that being a director was like playing the part of a god for a moment in time.

So I had become a professional actress at the age of nineteen. Calle glowed; it was his triumph too. Again and again I found myself going to him for guidance, for security. When I landed a leading role opposite Lars Hanson, my idol, I quivered with fright and it was Calle who reassured me and gave me the strength to stand up to the extraordinary power of that great actor. The play was *Shadow and Substance* by an Irish writer called Paul Vincent Carroll. It was a success, and sparks flew between Lars Hanson and myself, but I don't think, somehow, I would have been able to match up to that genius had it not been for Calle.

There was no end to the superlatives which greeted my début. It was overwhelming. Having been in the shadows for so long, I was now in the limelight and I was scared to death. I was courted by the press; I started getting fan-letters and film offers, and I was given grants – which helped, because I was still only a student with no pay, even if I got the big parts. It could have turned my head, but it didn't, and for that I'm convinced I have my 'rotten years' to thank. I have never regretted or felt sad about those years since growing up, because they enabled me to work on instinct. I used the pain of my past to communicate from the stage. In real life, I was still out of touch with people.

I had another letter from my Aunt Bad, warning me of the pitfalls of success. A second pair of socks accompanied a sad letter saying that perhaps she would have done better if she had been born in the 1920s. I was lucky, she said. She wasn't the only one to warn me – but somehow I knew the dangers instinctively. I pinned an aphorism up on the wall: 'The line between failure and success is so fine that we scarcely know when we pass it.'

Sjöberg was as fascinated by films as he was by the theatre, which was rare in those days, and it was through him that I got my first film part, in a movie called *Frenzy* (*Torment* in the States), which he was to direct. The script was to be written by a young unknown called Ingmar Bergman, who had asked to act as 'script-girl' in order to learn the craft of film-making from the great master.

This time I played a vulgar and downtrodden shop assistant. It seemed that Sjöberg was the only one who believed in my versatility and my talent for transformation; nobody else understood where I was taking it from. Though young in years, I was very old and worn inside.

Tutte, whom I met when I was about nineteen, was a breath of fresh air. He was a classical dancer and his full name was Isaac Samuel Lemkow: a small, dark figure with flashing eyes, with a hint of gipsy in his appearance, an ancestry reaching back into the mists of Russia, and a quixotic temperament. He had a remarkable talent for dancing and harboured all kinds of plans and ambitions. He was astonishing. But neither of my parents came to the wedding, since Tutte was not only a foreigner but also Jewish.

Tutte had escaped by the narrowest of squeaks from the occupied Norway in which his family had been living. Knowing how dangerous it was to cross the mountain barrier into Sweden, they had divided into pairs and crept over the border under cover of night. They were spotted and the Germans opened fire. In the shooting Tutte tragically lost touch with his mother and sister, who were captured by the Germans and vanished for ever. The rest of them, four brothers and the father, had to begin a new life in Stockholm.

Tutte was new, strange and talented – and he gave me affection. That was what I was really looking for, plain unadulterated affection, and for that I will always be grateful to him. Even in the first months of our marriage, we called each other 'mother' and 'father', like some couples do after years and years of marriage and children. About a year later, a girl-child was born. But how? I'm still horrified when I remember my total ignorance, my *naïveté* in all such matters.

I was in a rather posh clinic, a sterile and unfriendly place. I didn't say a word about the pains that came more and more regularly. I certainly didn't dare cry out. Tears and sweat mingled on my face whilst a cleaning woman, who was old and rough, told me hair-raising stories about her own experiences in childbirth. When I was left alone and felt that the baby was trying to get out, I was petrified: something must be wrong. I tried to push it back. A nurse came in by chance and seeing what I was doing she was as horrified as I was, and also angry . . . I had thought, poor fool, that I would be put to sleep, that they would cut me up and take out the baby!

I was angry that nobody had told me anything, angry that I hadn't bothered to ask about it, angry with myself most of all. I was to hate ignorance for the rest of my life, for what it had done to me, and for what it did to people living in the shadows: the manipulated ones. And I began to understand why so many people had tried to avoid my company in the past – because ignorance is contemptible.

I was born an unsatisfactory child. What I have tried to do is to describe my efforts to be reborn, in order to clear the decks. My sad truths were not lies, they were very much a reality . . . Finally I say this to myself: to understand is to forgive – even one's self.

Assembly Point

'It is a poor sort of memory
that only works backwards,' the Queen remarked.

Lewis Carroll, *Alice in Wonderland*

August, 1979   *Mas d'Aigues Vives, France*
We all have a place called Home, be it a house, flat or hotel. Yet every single home, resting-place or whatever we choose to call it, is different, even down to the quality of the dust that gathers.

Every dog is a lion in his home.
Every cock is proud of his own dunghill.

My abode – my own personal dunghill – is a very important part of myself. It is the place where I feel most alone, and therefore most alive.

I say that this is the place where I feel most alone, and yet I'm not. For the past three years, I have lived very closely with a person who happens to be twenty-eight years younger than myself. This young Frenchman, Glen, with whom I share my life, asks impertinent questions, does not treat me as if I were fifty-four and, what's more, makes love to me as if I was seventeen. Sometimes I believe he thinks I really am that age . . .

'You are old, Father William,' the young man said,
'And your hair has become very white;

60

Assembly Point

And yet you incessantly stand on your head –
Do you think, at your age, it is right?'

Lewis Carroll

I stand on my head a lot and, what's more, I like it.

I used to believe in the sentiment, 'Where you are, that's home.' I didn't believe in possessions or property. But right now I'm living in a large farmhouse in the main Midi in France, surrounded by some thirty acres. What made me change my mind? There are many reasons; perhaps one of them has something to do with being that Gemini person.

The road that leads to the house is rough, to say the least, and I need a Land Rover so as to be able to pass the first obstacle, the river. At first everybody complained about the road, said it was more like a track – they were sure I would have it fixed. But I didn't do anything about it, as I like the road that leads to the house to be (almost) inaccessible. I insist on my personal isolation.

You pass vineyards, wheat-fields, asparagus beds, cherry and olive trees; you get a glimpse of the gorge, with its green swirling river where the eagles nest and where we picnic and swim. In the gorge is a mysterious grotto called the 'Old Church', where I have spent romantic nights dreaming wild dreams, as wild as the place itself.

Finally, you see the great cypress, which must be as old as the house, a couple of hundred years or more. Facing the cypress and the house are the blue ever-changing hills. Because of the heavy erosion they have become like a part of my favourite country, Iceland – all texture. Mulberry trees make up an avenue towards the house. This is 'Mas d'Aigues Vives' – the Ranch of the Living Waters – which used to be a silkworm farm. This is my sanctuary, my hang-out. The place where I keep my bits and pieces, the place I love and call my home.

People thought I was totally mad when I bought the house some fourteen years ago. There was hardly a roof, and trees were growing where the bedrooms are now ... but it was *my* place, unruly wilderness surrounded by hills and mountains, with no other building in sight. There is no electricity or running water, but a well with a pump pushes two thousand litres of water up to the attic; there are big gas bottles behind the house which means that we have the great luxury of hot water, a gas cooker, gas lamps and even a refrigerator. There are twelve rooms and a giant fireplace that is like a small room in itself. I have no help in the house. I do it all myself, in fits and starts, not too much, not too little; there are always corners that are untidy, but on the whole it is fairly spick and span. It is simple and rustic as I wanted it to be, but it is also quite sophisticated.

It is a lonely place, so lonely in fact that some people give it a quick glance and run away, however beautiful they think it is. Many an angry taxi-driver has argued with my friends that nobody in their right mind would be living at the end of that appalling road and has insisted upon turning his car round in the mud, only to find out, back in the village, that it was the right road after all.

The music – madrigals and *chansons de danse* – that I like to play at the Mas fits in perfectly with this primitive terrain. I had no idea that I would ever come so close to the Middle Ages. With my Swedish background, I was at first shocked by what I saw; then I was fascinated, and finally I accepted it totally – except for the cruel aspects, like the tradition of hanging dogs or starving them to death if they prove to be no good at either hunting or truffling. And sometimes human beings are treated as badly, or live as primitively, as dogs. The local ditcher and hedger, so the story goes, gave all his worldly goods to the baker lady, hoping that one day she would look after him. They exchanged love letters for years, despite her six children by another man. But in the end he, a gourmand, was left in his cellar to eat Chum and Kit-E-Kat while she drove around in a brand new car bought with his money. Stories, stories, most of them hard to believe.

The rubbish dump is worth a detour, as they say in the tourist guides. It has the loveliest of views. It's such a romantic place that lovers meet there. Bras and panties hang in trees and bushes like trophies. But it is more than a hang-out for lovers – it's also a haunt for human scavengers like me. I once found a policeman's cape there that I lined with an old fur coat. I wore it in New York and somebody thought it so smart they asked where I had bought it.

In my house, I have no ornaments, no carpets. I have cushions to sit on rather than chairs, some beds and tables; only what is absolutely necessary. Apart from my library of twelve thousand books, I have tried desperately hard to free myself from possessions, but all the same I have been caught like everybody else. I hoard things despite myself. I may not have any priceless china or silverware but my collection of baskets grows steadily and I would hate to lose them.

To the locals, I am the mad, foreign woman of the 'Range of the Living Waters', whose herb-garden cures the animals in the village, who is seen walking her goats on leashes in all weathers, followed by a donkey, two white wolf-hounds and ten cats.

This reputation I have for being a witch-doctor seems to have spread even to countries I have never visited.

Respected Madam:

May God give you healthy and enthusiastic personality in all time to come. Here is a kind of request in favour of our family interest and for our happy marital life. I request to do something by which our interest in life strengthens. My wife is a little more worried than me as her breasts have gone down to NIL. Once she also tried to make suicide but somehow she is saved. She has got good physique and sharming fetures, she has good and loving nature also. All that desturbs her is no breasts.

She is very much worried because of that only. Once again we request you help us in our marital life. You can send us some medecines and good advice can also help us. We also request you to send your photograph with your loving letters, awaiting for the reply, yours loving . . .

P.S. I am sorry to inform you that India one dont get good doctors in this. We have tried that also.

October 21st, 1979 (Full Moon)
There is something haunting in the light of the moon, something spellbinding when it floats like a silver disc across a darkened sky, pregnant and ominous – 'the egg of the world', as the Eskimos used to call it. They never let their women contemplate it for too long, for fear it would incite them to orgies. It seems to incite me to decisions.

A few weeks ago there was a loud knock at the front door. I opened it to a well-rounded man with sharp features wearing an old-fashioned Borsalino. Without any formalities whatsoever, he said: 'If you ever are so stupid as to think of selling this place, I will not hesitate to buy it, because it is Paradise on earth.' Of course I agreed with him. We had a glass of wine and laughed together at the thought of anyone selling a bit of Paradise.

Yet I *have* made up my mind to sell 'Living Waters'. A most difficult, no, a horrendous decision, but the right one. First of all, too many ghosts still lurk here from a happy past, and this makes me not only sad and sentimental, but occasionally even tragic in mood. And then there are the economics; the mortgage that I cannot keep up much longer on my own. So we have agreed, Glen and I, to skim the coast all the way to Spain and Italy, to search for another, smaller place, closer to a village and with running water and electricity.

No other house or place has ever been so much a part of my life, and as the decision was made, something in me died.

December 3rd (yet another full moon)
Today I started the most difficult of tasks, namely trying to tell the story of my life. Glen looked at me in astonishment. I had stacked up wood for the night; laid a mattress down in front of the fireplace. I had decided to work through the night. If I hadn't made it a bit dramatic, I would never have started.

'Why can't you behave normally?' he said finally. The sky wasn't normal either. It was electric and of a rich purple colour with small, flamingo pink clouds all moving too fast. The sky is not always as mad as that. I decided therefore that it was a fine start. The music for the night would be madrigals; the fare light salad, cheese and wine.

December 5th
Colette wrote of those days and nights when solitude is like a heady wine that intoxicates you with freedom. I must say I don't feel any bloody intoxication, not yet anyway – only pain, going back into my past.

Assembly Point

SCHEDULE FOR MYSELF

1. Try to read at least 100 pages a day, something that has nothing to do with my work.
2. Concentrate on remembering dreams, however late I go to bed.
3. Keep myself tidy, not too many safety-pins in clothes.
4. Clean my nails at least twice a day.
5. A walk every day, no matter what the weather is like. Must look at horizons, not only concentrate on myself and the past.
6. One day off for friends, cinema, market and letters.

Today I looked for truffles in a blustery mistral and picked herbs for drying.

December 16th

I am losing touch with reality. Day and night merge into one another. I *like* this lopsided time.

Market day – the truffle men standing outside the café look like trolls, with their ugly caps and big pompoms, shouting to one another as if they were still in the woods, making big rude gestures. The egg man, on his small stool with his wicker basket in front of him filled with speckled eggs, is beginning to look more and more like an egg himself. Algerian women carrying flapping chickens under their arms look like wild birds, their shawls and long skirts billowing in the wind. Metre-long sausages and wild boars; hares and pheasants hang on steel frames in front of the café; it's for the Christmas lottery. Snow on the ground but spring in the air. Talking Nietzsche with Argentinian philosopher friend, buying tangerines from Corsica, smoked ham from Ardèche, shiny black olives from Provence, making *coq au vin* tonight.

December 19th

Glen cuts himself while machine-sawing wood. He bleeds profusely and almost shouts at me in anger: 'You and your herbs . . . haven't you got something that stops the blood?' Of course I have – yarrow – and it also happens to grow just where he is standing. I grab it and chew it before applying it to his wound. The bleeding stops at once. Almost inaudibly, Glen says: 'Not normal.' Yarrow has always worked when I have used it this way. It was not for nothing that old Achilles called it 'herb militaris'.

December 22nd
Colette once more: 'I have never had much to do with men whom other men called great. They seem so worried about their reputation and so frightened to lose it. I have always, it seems to me, preferred obscure people, be they men or women.'

December 24th
Christmas picnic by the green waterfall at the mouth of the grotto, and just outside it a huge roaring fire. The pinkest of all rosé wines cooling in the freezing water of the river. Tasty Algerian sausages smoking on the grill with herbed chickens, hot garlic bread. Suddenly, the bluest of all kingfishers flies like an arrow over the green swirling water. I decide it must be a good omen and I consider it my Christmas present.

December 24th – midnight
Autobiography an impossibility, yet I shall plug on nevertheless.

On Not Being a Star
...Being a Star

I know beforehand that my course in life
will be far from safe.

Vincent Van Gogh to his brother, Theo

In the autumn of 1945, the English film director Basil
Dearden came to Sweden to test for the leading female part
in a film to be called *Frieda*. The film tried to face the then
controversial topic of how to treat the Germans after the war.
A young British serviceman brings back a German girlfriend
to his rather stiff middle-class home, and the trouble begins.
It was typical that the film company had gone to Scandinavia
rather than to Germany; they were themselves prejudiced
against having a German actress in the part, feeling that it
was too soon after the war. I had forgotten all my English by
this time, but none the less I landed the part. Since I had
managed to follow his directing instructions, Dearden felt
that I would be able to pick up the language again without
too much difficulty.

My actor friends thought me completely mad when they
heard I'd be leaving the National Theatre for a year. 'What if
you are not a success?' they said. As usual I turned to Calle
for guidance, for security. 'Trust yourself,' he said. 'Dare to
stand up for yourself, no matter what change. Never allow
yourself to become too settled; learn that there is no security.'

I arrived in London in 1946 with my husband, child and

nurse. We had come by boat, train and, finally, taken a taxi to Ealing Studios, where we were ushered into Sir Michael Balcon's office and treated like VIPs, although we neither looked, felt nor behaved like them. We were more like Russian refugees, what with our wicker baskets, bags, bundles and tea-chests, all of which looked out of place in the well-upholstered room. As for the suitcase held together with string, even Martha-Stina, the nurse, had refused to have anything to do with it during the trip, although it seemed perfectly natural to me. There were many raised eyebrows and furtive smiles at our group and our belongings. I remember I was wrapped in a home-crocheted shawl that I had thought very special in Sweden. Here, I knew instinctively that I was wearing the wrong thing. I tried to take up as little space as possible, while Martha-Stina seemed to spread herself. In her smart, well-starched uniform, complete with hat, she was the only well-dressed person in our party and she knew it. She conversed in what seemed to me perfect English, while I talked in monosyllables. I was still shy and the truth was that I was rather scared of Martha-Stina. She intimidated me even then, when I knew that I was the reason we were all of us in England.

I was introduced to a Swedish woman called Siv-Inger. She was to be my interpreter.

In London at that time, I thought certain things were not very 'nice' – for instance, the flat that the studio had rented for us for the couple of weeks before we went on location. A bed-sitter in a basement in Victoria, so damp, dark and unfriendly that one wanted to get out as quickly as possible. Shillings for the gas meter, a mini coal fire in the lounge, the soggiest of breakfasts. What a difference from the neat little doll's house that we lived in on the outskirts of Stockholm, with its views of birch and pine. Here all I could see from the window was puddles and people's ankles and cats slinking through iron bars.

There were, of course, compensations. I was fascinated by the different attitudes to things, I loved the friendliness that people lavished on me, and I liked the eccentricity that seemed to be the norm. In my country there was no room for such things any more; you had to conform or else you were stared at, laughed at and pointed at. As a result, we had all become a bit grey and conformist.

Even so, I was glad to leave dirty London, which at that time had its fair share of yellow, pea-soupy fogs. Woodstock, near Oxford, could not have been more of a contrast. It reeked of tradition – which in theory I disapprove of, but can still fall for. Cobbled streets, beamed cottages, roses wherever you looked, a country inn; there was even, at the time, a little fair in the streets that made it all perfect, more like a film set than life. Then, behind the dolls' village, the castle, Blenheim – a fairy palace, with its park and lakes and bridges; I had never seen such a thing in my life. I was deeply impressed. And I was astonished at the behaviour of our leading man, who always seemed to be late for his morning call. When we, on time, went to fetch him in the morning, we would find him idly sipping champagne. Dear, was I shocked.

Perhaps all the stars lived like that; anyway, for the moment that's what I thought. They played golf and rode and seemed to be bored with their filmwork, not appearing to take it very seriously. Basil Dearden told me later that he thought me stiff and reserved, with no humour, no private personality, but that he was amazed by what came out in front of the cameras. I worked harder, he said, than any actress he had ever known. He was the typical tough director, with little regard for actors, and he treated people somewhat sharply. I believe that if I had spoken English at the time, we would not have got on any better – quite the reverse, in fact.

One day, to my great delight, we were all invited to the Palace and there I met a man that I got on with famously from the word 'go'. Basil sulked in a corner. 'I knew she could speak English,' he whispered to Siv-Inger. Well, I suppose I must have been able to communicate a bit by now, although I do remember Tutte helping out. Everybody was surprised to see me so gay and animated, so different from my normal silent self.

As we left, the nice jovial man kissed me on the cheeks.

'You'd better watch out – in the old days women used to be burnt for such things as you say,' he laughed. 'But if you ever get into trouble, tell them that I approve.'

That was the first and last time that I met Churchill. Having no interest in politics then I'd had no idea who I'd been talking to and had not been overawed like some of the others. To me, he was just someone with whom I was able to open up and be myself. I was told by Siv-Inger, later, that I had been playing a smart game. But names, including my own, have never meant very much to me. No, I can't work myself up to be excited about a name. It has frightened me when I have been introduced as a sort of celebrity; it has made me feel uncomfortable and unreal, as if something was expected of me, as if I was being judged for my name and not for myself.

The studio managed to do a bit better for my second home in London, as I had absolutely refused to go back to the bed-sitter. This time it was a flat in Dolphin Square, also near Victoria, with long, arching corridors, rather hospital-like but with three rooms and two bathrooms, so that Martha-Stina had her own quarters. I remember distinctly that the baby slept in two armchairs pushed together. God knows why we didn't buy a cot.

I still went to the studio by underground. It took me about an hour. I had refused the offer of a car from the studio because of my fear of having to talk to the chauffeur. What on earth could I have said to him? I don't remember if I met people on set: being so shy, I didn't dare to make conversation. I stayed small, talked in a hushed voice. I think that deep inside me lurked a midget that refused to grow up. I worked hard, got up before dawn and returned late: there seemed to be a lot of overtime in those days. Six months it took to make the film; that was yet another surprise to me. In Sweden, four or five weeks was the usual time allocated. The machinery seemed cumbersome and there were a lot more people around, which slowed things down.

As for my private life, I have no idea what Tutte did during this time, only that he spent a part of every day training at Sadler's Wells. I tried as hard as I could to be interested in Tutte's ideas, his struggles, went to ballets with him, became friends with his friends, all connected with the dancing world, which wasn't really my scene at all. I began to realise that I had put him in an awkward position. Perhaps in order to join my world, he had decided to become an actor. Producers helped out for my sake, which I found embarrassing, giving him small parts in movies that I starred in. Tutte found it equally embarrassing, of course, but could not admit it, and so, naturally enough, took all his anger and frustration out on me. For my part, I was not sure that he was as good an actor as he was a dancer. Actually he did make it, but not until some years later, as a character actor in British films.

Some of the other stars in England at that time were Margaret Lockwood, Anna Neagle, Vivien Leigh and Valerie Hobson. I met them all at the very first Royal Command Performance after the war, with me looking like a milkmaid in her first long dress in comparison with all the finery, the feathers and the jewellery the others wore. Even the girls from the Rank Charm School looked more sophisticated and glamorous than I did; they had an assurance and poise that I envied. I was told later that Vivien Leigh had said how very clever it was of me to dress so simply; that in my black and white dress I had stood out against their sequinned ball-gowns. At that time I didn't own any jewellery, I wore no make-up at all and I hadn't even bothered to go to a hairdresser, though being the hygienic Swede I did have my dress cleaned. It's important to remember that, coming from a country that isn't overawed by royalty, I wasn't that impressed or nervous at the thought of shaking hands with the Queen – and, as for hairdressers, I never went to them, nor do I now. I didn't do the simplicity bit for effect; it just didn't occur to me to get a new dress for such an occasion. When David Henley, director of the Rank Charm School, found that it was the only long dress I had, he said: 'My dear girl, if I had known, we would have sent you to Hartnell.'

I could not have been further from what a film star should be or act like. I was, according to public opinion, so untypical that it wasn't even *funny*. The boys who did the publicity at Ealing studios were forever tearing their hair at my antics and my sincerity, which they called 'simple'. To them, I was doing a dumb thing, trying to be honest whenever I had an interview. I was so 'blue-eyed' that, when thinking back on it now, I shudder with horror. As for my appearance, even my best friends said that I ought to try dressing a bit better – that I looked as if I had dressed against the wind, and if I did put on a new dress I would somehow manage to make it look worn and crumpled in a matter of minutes.

This uncompromising me was not easy to grasp, not even for myself. The exterior was simple enough, but the interior person was complex, still half-developed and stuck at the awkward age. I didn't really communicate with anyone, not even Tutte, who was the person closest to me at that time. We had grown more apart over the years. He had become as opinionated and aggressive as he was unsure of himself. Not being able to earn his living had begun to destroy him, little by little, and when he began to take it out on me, I started to feel it was all my fault. As a result, I became increasingly timid and had very little to say for myself. Our physical relationship was almost a total flop. Even though we had produced a child, neither of us knew anything about sex; we never talked about it and we certainly never read anything on the subject. I didn't even know what an orgasm was. We just played the mum-dad act and held hands from time to time. I was intensely anxious in those early days and kept myself to myself far too much.

I also had the public pressures to cope with. At this time, I did feel like a foreigner in England, and the star system was quite alien to me. I was being pushed, however gently, into a position that I didn't like, or, for that matter, approve of. It seemed to me a bit silly to try and live up to something that I wasn't. For the first time, I was encountering the kind of hysterical worship that gathers round popular actors and actresses. Since I not only felt rather ordinary but actually was rather ordinary, the publicity people had to do their damnedest to make me *extra*ordinary. That is, they tried to convey my very simplicity as being something strange and rare. It was all they could do, in order to make me appear more interesting than I was.

Every Swedish actress in those days was compared to Garbo and Bergman; it was all too easy. I was the first to see that I did not have Garbo's austere, tragic beauty; nor did I have Bergman's cosiness or, for that matter, her naturalness – that fresh outdoor look that was regarded as a Swedish characteristic. As a matter of fact, I was not at all a typical Scandinavian. My hair was mousy rather than ashen blonde (or Swedish blonde, as it was called), and I was small-boned, not tall like the other stars.

But I came first in the poll of the year's best actress: the English decided that they would like to take Frieda into their homes. It was a fair and honest film and very serious indeed: the *New York Herald Tribune* commented that while it was not a film for ordinary people, it was certainly useful for students of sociology. But now I had to go back home and fulfil my contract with the National Theatre – and also make a film with Ingmar Bergman.

On Not Conforming

Pray that success will not come any faster
than you are able to endure it.

Elbert Hubbard, *The Notebook* (1927)

Music in the Dark was to be my first and last picture with
Ingmar Bergman directing. It was 1947.

Tutte had gone to Norway on a job. At Ingmar's suggestion, I moved to a cheap little pension where he and the
leading man were staying. It was there I was unfaithful for
the first time in my marriage. It's not really surprising that it
happened. I was still a blank page, so much to be filled in – a
star perhaps, but also only a child.

I had met Ingmar when making *Frenzy* but he had been
quiet, evasive, and charming, in a way that I didn't quite
trust: there had been no communication between us. Now I
suppose he wanted to remedy this, to have me at close
quarters so as to be able to observe and guide me more
directly. I was quite happy to comply because I had recognised how good a director he was. We needed each other;
the nets closed in. I was with him and the actor from morn to
night, every single day except week-ends, when I fled back
to doll's-house-ville. Ingmar threw his hands up in horror
when he heard about my little life in the suburbs.

I soon realised that Ingmar needed a close relationship
with his actors, to try to get to know them inside-out.
Sometimes I feared those searching eyes that wanted to

know our innermost secrets, and I would withdraw. I felt he wanted us to be dependent on him emotionally. He seemed to want to understand me both as an actress and as a woman, but as I was not yet mature, I can't have been that much of an inspiration. This was Ingmar's fourth film and he was finding his way with the medium, as a director too. It was not until a few years later, in 1955, that he had his big success with *Smiles of a Summer Night*.

On the first day of shooting *Music in the Dark* we celebrated an ancient Swedish custom which takes place every December 13th in the early morning. A woman is chosen to be Lucia, the bringer of light into the darkest day of the year. I was Lucia, with a crown of candles on my head; Ingmar was one of the choirboys, dressed up in a white night-shirt and a tall paper hat with stars. A strange sight: his diabolical laugh and strange half-smile didn't fit the costume . . . It was also odd to see him at night in bed, dressed from top to toe in a white, or was it pink, flannel romper suit, the kind that babies wear, complete with feet, all zipped up. His current wife had made it for him; he said he felt safe in that kind of clothing at night. It was not exactly sexy but it was funny and endearing. What's more, he was very proud of his night-gear and he didn't mind us seeing him in it – it made him appear vulnerable and childish. What I think surprised me about Ingmar more than anything else was the old-mannish habits he had acquired at such a young age.

He frequented an old-fashioned restaurant which was not all that good, although it had a certain reputation. He ate very Swedish food, drank his bottle of beer, sat always at the same table, talked to the same people. He was very choosy who he talked to and, when he did, it was always at his instigation. Most of the time he listened; he is the best listener I have ever known. He attracted me and repelled me at the same time. But if you got his attention, you could not help being excited by him. His descriptions of people were accurate and sometimes cruel: he had a slightly acid brand of humour, and when he had a remark to make, it came after a long period of silence. His language was full of slang expressions – but it was a rich vocabulary all the same.

There were so many stories about him – a lot of them fabricated, I'm sure, by people who both hated and loved him. He made a point of avoiding the limelight. He gave only one big press reception before he started the film, and after that the studio was closed to visitors. But sometimes he would grant a personal interview in his home and shout his mouth off about his latest love. Somehow, that image of him acting up to the media didn't fit in, it seemed out of character. He was playing games, even with his public, in order to confuse them, as he did with all of us, however close we came to him. But his complexity was fascinating: it made you alert, it kept you on your toes, because you never knew when the sting would come, or the loving embrace. Everyone tiptoed in the studio while he rehearsed the actors, a deadly hush like a funeral parlour. Nobody dared to yawn, even if time was dragging. If he saw anyone beginning to slacken off and taking on a sleepy expression, he would watch them intently and then, when the mouth showed the first dangerous symptom of the beginning of a yawn, he would pounce and show the criminal the door . . . His temper was something that we all feared: an egotistical anger that was able to change the atmosphere in the whole studio.

A dictator, yes of course. But he managed to get amazing results from his actors and his staff, who idolised him and stayed with him picture after picture, however badly they were treated sometimes . . . And he could be fun, too, in his very special personal way that made you forget the blows. And then of course there were those romper suits that endeared him to me, the lonely frozen child in him that not everyone was to see. The god-fearing, doomsday-ridden son of a priest that he showed us in his films was really a home-bird who hated to travel, to live in hotels, to eat foreign food. When all was said and done, he needed his lot of hens where he was the king rooster . . . In the studio, for lunch, he would withdraw to his room to drink his cup of tea and eat a piece of rye bread, a boiled egg; he would hardly ever come into the canteen. When he did, all life would suddenly stop and soon only his voice would be heard, his voice and his satanic laughter.

Ingmar can be extraordinarily close to people, too close for comfort. A demonic closeness; you don't feel safe. It is as if he could take you with him into his own remoteness. Yet it has nothing to do with true communication. It's more like a laying on of hands, or hypnosis, or witchcraft.

He is a formidable, intimidating person, who can put on the charm at one moment and leave you out in the cold the next, who draws out both good and bad in people and can make them very dependent on him. I had a certain reserve with Ingmar, a reserve that I never got over, however closely we worked together. I didn't want to be one of his puppets. Although I will never deny his mastery, I didn't feel that excitement I had experienced with Alf Sjöberg, who really inspired me and got the most out of me without doing a Svengali act. Whenever I am asked what I think of Ingmar Bergman, I always say the same thing: 'You don't necessarily need to like genius, but you can stand aside and admire it.'

Music in the Dark was basically a rather sentimental love story about a young man who goes blind through an accident and a young girl who falls in love with him. What Ingmar was interested in was the man's loss of identity, his loneliness and his despair.

In an earlier film, Ingmar said, 'You can't be alone. You have to have someone to love and take care of. Otherwise you might just as well be dead.' In this film, Ingmar wanted to show that he could be positive for a change; mind you, he couldn't help squeezing in some anguished scenes that the critics felt were artificial and not necessary to the story. All in all, it was not the lyrical, poetic film that Bergman had promised. As an actress, I came out of it well, mainly because I had been typecast as the sensual robust peasant girl. It was the perfect *anima* part . . . the mother figure, however young – the madonna, the typical feminine that yields, gives, and takes any kind of punishment – the typical woman.

There is no doubt that Ingmar drew a good performance out of me but he could have got more depth, perhaps. There was something missing in our relationship, something very important to both of us – which was *trust*. We eyed each other with suspicion. But also, at that time, I didn't really respect the cinema as I came to do later on. At the National Theatre, they despised, or anyway looked down on, film actors. You played in films for the easy money, not for love or as a vocation. Perhaps some of these things smeared off on me. I was easily swayed by strong opinions when they came from people I admired – and at that time, the theatre was my life; I was passionate about it. It had, after all, given me what little strength and confidence I had. The theatre was my real world, where I could dare to live out all the feelings I had kept hidden under my demure façade.

While I was working on *Music in the Dark*, I hired a cook-cum-housekeeper who frightened me more than Martha-Stina did. She had obviously seen better days and she talked endlessly about her noble ancestry. She treated Tutte and me like dirty 'proles'. In her eyes, we were just children and upstarts, and if we dared to be late for dinner, oh dear, the scenes she created. I somehow managed to get up enough courage to give her the sack. '*Nouveaux riches*,' she shouted, 'vulgarians.' Meanwhile the Swedish press was still harping on my 'simplicity'. I was good copy – the new star who had made it both at home and abroad. 'The same old Mai,' they wrote. 'You would think that she was on the way to the factory, not to the National Theatre. She is so unassuming that she almost obliterates herself.' And then they would scold me patronisingly: 'It's about time you grew up a little, Mai, you are a big girl now.' 'If she has money, which she must have by now, she certainly doesn't show it; pity, a little more poise, or at least neatness, would pay off.' 'She is a terrible disappointment in reality,' screamed another. ' "I live a very ordinary life," she said, looking like any old housewife. Perhaps Mai will have to change her tune when Hollywood knocks on the door. They will never accept you as you are now, Mai.'

That haunted refugee look that they had prepared for me in England, I now adopted for private use – the scarf and the mackintosh became my permanent outfit, both off and on the screen. For years to come, I encountered people who thought they recognised me as 'Mai Zetterling'; if not, I must at least be her sister. I was often taken for the maid as I opened the door in my home, or for the nurse when I walked the child in a park, but I was relieved when people didn't recognise me.

I was supposed to go back to England to make another film with Basil Dearden, *Saraband for Dead Lovers*, but to my great dismay I found myself pregnant again. David Henley of Rank came over to Sweden and I had to break the news to him. He was shocked: 'Are you that little concerned about your career?' I *was* concerned, but I still knew nothing about preventatives: my whole attitude towards such things was mind-boggling. I didn't really want children, was not particularly interested in them; nor was Tutte. I was hooked on my work, which made me feel more alive than anything else. I didn't understand the responsibilities of motherhood: my daughter was a doll that I hired someone to take care of, whom I sometimes played with and basically cared and catered for but whom I didn't miss if I had to be away from home. And now I was having another. I had not the slightest intention of stopping the pregnancy, and no one suggested it to me, though I do remember David Henley asking me if I really wanted another child at such an important juncture in my career and pointing out that I would have plenty of time for children later, as I was so young – but that is as far as it went.

Tutte was overjoyed – largely, I think, because he wanted me to slow down, to have me at home for a bit. I tried as hard as I could to become dependent on him, to make him feel better about my success. There was a lot of game-playing for the sake of staying married. I did actually believe, when he told me that he had been the reason for my success, that without him I would be nothing.

We lie loudest when we lie to ourselves.
                                    Eric Hoffer, 1954

As for pregnancy, I just hated it. The supposedly greatest experience in a woman's life was the worst thing that could have happened to me.

It was a boy this time and, as before, the child was brought
to the theatre and fed in the wings at rehearsal. I was playing
Electra in *The Flies* by Jean-Paul Sartre, a fury of hate and
passion. It was a wild role that took all the energy I had left,
only two months after the birth. On the first night, when the
author was there, I fainted between two long speeches and
yet again when I ran into the wings. Nobody seemed to
notice except the prompter, certainly not Sartre, who described me as 'an important *tragédienne* of the century'.

I must admit that I was now becoming scared of all the
acclaim. What's more, I felt guilty about it. It didn't help that
I lived in an environment that seemed to be based on guilt. A
Calvinist lurks in the soul of most Swedes, and I was no
exception. Tutte withdrew into himself, becoming more and
more depressed. 'Do you think I like being called "Mr
Zetterling", having to ask you for money, living on your
success?'

Finally, I decided to accept a seven-year contract with
Rank in England. There were many reasons for this decision,
however much everyone warned me against it. I knew that I
wanted to go further afield and not stay in Sweden, which
already seemed to have grown smaller after my interlude in
England. I did not want to end up at the National Theatre,
with all its inbuilt security, and be pensioned off at sixty –
becoming a sort of monument to Swedish theatrical history.

Tutte shared my decision. Perhaps he felt that it gave him
another chance; perhaps England would be kinder to him.
He went eagerly to London to start looking for a house for us
all to live in, while I began rehearsing Federico García
Lorca's *The House of Bernarda Alba*, a play with only women
in the cast, all yearning for a man to change their lives. This
time I was to be a dark, sensual Spanish girl; acting against
type. If I succeeded, it was mainly thanks to Sjöberg – but
also, perhaps, because of all the locked-up passion that I still
had within me.

I was intrigued by the actress with whom I shared a
dressing-room. She was a real 'femme fatale'. In the old days
one would have called her a vamp; she was a beauty, with a
striking personality and an amazing figure. All the boys

were in love with her and so was I. I looked at her with astonishment, perhaps in awe more than anything else. Sometimes she would treat her admirers with an iron hand, after having been all milk and honey, cajoling them until they followed every one of her whims and orders without hesitation. She flirted with one and all and she flirted with me. I became one of the admiring court, one of her little slaves. When she called me her 'little white dove', I was in heaven. She was generous: she gave me presents and big sensual wet kisses, smack on the lips, no little dry pecks on the cheeks. She was lovely and friendly but she got me to do all the dirty work, like pushing away the more boring of her admirers and making me run errands for her – which I loved doing. She was a very talented actress and I dreamed of being like her, but knew I never could. I didn't understand what she saw in me, why I was her friend. I was nothing to look at – I wore little Edith Piaf dresses, black with white lace collars; I was small and bony with tiny breasts and short stocky legs; though some called me pretty, I faded to nothing in the company of the majestic Valkyrie.

One of her pet names for me was 'my mousy angel'. I played that part perfectly; I had a schoolgirl crush on her, but it didn't go further than holding hands which, however innocent, was too much for me, as I spent such a lot of time dreaming about her. The word 'homosexuality' was not part of my vocabulary. I had no idea what it meant and the mere thought of it scared me.

She wanted to be my friend and, being quite friendless at that time, I hankered after warmth. I wanted to share laughter and secrets, to have a real friend; but deep down, I mistrusted her friendship, seeing how she misused people around her. I fitted in as one of her slaves, no more than that, so I started to withdraw, although it hurt. I began to wonder if she was more fond of my so-called reputation than anything else and I didn't understand the feelings she had awakened in me. I was still very much an adolescent, although I was twenty-three and the mother of two children.

Central Casting Office: Stereotypes Wanted

Abnormal, *adj.*: not conforming to standard.
In matters of thought and conduct,
to be independent is to be abnormal.
To be abnormal is to be detested.

The Devil's Dictionary, Ambrose Bierce (1881–1911)

The house Tutte found for us in England – 'Woodlea', mock-Tudor, small and compact – was certainly a lot larger than the doll's house in Sweden, and the seven acres that went with it seemed immense in comparison with our grassy patch at home. It had two fair-sized rooms downstairs, three bedrooms and a kind of cubby-hole. It lay north of London near a village called Bovingdon.

Martha-Stina was still with us and as bossy as ever. Tutte's brother, Thorleif, came to live with us, in true Jewish family tradition, and in fact turned out to be a splendid substitute father for the children. Tutte day-dreamed, had impossible maniac expectations from life and did not want to get up in the mornings.

Tutte and I hoped we could live inconspicuously in this house as respected members of the community. But although I was a trained actress, in real life I was totally useless at pretending to be anything other than what I really was. That's why I was so laughably inadequate as the English housewife that I was determined to be in between film engagements.

My seven-year contract was well paid but not as well paid as one might think. It meant a certain security for the family, which I was completely responsible for as Tutte could not get any work in England, mainly for work-permit reasons. The only trouble with this new contract was that I had to do what the big bosses decided, which was disastrous.

It began with a film called *Portrait from Life*, in which once again I played the refugee part. I had been typecast; my image was set. I must have trudged, looking pathetic, through more bombed cities and rehabilitation camps than any other living actress. In the meantime, I was among the US nominations for best actress of the year for my part in *Frieda*. I was amazed, because the role of Frieda, for an actress, was a poor five-finger exercise, but I had begun to realise that the cinema did not expect great acting talent as much as a personality who could become a star.

For my next role, I was pushed into *The Bad Lord Byron* as Teresa Guiccioli. I could not have agreed more when the press shouted: 'Bad Lord Byron, Too Bad.' 1948 wasn't one of the cinema's golden years.

It was the theatre which saved me from utter despair. I realised after a year or so that I had made a terrible mistake in signing that damned seven-year contract. The British film industry was just trying to ape the American one. I was thrilled when I got the part of Hedwig in a revival of Ibsen's *The Wild Duck* at St Martin's Theatre, with Anton Walbrook, Fay Compton and Miles Malleson. To everyone's surprise, it was a knock-out success, and ran for almost a year.

In the middle of the run, I met Jacob Epstein. Actually, it was Kathleen, his wife, who made the overture, and told me that he wanted to sculpt me. I had no idea who Epstein was – it was Tutte who said, 'Of course you must say yes,' and informed me that he was a very famous sculptor. At the first meeting, I was totally bowled over by him. He greeted me with hands full of clay, in baggy and well-worn trousers, with a funny cap over the curly grey locks, which made him look like an elderly cherub. He had twinkling, sparkling eyes, and he was warm and kind. I had never met anybody like him. He was the simplest of men; also the most complex.

He had an accent which I later recognised as that of a Bronx cabman and he was full of the most extraordinary stories about people whom he had met: Isadora Duncan, Bernard Shaw, Einstein, Picasso, Augustus John, Tagore. I was enthralled . . . I was in love.

At that very first sitting, he made hundreds of little clay worms. I can't describe them in any other way, and he talked to them as if they were his friends. There was nothing on the stick that seemed remotely likely to become my head. Slowly the first little worm got caught on it, then another, and each was given a message as it was added. After an hour or so I suppose a hundred or more of those little worms were on the stick. The next sitting, the same procedure. In the end I found the courage to ask him – why all those worms. 'Why?' he said, surprised. 'I must find your soul, don't you see.'

I did see what he meant – and so, slowly and very carefully, I emerged out of the clay worms.

Then there were the musical evenings in his studio, sitting between the giant sculptures, the 'Resurrection' group, 'Social Consciousness'; he seemed larger than them all. He would dissolve in tears or laughter, depending on what the concert was: Bach, Schubert or bongo drums. I don't know if I have admired anyone as I did Epstein; he taught me more about humility, I think, than anybody else in my life. When he met a person, he would say simply, 'I sculpt, what do you do?' He came to me at a very important time. He was a kind of father figure, so much wiser than anyone I had ever met, and yet we had many things in common; like me, he was an instinctive rebel, and he too had left school in his early teens. Kathleen, his wife, I didn't understand, or was it just that I didn't want to understand her; was I slightly jealous, perhaps? She had him all to herself. He loved the *St Matthew Passion* and tried to make me go and listen to it, as well as to Bach's B Minor Mass. Now I love both these works, but at that time I was not ready for them.

Sometimes I went with them to the Caprice Restaurant, which was very posh, but he never changed out of his old working clothes when he went out and would hand in his shabby old cap to the cloakroom attendant.

I romanticised and dramatised – but Epstein was certainly a very important influence on my life. Whenever I have come across his kind of greatness, I have encountered the same simplicity, and I find that immensely moving. My vocabulary was too scant at the time, I was too childish, and in the end we lost touch. Also, he had many guardians . . .

My bad-luck contract with Rank continued. They made me say no to a film of *Miss Julie*, which Alf Sjöberg directed; it almost broke my heart, I so loved working with him. Instead, I played yet another refugee in a charade of a film called *The Lost People*, with Richard Attenborough, prompting one critic to comment caustically: 'In view of the poor parts she has been getting in English studios . . . Miss Zetterling begins to seem like something of a displaced person herself.' And then, dressed up as a doll in a film version of Somerset Maugham's *Quartet*, I played a naughty girl in Monte Carlo. But for some reason I had become popular in Britain, in spite of my run of bad parts.

In the village where Tutte and I lived, I was classed as half-funny, half-mad. To cheer myself up, I bought a small monkey. It was in a pet shop opposite the theatre and looked as sad and forlorn as I felt. I called him Chico; he was minute and loved me desperately and I took him everywhere with me, even into my dressing-room in the theatre, to the consternation and horror of my dresser.

Once, Chico escaped from the house. A sedate little tea party was going on under some trees a few gardens away: three old ladies with the local vicar. Suddenly Chico jumped from the trees above them and snatched the most delectable of the cakes. Two of the ladies fainted, certain that the devil in disguise had visited them.

To complete the menagerie, there was a goat and my Harrods chickens. There was still a great shortage of food and I had thought that a few fresh eggs would be good for the children, so off I went to Harrods pet shop and chose the most decadent-looking hens, snowy white with great tufty furry feet. They didn't look a bit like chickens; they looked positively indecent, and that's what I had liked about them. As for the cock, I was still ignorant about all matters of sex; I thought he was necessary so that eggs could be produced. Well, he nearly killed the two hens that I had bought at such great expense, with his ardour or his chauvinism, or whatever you want to call it. And no eggs – except when Tutte played a joke on me.

Every morning about five, before setting out for the studio, I would creep into the chicken hut armed with a torch, and see if there was an egg to collect. One day, to my delight, there was. I ran back with great excitement but when I saw the faces of the Lemkow brothers, I began to be suspicious and quite rightly so because, on the back of the damned egg, which was made of porcelain, it said 'Harrods'.

Woodlea didn't seem a lucky place. Our Norwegian housekeeper got raped in a ditch by a soldier; Tutte was constantly refused work-permits, which meant that he had to stay at home training for ballets that he could never dance in, feeling useless; and there were continual problems with our daughter: she didn't seem to fit in, not wanting to play with other children, and was moody, difficult and backward for her age.

I fell in love easily those days – I was on the look-out for 'happiness'. I was twenty-five, he was a Frenchman some fifteen years older. We went together to France for a holiday and for the first time in my life I looked a bit like a star because I had bought up the glamorous clothes from my last picture at less than half the cost. We went to Le Cannet, above Cannes; it was fashionable at the time and I was happy in my body for the first time in my life.

Despite my feelings of guilt, because I had, as it were, run away from home, husband and children, I was grateful. Here was a man who put me on the map, physically, someone who was able to bring out my sensuality for the very first time. The seemingly cold Swede was after all a full-blooded woman. I was a late developer. I felt that I had just begun my life; the only time I had felt truly alive before then was when I had been on the stage.

But despite the ecstasy, my guilt won through and I left him, taking a train from Arles back 'home' to Bovingdon, England. There I discovered that my most recent film, *The*

Romantic Age, was a resounding flop too. 'What a tragedy, what a travesty of star-building,' one critic wrote. In 1950, numerous articles were published about the eighty Rank stars being more or less totally wasted, if not destroyed.

I found myself pregnant yet again and this time I knew it would have been very wrong indeed to have had the child. In England in those days an abortion was hard to accomplish; it was strictly for people with money. Mine was done by two Hungarian peasants on a kitchen table with a local anaesthetic. The next day they rang up and asked: 'Are you still alive?' Hungarian humour, I suppose. I was miserable and very alone and confused as to what to do.

I hadn't told my lover about the child until after it was all done. He was upset, so was Tutte; so was I. I packed my bag and left them all. I knew that, for the moment, my children were taken care of by people whom I paid, and I went off to sort things out for the future. I hoped it was not going to be too long. It was a low point in my life and my way was lonely, independent and sad.

I moved into a strange little family hotel run by an ageing opera singer and her sister. There was always somebody singing Italian arias, or practising on the piano. It was a noisy and friendly atmosphere and a lot of lonely frustrated ladies seemed to be living there, who met in the kitchen at all hours of day and night.

Lonely men meet in pubs, bars, clubs to tell about their misfortunes or brag about their conquests. Women do it differently. They seem to congregate in second-rate hotels or pensions run by ageing spinsters. I have come across these places in London, Paris, New York, filled with ladies gone bulky and blowsy and bitter. In these establishments the cocktail hour seems to extend for ever. Sad places full of gloom, with no difference between night and day, as the heavy curtains are always drawn against the cruel light.

At least I was never alone in that family hotel, or, let's say, I didn't need to be alone; everyone seemed to have love problems of some kind and needed to talk. It was grisly comfort but it *was* comfort. My heart-strings were being pulled all the time, mainly because of not seeing the children

87

but also I was, of course, feeling guilty because I was told that I was wicked and bad and cared more for myself than my children . . . What was wrong with me? Why could I not put up with a mediocre marriage for the sake of the children like so many other women? I started to believe what I was told, that I was an unnatural mother.

I had been 'allowed' by Rank to take a short-season engagement at the Lyric, Hammersmith to play Nina in Chekhov's *The Seagull*, with a cast headed by Paul Scofield. I was treated with respect again by the critics, but I was a stranger in the company. I felt they didn't take me seriously because they saw me as a film star rather than as an actress. I also worked in a way that was totally foreign to them. The Stanislavsky method had never really caught on in England, and although I didn't pursue the topic, they knew and found out about it through my behaviour before and during performances. I would arrive several hours before curtain up and would hardly talk to my dresser when she arrived. I had tried to warn her that this would happen, but she probably thought I was stuck-up and didn't want to converse with her. I had made lengthy notes about the childhood of Nina, with masses of detail, and during the performance I would never talk in the wings to the other actors. I wanted to keep my concentration and be Nina in between the scenes as well, which I acted out in my imagination.

This method of acting was, for me, very important. It was a way of forgetting myself and becoming another human being, if only for a few hours, and it gave a springboard to inspiration, this tightly-drawn circle. The method had been taught to me by Calle in Sweden and I carried it with me all my time as an actress on the stage. It helped me no end, as I was basically desperately shy and couldn't bear the idea of walking on to the stage as Mai Zetterling. And I think it worked for me. It certainly was exciting. Through my concentration I would almost, in my mind's eye, have visions of the various kind of Ninas I had been and see her childhood with tremendous clarity. It helped me to build up the character vividly for myself, and I believe for the audience as well.

At that low ebb in my life, I met my wizard accountant, Arpad Rosner, who wrote poetry at night between the ledgers, who was passionate about life, politics, dance, art, who told me funny stories in broken Hungarian that I didn't understand; who complained about me not having enough humour and about my total lack of organisation when it came to money matters. 'Where has all the money gone, Mai?' he would ask, and dance about the room, showing me the ways in which the great master Laban, whom he had worked under, made words and movement into a special art form.

I remember I paid a lot of bills in those days. I was in charge of seven people, had a big car which I couldn't drive, a flat in London, a half-time secretary for the company that my husband and his brother and myself had formed with David Henley (whom we also paid). Then there were school bills and maids, gardeners . . . 'You are living beyond your means, Mai,' Arpad shouted. 'You must wake up to reality, look at facts, sums, you must stop being a child.' By this time, he would be foaming at the mouth with excitement, spitting out the consonants so hard that you almost needed an umbrella – and then he would recite his latest poem. Dear Arpad, what would I have done without you?

Not only did Arpad come to my rescue, but also the theatre helped me beyond anything that I could have done for myself. I was asked to appear in a play by Jean Anouilh called *Point of Departure,* based on the Orpheus and Eurydice legend. In it would be another Rank star, Dirk Bogarde. Just at that time, we, the eighty Rank stars, had all of us been given a chance either to break our contracts or take a much lower salary. There was no doubt in my mind, nor in Dirk's, that we should get out. The British film industry was at a very low ebb. They had done their best to destroy the future for their so-called stars. As for myself, I was rather less sought-after now that I had made those bad films: *The Bad Lord Byron, The Lost People* and another terrible film called *Blackmail.* I was frightened but I was free.

I had found myself a small flat. The children were at boarding-school; I could not yet afford to have them with me. I needed more money, as I seemed to be paying out more than ever: lawyers, accountants, the annulling of the company.

Whilst the film *Blackmail* sank without trace, the production of *Point of Departure* ran for almost nine months, and stopped only because Dirk Bogarde could not take the strain of a long run. For a hypersensitive actor, as he was, it can seem like a prison sentence, however deeply committed you are. It is a hard thing to explain what actually happens to your brain in a long run. You are stuck in a routine, you cannot move away from the play's construction, lines have to be delivered, the same pauses given for effect. You become dehumanised, despite all the moments of inspiration. That's when a certain madness creeps into the brain, and the fear that all actors have becomes reality: you no longer know who you are, where you are, you temporarily lose control of yourself. It is even impossible to take a prompt from the stage manager, that is, if he is there at that very moment – he is so sure that you won't fluff your lines after thirty performances. It seems that the deafness in your brain lasts for minutes, when it most probably is only a matter of seconds. Dirk got physically ill from fear and nerves, so much so that he had to leave the cast. The play was never the same for me, even though as good an actor as Peter Finch took over.

Dirk and I had had an extraordinary relationship on the stage. In real life, we somehow avoided each other and were afraid at the same time. Everyone who saw the play was sure that we were having a great love affair. We were, but only on the stage. We loved one another passionately for three hours every day, lived out one of the greatest love stories of the world, in such truth and depth that life outside the theatre seemed shallow and unreal in comparison. In a sense, we could not have had a real love affair, even if we had wanted to. But it was also impossible, as Dirk had other interests outside the theatre which I could not compete with. I do believe that we were satisfied because we both lived out an unfulfilled dream of love.

When Dirk left, I was heartbroken, as if my lover had left

me in real life. Nobody could have taken his place; as I said, not even Peter Finch, who I did not have much of a *rapport* with on the stage but who, in real life, became my lover. He was a roaming fellow and had no bonds – neither had I, any longer. I truly liked Peter, an Australian outlaw character, wild and unruly, who despised himself for having become an actor. He hated the idea – it was not a man's job, in his opinion. He was a haunted, unhappy man, almost Swedish in his *angst* about life, angry with himself for having been caught in such a cheap trap: being an actor, even worse, a film star. Our relationship was brief. He was seducing women to prove something to himself; his heart was not in it, and for me he boozed too heavily, which I found hard to accept. It became a bit pathetic; it left me sad and tired.

Divorce cost money in those days. I was in a panic, and it was then that I made yet another blunder arising out of that damned insecurity as to where the money was going to come from. It had to come from me, but how? So I signed yet another fatal contract, this time with a freelance producer who made his private publicity lady write about me: 'She is out to put passion into 1951's pictures' – 'Passion girl of 1951.'

I had now become, as someone put it, 'Britain's Swedeheart'. I hated it.

It's such a cuckoo business. And it's a business you go into because you're egocentric. It's a very embarrassing profession.

Katharine Hepburn

I had to start playing the game. It felt all wrong, what I was asked to do, but I agreed to model clothes for Marshall & Snelgrove. I looked silly and was totally unsuitable as a model. I was in a full-page spread in a Hartnell dress in *Harper's Bazaar*. I opened the Ideal Home Exhibition. I presented prizes at a star ball, a dance competition. I opened a show in Wakefield, was a star at a garden party. Dangle Dolly Days, I call them now.

I met Herbert Lom when we co-starred in the second film

on my new contract, and 'Herbert Lom as a lover' were the newspaper headlines that soon were to become headlines in my life.

I had worked with him before and had feared him slightly. He had been aloof. He seemed super-intelligent and fascinating; he also happened to be extremely seductive, and now that I was living alone I did not feel guilty. Although he was married and had a child, there was an agreement, apparently, so I didn't hesitate. I did not want to live a spinsterish life now that I had finally found my body. He made me find it even more. I fell deeply in love with him as never before; it was to last for a couple of years . . .

Herbert seemed to do all the right things. He was impeccably dressed, gave parties for directors, writers, producers, hired servants and silver trays, and owned a super-special car which always attracted a mob. He had a rubber stamp of his signature and thousands of photos his secretary sent to his fans. I had never bothered to do that. He made me – and got me a stamp signature for my birthday. He also said I ought to do studio photos for my fans. So I did.

Herbert's friends were mainly professors, scientists, artists; he was political, he cared, and he tried to make me care as well. He encouraged me to read, and started me off on Shaw. He even tried to send me to his analyst, who advised him on his film roles as well as his marital problems.

I was in the culture-vulture set; it was above my head. I lived on borrowed intellect from Herbert. I was still such a greenhorn, I tried to change myself, to be somebody I wasn't, in order to please. My own character was still not there; I was too easily blown by the wind. I went on marches, gave money and support to the Theatre Workshop in the early days of Joan Littlewood. Herbert tried to sort out my life and found me a place to live with my children in one of the first communities to grow up outside London. Architects, analysts, designers, a film director; it even had its own school. It seemed perfect. I would have a flat where we would live together. If I had to go away, the children would be looked after by the staff, and they would not feel lonely because of all the other families. In theory, it was a good idea

– it was very much designed for the woman with a job and children – but I didn't find it a happy place. Communal living seemed to mean nobody caring a hoot about the others. I tried to cope with it but have to admit in the end that I hated it, as did the children. To this very day, my son groans about that awful year.

But I was in such awe of Herbert that everything he did seemed right. And he was playful and loving and I was so infatuated that I found myself sitting alone for Christmas and New Year when he was with his family. It was lunacy, utter madness. Why didn't I use my intelligence and common sense? Why didn't I take myself in hand? He lived a double life and had no intention of leaving his wife for me. I did everything I could to make him stay with me, so as to keep him away from his home. What childishness it was.

I didn't go to see the Hungarians this time but went to a doctor in Park Street – to be absolutely horrified as the doctor started to play with my clitoris instead of doing a proper investigation to see if I was pregnant. I was equally surprised in Harley Street, where I encountered a most curious specimen of a surgeon who specialised in making dwarfs grow; he kept dirty books in his desk drawer and read passages aloud to see if I was shocked. I was, but I needed his help. Afterwards, he fixed me up with a coil, which I kept for a few months – but then I found myself pregnant again. It had fallen out. 'Impossible,' he said, and put in another one, and the same thing happened again. I tried all there was to try. I got desperate and the situation with Herbert did not get any easier, although I was as much in love as ever. Then came the big surprise offer, to make a film with Danny Kaye. I accepted.

In the Monkey Cage

The toughest thing about success
is that you've got to keep on being a success.

Irving Berlin

I was even now playing childish games with life. There was still a lot of troubled water I found myself trampling in. Now I wanted to adjust to the world, comply with its rules; didn't want to be the oddball any longer, the unclassifiable, the unusual. I wanted sameness, so I sidestepped what I believe was my true nature. As a result, a rather wishy-washy personality emerged. I became too obliging, borrowed mannerisms from other, more famous stars. I joined the Stars' Band Wagon, adapted to its unwritten codes of behaviour and became what I had tried so hard to fight against: a product of the star system. Trying to sidle up to the jet set, singing the same songs, instead of sticking to my own very personal tune, however odd. Trying so hard to be conventional that I wasn't one bit convincing, even to myself. It is funny, looking back: having had no respect for fame, here I was seemingly star-struck, a victim of my profession and yet vulnerable too. I was riding two horses, pulling in two different directions. The trick was to get off before being pulled apart. Striving for a false position I got stuck, cornered by none other than myself. At the time I wasn't aware of the game I was playing: game-playing was, in fact, part of the search for myself.

A Misfit in Hollywood

Mai Zetterling had no intention of going to Hollywood. But there she was. The fact that I had got there was something of an accident. I was cast for *Knock on Wood* when the Paramount Company planned to make the film in Britain. At the last moment, it was decided to switch the production to a Hollywood base. I went too.

She is nearly thirty, in mid-career, with a list of good but not outstanding film credits. She is pretty, photogenic but she has none of the breathless Hollywood-type allure. At a send-off party in London just before she left for Hollywood, it took me fifteen minutes to find her. First I encountered every Hollywood star now in London and every British starlet who hopes to leave London for Hollywood. SHRINKING. At last, standing unobtrusively in a corner while cameramen photographed the other stars and starlets, I heard the shrinking Mai Zetterling make unstarry conversation.

Will Hollywood change Mai Zetterling, make her even more retiring – a professional recluse like Garbo – or transform her into a conventional glamour girl?

LA REPORT: She is getting on well with Mr Kaye. He says: 'She is refreshingly different from my usual leading ladies.'

The surprise casting of the year is, by all odds, the selection of Mai Zetterling as Danny Kaye's leading lady in his newest movie musical *Knock on Wood*. Miss Zetterling is in the best Swedish tradition, an unsmiling but exceedingly lovely young lady, deadly in earnest about everything. She is not exactly without humour but she does have to be introduced to a joke properly before she acknowledges it. 'Ah,' she says, 'you are making a joke.' Then comes, if not exactly a smile, at least an upturning of the lips and a nod of appreciation.

Mai Zetterling pips the glamour girls.

The blonde who usually wears the wrong clothes has gone to Hollywood . . . it's amazing.

For easy on the eye though she is, with her silky ash-blonde hair round her finely modelled face, her large blue eyes and her trim little figure, she is no showy 'look what I got, boys' cutie. She does not, either on the screen or off, look like a home-wrecker.

She is no camerman's delight at a première in some carefully revealing and eye-catching creation. She usually wears the wrong clothes, the wrong colours, with as unhappy ideas of what suits her off the set as British dress designers have had of what she should wear before the studio cameras.

In New York, I was met by a Paramount representative, a real smoothie. The car was black and long, like a funeral limousine. He was full of wisecracks but after a while he stopped, obviously disappointed, both in my appearance and my questioning eyes. The only thing he said to me as a parting word was: 'Keep smiling, Mai' . . . At that time, I felt more like bursting into tears and taking the first plane back home, which was England now. What on earth was I to do with a four-room suite during the four-hour wait between planes? They had put me at the Plaza Hotel, one of the ritziest places in New York.

Today, of course, I know about all the unwritten bits in the contracts for the stars: you wine and dine them lavishly, give them the full treatment in circumstances like this; you never know, she might be the next box-office hit. I don't think that the fellow from Paramount believed it after our brief meeting. Neither did I, actually.

In LA I was met by the directors, their children and wives, and Danny Kaye. They all looked so healthy, so suntanned, so chic in their unchic wear, so at ease that they seemed ill at ease. Jokes, laughter, more jokes which I didn't understand. I felt intimidated, of which Danny Kaye was well aware.

'Great to meet you, Mai,' was the greeting from the publicity bloke, who was a slick operator. Hired for the picture, he was to take me to my hotel on Sunset Boulevard because I must be tired; the others had to go off to some party or other . . . I was relieved. 'You'll find she is a great human being,' they told him. I was shrinking visibly . . . what on earth had I got myself into? I was to ask myself that question many times during those three months. It felt like being on another planet.

So much neon, so many garages. The publicity man chatted non-stop to me, answering his own questions, never bothering to listen to anyone else. As for me, I was still up in the clouds and couldn't really believe that I was in Hollywolly-wood: the town that had given birth to King Kong and Mae West, to Dr Jekyll and Mr Hyde, to Tarzan, Batman and my old friend Shirley Temple, and to my idol of teenagery, Tyrone Power.

I was in the land of Ku-Klux-Klan, heading towards the famous Strip, Sunset Boulevard, a freaky, Hieronymus Bosch place, I was soon to learn. They had put me in Château Marmont, a place where Garbo sometimes stayed, and smack opposite was the Garden of Allah, which was even more well known and beloved of all the great writers who had come to the Coast – it was known to be a classy hangover place. I had been given a flat of two rooms, a bathroom and a small kitchenette with a view over the Strip and the swimming pool.

The publicity fellow, who looked worn out, opened an album all covered with glossy photographs of pretty boys between twenty and thirty: blond dandies, swarthy fellows in Tarzan swimming-trunks, pale supermen, muscle beach-boys, oiled for effect, the kind of body-building types that inhabited beaches, baking their bodies in the sun with matches between their toes so as not to show the smallest bit of white flesh.

I waited for him to start the conversation as I had not the faintest idea what the pictures meant – what was I supposed to see in all these unlived faces? 'We would prefer that when you go to openings you choose one of our contract boys. I can leave the book with you here – so you can look at it at your leisure.'

I couldn't believe my ears when he continued, with the blandest of smiles: 'Of course, they are available, if you are interested.' I had been polite up to then, quite silent but polite. 'You mean they are put-up sex jobs, they have no objection?' This time I didn't wait for an answer. 'First of all, I don't go to premières and, as for sex at the moment, I have no problem – if I need it, I prefer to find it for myself.'

The publicity man didn't speak to me again during the whole picture, though he left little polite notes on my dressing-room door that I didn't take the slightest notice of because they were usually about doing pin-up pictures in bathing suits. I was difficult, he complained and, what's more, totally miscast for the role in the picture.

I was ill at ease in Hollywood. I didn't understand the jargon, the jokes. Oh Christ, those endless jokes: jokes about anuses, cunts, balls, fucks, cunts, anuses and yet more anuses. The anal jokes bored me – all those dirty words said for shock effect had a deadening effect on me, of yawning boredom: it was so poor, so desperate. One day I just couldn't take it any more. I took Danny by the arm, closed the door and (I suppose very earnestly: in my press cuttings I was always described as so very earnest in those days) asked him to stop all that dirty double talk. I just couldn't work in that kind of intimidating atmosphere. If I spoiled my chances by talking to him in this way, never mind; I wasn't really set on a Hollywood career.

I did not want to be one of his entourage, one of the followers all the great stars seemed to have. He had plenty of them around: agent, manager, secretary, chauffeur, producer, analyst, wife, and so on: a very long tail of dependants. It made me think of those parasites which live on whales and rhinoceroses, tolerated by the big beast. The yes-men who spent so much time in the shadow, so much energy keeping up pretences, smiles, hollow laughter, got only kicks and insults in return – yet always they came back for more. Perhaps they were all masochists. If so, there were a hell of a lot of them in Hollywood. A masochist's paradise.

In one of the first letters from Herbert he warned me of the dangers that I had already discovered for myself. He told me that I would have to learn to read people's motives very carefully and to gauge their sincerity by keeping my wits about me at all times.

My private little session with Danny changed our relationship completely, for the better, and I began slowly to comprehend the dilemma of a great star in a star factory. Too much flattery, too much notice taken of every little detail, everybody nosing in on your private life. As for the money, someone like Danny didn't want to have anything to do with it; certainly nothing as squalid as carrying loose change, so he always had someone following him around with a wad of notes and change for tipping. You have to be very rich indeed to go around empty-handed.

Danny thought me quaint, too serious. He said: 'Don't be over-modest, Mai, it doesn't pay in this town.' But he came to respect me all the same, as I also grew to respect him.

The only one who does not understand Mr Kaye's jokes is Miss Zetterling. Between camera set-ups, she recalled that she had financed her dramatic studies in Stockholm by selling men's underwear in a local department store. 'Oh, you've come up in the world,' remarked Kaye sweetly. 'What do you mean?' asked Miss Zetterling. 'You've graduated from shorts to features,' grinned Kaye.

Hollywood treated its stars rough, not like humans but like monsters, goddesses, heroes. To be admired for your beauty, your sexiness in that crazy public way is both dangerous and disconcerting. In comparison with Monroe or Garbo, I was small fry, way down the list, when it came to beauty and that near-hysterical attitude the public had showered on them. Often there were desperate people inside those blown-up heroines, searching for their own identity, becoming more vain and at the same time more insecure, suspicious of all the people surrounding them, accosting their privacy.

At that time, I didn't realise that many people there were like me, some even more frightened and insecure. Everyone seemed so self-possessed, so in command. To say I felt stupid is an understatement. Dumb, dumb, dumb, I thought was written all over my forehead. Surely anybody could see that. So I talked banalities and avoided serious discussion. But I was even bad at banalities, and I had no sense of fun and humour. Do I paint a dull picture of myself? Yes, but it is true that I felt all these things, which certainly did not make things easy in the kind of world I had chosen to be part of. I was on show, my sexuality was fingered and stepped upon by a public who did not care what became of me once they had had enough.

As for the place itself, it seemed like a big joke to me, one of the ugliest cities I had ever seen. My disappointment was great when I began to look around. All those freeways which were a nightmare to drive on. And all the petrol-stations, the Hamburger Heavens, drive-in cinemas, bars; tours of the stars' houses in great air-conditioned buses; maps of their homes, people collecting the stars' garbage and re-selling it; drugstores with drugstore blondes, dark air-conditioned places to catch cold in. A town without a centre, a town with bungalows, stores, parking lots, posters, and no people in the streets. Everything seemed cardboard; something that wasn't intended to last. Swimming-pools and plastic blue-green lawns which did not match the turquoise pools; artificial-looking palm trees and sprinklers, forever squirting water in a seemingly waterless place.

They dyed my hair – first to Swedish ash-blonde, then closer to Danny's colour, a rather carroty tone. The lady was a very famous dyer of stars' hair, feared, revered and gossiped about, she being the worst gossip of all. She had them all eating out of her hands. She was important, she changed their looks, transformed them into glamorous, sexy beasts. She took one sidelong look at my hair and made an ugly face. She was smeared in every colour of the rainbow; she was running from booth to booth with tremendous vigour, her gloved hand dripping with red, henna or black, a girl running after her, brushing the floor as she went. In one booth was Olivia de Havilland, in another was Rita Hayworth; she came screaming with anger from one booth, laughing like a hyena from another; she joked, provoked; she was extremely rude to her assistants, who seemed to be in awe of her. Her salon, or whatever you could call it, was not smart, not clean – hair, hair, everywhere – the girls who were supposed to tidy up could never match her speed. It seemed like one of the madhouses that Peer Gynt visited, or a scene from Peter Weiss's *Marat/Sade*.

I sat in total astonishment looking at the scene and didn't dare to say a word for myself. Nor did I feel real when I went to dinner that night, one of my very first dinners during my stay in Hollywood.

August Strindberg, a fellow countryman of mine and a sick genius, used to write plays and novels about marriage and against women. Well, here he would have had a field-day. Perhaps he might even have been a bit intimidated by the scene that I encountered. The insinuations, the downright rudeness to the partner in front of the guests, delivered with devilish smiles and not much subtlety, was incredible. After such an attack, no one would dare to speak: the silence would be almost unbearable, except for the one who had created the scene . . . and of course he himself would break it after the right length of embarrassment, by a rude joke, another insult, or a loud burp. Then relieved laughter, high-pitched, hysterical; I don't think I have ever heard so much high-pitched laughter anywhere.

Later, swimming in the pool was no fun because it had to be in the raw. 'I thought you all walked around naked in Sweden all the time.' I retired deep into the garden with its plastic grass, while the men compared the size of their penises in the water. I went home very depressed.

My letters and our telephone conversations made it apparent to Herbert just how desolate and isolated I was feeling at this time. He was worried that I wasn't able to fit in to this totally alien way of life and that I could only see myself as being out of the ordinary. The problem was that I tended to idealise everything. He urged me to pull myself together and to make the best of what I had. After all, I was a constant focus of attention, I wasn't short of money and could afford to live comfortably, and I had the opportunity to mix with all sorts of interesting people. Despite all this, it wasn't enough for me. Why didn't I think more positively, cast off the despondency which clouded my vision? It was a waste not to appreciate those who loved me, and if I didn't take stock of my good fortune now I would stand no chance of ever being happy.

'Isn't she just the greatest doll you've seen?'

'She is just going to be great in the picture.'

All that salesman talk was embarrassing. What are you supposed to do – smile gratefully, lower your eyes? Do you get cynical and put on a tired expression as if you had heard it at least a hundred times, or do you pretend not to hear? That's what I did, rightly or wrongly. Deaf and dumb I was. Innocent eyes scanning the horizon, or staring into a wall. Deaf and dumb and terribly embarrassed. I was not the Scandinavian dynamite they had expected.

Don't forget, it was the 1950s, the time of the pin-up, the Oomph girl, the cheesecake and the cutie girls. Busty blonde bomb-shells were being discovered by the hundreds, and especially in Hollywood. The bikini was launched and designers were earning fortunes on minute pieces of nylon string and elastic, just enough for covering the essentials.

It was the time of the sweater-girls with prominent tits. Your knockers really had to be knock-outs. (The producer Howard Hughes designed a very severe uplift for Jane Russell, who was the perfect sweater-girl.) Every girl worth her salt had to have something in front. Not everyone was so lucky as to have the real thing, hence a great big booming business in a contraption called Gay Deceivers, complete with steel wires and trays to lay the goodies on.

I remember standing in the Champs-Elysées gaping in wonder and surprise at the great tits that had suddenly grown on the poster of *Frieda*. My breasts are of normal size, nothing outstanding, or should I say upstanding, but on the poster they certainly were, quite out of proportion to the rest of my body. If I had had such ornaments in reality, I would have been quite dangerous, as they were pointed like needles.

I was the wrong kind of property for Hollywood, ill-suited to playing the cutie-pie, the piece of ass. According to the Press Boys at the studio, I was more of a sour-puss than a glamour-puss 'putting on airs'. They thought I was 'doing a Garbo', as they put it, the 'I want to be alone' bit. I was a very difficult character who refused to obey orders. 'Hi, Mai, show a bit of leg' – and when I said no, they said, 'All the stars do, what's wrong with showing a bit of leg, Mai?' 'Keep on smiling, Mai.' To them, I was a real flopperoo; they were only polite because of my dressing-room romance with the great star. In front of him they tried to outsmart one another and accepted every kind of humiliation from him in order to obtain favour. Danny called them a fine pack of ass-lickers, cunning foxes; he only got a crooked smile in answer.

You might say that I was quarrelling with my bread and butter, not conforming to the set-up patterns of so-called stardom. I was standing in my own light, as I didn't play according to the rules of their game. No, the Swede didn't do a thing right in Hollywood. Actually, I behaved according to the slang interpretation of what a Swede is like. SWEDE: a blunderer; a clumsy piece of work.

How did I have the nerve to behave as I did? Perhaps it was because of my run of luck in the past, success beyond my wildest dreams. I had not known the true meaning of failure. I was still living with the secure feeling that success would always be around the corner. What a dangerous little thought that was – but what it undoubtedly did was to save me from Hollywood, because one is but human and it can be very difficult to resist the money that is offered, which has nothing to do with reality or what one could earn anywhere else in the world. I so often heard the phrase from writers and actors from New York: 'We will just take a year or two of this whacky place, grab the money and run as fast as we can back to sanity, to act in proper plays, talk to real people and write the great novel that will show up this place for what it really is . . . you just wait and see.' But many got stuck, couldn't resist the sun and pool bit and all that goes with it, couldn't resist the Goose that lays the Golden Oscars. So they joined the club and became smooth operators in order to survive, with big analysts' bills. They became ink-slingers instead of writers. I could have sunk without trace like so many others; so many ended up serving in seedy joints or became cocaine-eaters, or went on the needle or into institutions, or died by their own hand. Perhaps I could have been a star. I turned it down. It was not for me – I preferred a simple life and a somewhat freer existence.

The good people of Hollywood did exist, and what's more I met them, finally. There were Arthur and Gail Ross, he a script-writer, she an elocution teacher. They were worth waiting for. They were simple, direct and unassuming, and had a way of enjoying themselves that I could appreciate. We went to the beach-hut that they had rented, a somewhat rustic place with a huge white sand-dune rising plume-like up the sea-cliff, as Arthur liked to describe it. I remember having the best chicken ever in my life there, roasted by Arthur, with butter and brandy: it has never been recaptured.

We talked, we spoke of passions for food and eating and tasting and savouring . . . the art of eating in good company. But of course, dear Arthur, we also spoke of other passions, intellectual and political . . . Conversations with you were never finished. 'You and your solitude,' you used to say to me, determined to make me laugh.

Then there was Salka Viertel, who wrote a number of Garbo's scripts and was her best friend; what a lovely serene lady she was. How she could have stayed like that in the film racket and the hyped-up atmosphere is beyond me. It was at her place that I met Jean Renoir, the film director, and his large, noisy, sensual family. I was soon accepted in their house for lunch on Sundays that were very French indeed, as lunch was just about finished at tea-time. His old nurse, who spoke nothing but French, was still with him, looking after his children. She had been his father's model and one of his great loves. Actually, the house and the garden were like a

Renoir painting; it was as though they had carried a bit of France with them to this far-away coast. And there was music. Satie, Darius Milhaud, Poulenc – composers that I was going to love very much in the future. The food was straight from heaven, the bread was home-made, the wine was French and there was lots of laughter, and jokes of a kind that I could understand. So in the end I did encounter generosity of spirit and happy homes and sanity. Renoir didn't much like it in Hollywood, though, and hankered after his homeland.

Sometimes I would go to Malibu at week-ends, to avoid the sterility of Hollywood. I didn't care a damn about deep-sea fishing but it was a change of scene and it was fresh air. On the big boat that you went on for the day, the jargon was rather crude, but it was different: nobody talked about Hollywood and nobody guessed I was an actress. But in the end I had to stop going out on the boat because I got too sunburnt. All film stars wore big-brimmed hats against the sun so as not to destroy their complexions.

As for Danny, well, we became friendly, if not friends, and the way he worked was a challenge, because it was a way I had never worked before. He was totally unpredictable, would change his lines around and expect you to follow him. Of course, I realised I was a stooge, as it's called; to play opposite a comedian is to give him the support to hang his jokes on. My part was therefore not much of a part. Danny wasn't really serious until the cameras turned; before that he would be fooling around. Without being deliberately selfish, because of his strong personality he was liable to swamp the other actors completely. He would switch both action and dialogue in the middle of a scene. He was a natural actor; he didn't want to get stuck in a certain pattern. If you had to do the scene again and again, he needed and wanted to be spontaneous. I learnt a lot from him this way: I became more natural and spontaneous too.

One day, Danny asked his chauffeur to bring his daughter to the studio. She arrived in an enormous limousine, sitting forlornly in the back. She was brought on to the set and lifted up on to a table by Danny: a shy, silent child. He stopped the filming and started to clown for her and for the crew, who laughed politely. He stared at the child; she did not even smile. Finally, he could not bear it any longer – he lifted her down from her elevated place and asked the chauffeur to take her home. The rest of the day he was gloomy, disturbed and a bastard to most of the people who dared to come close to him.

Danny was a lonely clown, in deep trouble with himself. Passionate by nature he hated passionate people, if they were women; scared stiff of himself, he feared his likes. He had mapped out a very lonely road. Apart from acting vigorously in front of the cameras, he spent most of his energies and spare time on golf courses, chatting aimlessly behind a joky façade.

He did, however, devote a big part of his life to the cause of the poor children of the world. His work for UNICEF was a great success. The children trusted him and he them; perhaps only with children did he dare to be himself.

Hollywood was in trouble but trying to pretend that all was well. Every studio had to cut down on staff, they were all forced to change management – but that was really nothing new: it had been going on ever since Hollywood was on the map as a film city. All that wheeling and dealing, all that struggle for power, all that chopping off of studio heads. There was always somebody else who was going to be greater.

Towards the end of my stay, I had a letter from Herbert. He had been having sessions with his analyst about our relationship. He was feeling clearer in his mind and more positive about our future and was looking forward to seeing me. But he was still rather ambivalent towards me. I made him feel inadequate because of my strength and determination and he was aware that there were many things I needed which he could not give me or did not believe in himself. Whereas I was a believer in marriage or at least an intense relationship between two people, he was not so sure. He did see that marriage was necessary in society's eyes and that children born outside wedlock might suffer needlessly. Although half drawn towards marriage, he was held back by the thought that, even with someone like me, the ideal could not last long. For this he blamed society's old-fashioned ideas about, and expectations of, the institution of marriage, which would always destroy two people's love for one another in the end.

I was asked to do a film with Gregory Peck. I read the script, which was a thriller of sorts, and I turned it down – to the horror of my agent. If it was more money I wanted, he could fix that; 'You're playing a smart game, Mai. You're a real smart cookie,' he said, and was impressed.

'It's not the money,' I said, and added very earnestly, 'I don't like the script. And anyway, I told you I was going to work in the theatre in London when I finish this film.'

'Oh, don't worry your pretty little head, dear, about that, we'll fix it. As for the script, you know it was written by a fellow who is the greatest and has done sixty scripts, every one a winner.'

'No,' I said, 'I really don't want to do it, even if I had been able to.'

'How much will you be paid for this play?'

'Forty pounds a week,' I said.

'Four hundred, you mean, oh, we'd easily treble that for you. Money really talks in this town, Mai, and can buy anything and anybody, even you.'

'No, forty pounds – it's theatre, don't forget – and it's Ibsen's *Doll's House*.'

I was reminded of what Dorothy Parker had said: 'Hollywood money isn't money. It's congealed snow, melts in your hands, and there you are.' And of J. O'Hara on the subject of Hollywood: 'I have never heard so much crap in such a short time in my life.' I am apt to agree with him; too much ubble-gubble talk, too much buttering-up, too much hot air and energy spent on celebrating yourself. The rustic in me rebelled, and I became indeed what Danny had warned me of – overmodest. I underplayed myself as a kind of reaction to all that balloon juice, arm-twisting and back-slapping.

So, to the bosses, I was definitely on the shit-list, especially as I had dared to turn them down. Later, what came back were things like: 'She is an introverted oddball. She might be a great actress but she isn't a man's idea of a sex-job. A prim and proper Miss will never really make the headlines.' And they had got it all wrong about Ibsen's *Doll's House*: they thought I was doing a children's play called *The Doll's Palace*.

I was never asked to do a film in Hollywood again . . . *Knock on Wood* was a great success, but I never followed it up. Hollywood's jungle laws were not for me.

The only thing that makes life possible, is permanent intolerable uncertainty, not knowing what comes next.

Ursula K. Le Guin

Meanwhile

What lies behind us
And
What lies before us
Are
Tiny matters
Compared to
What lies within us

Indian Graffiti

February 3rd, 1980   *Mas d'Aigues Vives* (Living Waters)
Sitting in the office at the Notaire's in Uzès (my nearest town), I'm
trying to hide my unpolished boots under the table – I walked the
goats this morning and it shows. Says I: 'Just two months to go
before we move.' Says he: 'One month, you mean.' That turns out
to be correct. Panic, chaos in my head, the packing has to start right
away. Perhaps it's just as well we don't move on April Fools'
Day . . .

But I am certainly disturbed in my mind – I didn't really want
ever to leave the Mas. The Mediterranean sky turns a dismal grey. I
feel out of joint with myself.

February 10*th*
Spring is naughtily early this year and it makes this a very hard
place to leave; the place I have loved more than any other I have
lived in. The thirty acres have been fully explored. So much

happiness, so much pain. Contractions in the belly when I think of leaving it all.

Books, books all day and half the night, up to my ears in books. Twelve thousand of them. Dusting, packing, sealing the brown boxes I have picked up like a thief, outside shops or from rubbish dumps. The one hundred almond trees that I planted are blossoming more abundantly than ever before, as if they knew of my departure. The blue globularia in the hills are trying their best to convince me that this is the best place in the world. Dear God, you don't have to try, I know it to be true. The silver-grey tassels of Garya Elyptica sway in the herb-garden that otherwise looks sad and neglected.

February 16th
Books for breakfast, lunch and supper. Today's fare is travel, sailing, adventure; it suits me fine. Kipling on success and failure: 'These two impostors should be treated just the same.'

February 20th
I sort through the personal books in my work-room. Herbal medicine, goat-breeding, gardening; the supernatural, alchemy and cookery-books. Mai, oh Mai, you are mad. What do you want with three hundred cookery-books? Cooking for lovers. . cooking with roses ... with violets ... pauper's cook-book, witch's cookery-book, a book of cooking for the working classes. Poshfood, gourmet food, vegetarian, Japanese, Chinese, and so on and so on. Why do I always go too far?

This morning I woke up furious with myself and promising faithfully never ever to make jams, pickles and chutneys again, as yesterday I had to throw away dozens of old jars of sweet gooey stuff. Still, I enjoyed making it.

February 22nd
I dreamt that my sunflowers have all been burnt down. I see a field of black, wizened, still smoking sunflowers. I try to cry but can only open my mouth in agony; nothing comes out, not the smallest sound.

I wake up deeply depressed about leaving my own creation of a worldly paradise. There is only one consolation – that the suffering that I will feel will, must, come to an end.

February 28th

I go for a last walk; taking the old path I used to go along with the goats; the happy walk, I used to call it, where I used to sing crazy made-up songs. Today I can't even hum. If I could, it would be a sort of funeral march. It is the kind of day when I want to burst into tears all the time. Instead, I put on my efficiency mask. Last pie in the oven, the last fire which I make out of all the flowers left in the vases and still not dead. Almond and heather, miniature daffodils. The mosquito net still hangs in the bedroom like a bridal veil. The sky is indecently blue and shining. It is the perfect going-away weather, as we used to call it, with typical English irony. It all hurts like hell and Keeper, the wolf-hound, is ill; it's cancer.

March 3rd   *Le Mazel, Ardèche*

The next house of mine is also a ruin, with no hot water, toilet or bathroom. And it is at least twice the size of 'Living Waters' . . . 'What folly,' say my friends. 'She has become a megalomaniac,' says another. I have to admit; it all seems a bit mad.

When I saw the house I recognised it at once, because I realised that I had seen it before in a precognitive dream . . . how could I refuse it?

The electric light hurts my eyes, so I unpack the candles first. 'Typical,' says Glen. 'I suppose you want me to cut off the electricity now.' It is cold and damp. I'm full of apprehension; I have bad dreams, full of ghosts. One of them was even sitting on the bed trying to get in between Glen and me. Keeper is very ill and whimpers in his sleep.

March 5th

The moon pours in through the window. I lie awake until a red strip of sun shines into the mirror and casts reflections on the

111

peeling walls. It is rough living here and it is getting colder. *Do I really want this?*

March 6th

Bad dreams continue. Cleaning, painting, planting roses that I stole from my own herb-garden. Cats are beginning to settle in but Keeper does not improve.

The people here look like mountain people; so much tougher than the other place. There is no sophistication whatsoever. They come mainly from coal-mining stock. There are several butchers in the small town; I chose the one named Platon. Told him I preferred philosophical meat but I'm not sure he understood what I meant. Unshaven old hippies hug the walls in the big café, sitting like a flock of black birds that have flown in from some nasty polluted spot; they stare at us rudely. In the town there is another group: the political radicals, gipsy-clad, eager, protesting against pollution, the digging of uranium. Near my village, a different crowd: frozen black and grey people, huddling together for warmth, march under a torn red flag and a banner saying 'The people from under the earth' – it is the funeral of a coal-miner.

March 9th

To get to the new house, 'Le Mazel', you have to go through a small village called 'Be careful with yourself', then there is a very steep and bendy climb through a forest and a breathtaking view over mountains and snow-clad Alps. Mountains lying like waves in front of my feet, casting deep blue shadows. Sometimes it reminds me of Japan, misty and mysterious. In the midst of all that beauty there lies a misshapen house in garish colours, and in it lives an Alice in Wonderland character, madder than the maddest Hatter. He laughs like a rogue, which makes his substantial tummy shake like jelly. He has a glass eye, which he sometimes takes out and tosses in the air, waiting for a reaction. Sometimes he asks us in for a *pastis*. We are given glasses which have never been washed; they are red like wine. Our drinks are topped up with water straight from the garden hose. He lives alone with a servant whom he hired when he was young and rich. Now the land has been sold and all that's left is the lop-sided house and a few goats and the servant.

Meanwhile

March 19*th*

It is freezing cold. I warm my bra in the oven before putting it on and afterwards make croissants. I wear old-fashioned carpet slippers which heat like hot-water bottles. I wear football stockings and layers of sweaters which I peel off as the heat begins to spread in the room. I look a funny sight. The star at home; nobody would recognise me. I always have a roaring fire and many candles when I have breakfast. And today I saw Mont Blanc from the bedroom window, four hundred kilometres away, shining and majestic and slightly unreal, as in a dream. A vision of great beauty – but it could not take away my sadness at Keeper's death.

March 20*th*

Floods. It is as if the Gates of Heaven have opened. It is a violent climate, small rivulets everywhere. We go to a big city to see a movie but as there is nothing worth seeing we buy a small television instead. We are both terribly depressed because of Keeper. Life is rough and raw up here at the moment. 'Flee to where the raw rough breeze blows' comes to me – I have, dear Nietzsche, I have.

March 30*th*

The whole valley seems to be full of flowering mimosa now. Sudden spring. My work-room has been nicknamed the 'star chamber' but I certainly do not feel like much of a star these days. More like a misfit in this wild mountain place, trying to piece together what was me, is me.

The brain upon which my experiences have been written is not a particularly good one. If there were brain-shows, as there are cat and dog shows, I doubt if it would get even a third-class prize. Upon quite a number of points it would be marked below the average.

H.G. Wells, *Experiment with Autobiography*

Me for Myself Alone

I can only make direct statements, only 'tell stories'.
Whether or not the stories are 'true' is not the problem.
The only question is whether what I tell is MY fable, MY
truth.

C.G. Jung, *Memories, Dreams, Reflections*

Was it intuition, a sudden inspiration, that had made me go
and see Binky Beaumont after accepting the role in *Knock on
Wood* in early 1953? Binky, the undisputed King of London's
theatreland. What I needed at that moment in my career,
only Binky could have helped me to achieve.

When he asked me what I wanted to do after my Hollywood bit, we giggled, as we both knew how unsuitable I was
for a permanent role in that dream factory. Without hesitation, I had answered: 'Nora in Ibsen's *Doll's House*.' It is a
play about the predicament of women and Nora's escape
from her delusions about marriage. It is also a plea for
women to be regarded as human beings and not just
playthings – yet there I was, going off to Hollywood which
had made a point of keeping women in just such a situation,
working desperately to keep them as dolls and babes.
Hollywood had nothing whatever to do with the new and
commanding femininity that I wanted to be part of. So Binky
and I giggled again at my choice of play and role. It certainly
was in sharp contrast to the world I was going into.

I had been feeling for some time that I had come to the end

114

of an era in my life and that there had to be a turning-point if I was to go further. I wanted to evolve as a more complete person. I felt I was leading a false existence. Before, I had not had the strength to rebel against it; now, I felt the time had come to try to live more according to my own nature. Unconsciously, I was making arrangements to help me on the way. Nora was a kind of scapegoat, a way of finding myself.

'We will do it at the Lyric, Hammersmith,' Binky said simply and in a matter-of-fact way, after we had talked for an hour. 'As soon as you come back from having put your footprints in the cement outside the Chinese Theater in Hollywood.' (In fact, I never did achieve that honour.)

Nora, little slavey, vamp and doll's-house wife, all the things that I myself had been and still was, in many ways. Like her, my identity had been swamped; I had allowed it to happen. Why? Mostly for the sake of love, also out of a need for guidance, for fathering. In my personal relationships, I had played as many games as Nora. I had not been a bit self-sufficient, although I had proudly thought of myself as a free bachelor-girl. What self-deception. I was nothing of the sort. In order to gain self-realisation, I had to get rid of that old *persona*, which was torturing itself in a morbid way. Leaving *him*, Herbert Lom, the man who loomed so large in my life, would be dying a long slow death. But I had to stop the feeling that I was a martyr, the misunderstood one, which was the part I had been playing those last three years. I had spent far too much time yearning, day-dreaming about him, always feeling unsatisfied, however much we had been able to be together. I disliked the kind of two-faced diplomat I had become; the cunning sly-boots, which was against my will and temperament. To keep him, I had been prepared to do almost anything. But now I had become tired to death of my mean and freakish little games. I decided I had shed enough tears, had done with self-torture. Did I not have the master key to myself? After all, I and I alone did the choosing of what kind of person I was to be. I had to find a new road. On that road, Nora in *A Doll's House* was a character who taught me a lot.

Ibsen wrote the play when emancipation was a serious and daring subject. His play had been taken as a social comment at the time. It won him laurels as well as protests. It had not been performed in England for over twelve years and now it was considered out of date, irrelevant. Surely, by now, women like Nora had nothing to complain about? Women had become emancipated; they were no longer chattels, and their husbands seldom tyrants. In fact, very little had been accomplished since Ibsen wrote his play. Women were just as stuck in their roles as wives and dolls, myself included. Yet for all that, I felt guilty about not being a perfect mother and wife, which was the role that Nora in the play had chosen for herself. But Nora manages to change and to realise that motherhood is not the first step to herself, that first of all she has to grow up and become a person in her own right.

'How can I possibly educate my children,' Nora asks, 'when I myself am not educated or grown-up?' For a man, such an idea is perfectly acceptable but for a woman, even today, it seems abnormal. Nora leaves, slamming the door behind her. Self-realisation takes priority over her love for her children.

The slamming of that door by Nora became the great symbolic gesture of all women's movements ever after. However, when the play was first performed in Germany, the final image so shocked the public that Ibsen was more or less forced to write a new ending. In the German version, Nora looks at her sleeping children and says: 'Oh I sin before myself but I am unable to leave them.' Later, in the printed version of the play, Ibsen forbade this ending.

Like Nora, I had been a sort of child bride, not a bit ready to educate my children, only to play with them like dolls. I could identify completely with Nora on the stage, because like her I had slammed the door, for more or less the same reasons: the need for more open skies.

I had a sense of shame about myself, about not living up to my standards. I felt unbalanced. My dancing accountant, Arpad, even went so far as to call me neurotic at this time in my life. He was probably right; I wanted to lay bare the real human being which I had been hiding behind a self-sufficient mask; I was no longer willing to conform to the pattern which most of us still did. I did not want to be a stereotyped female; I wanted to be myself, complete with all my faults. I had been both too submissive and too arrogant. This had to stop. All my life I had done just this, gone to the very limit of a situation, and the changes had always been abrupt and painful. This was one of them? Basic laziness and fear of change was, I suppose, one of my main weaknesses.

From Hollywood came a woman in fighting spirits, determined to be able to stand alone.

A clean break. It was a hard and horrible phrase, one that Herbert had used when talking about other people's affairs. And now ours. How hard it was to resist him. That heavy Slavonic charm was devastating. For weeks, having made up my mind to put an end to it all, I was still waiting for his calls at any time of day and night. And when the call came I would pretend not to have been waiting. I was still game-playing at being understanding, sophisticated, while at the same time trying to change my life. A very contradictory lady indeed. In the name of love or whatever it was, I was ready to give myself a kick in the ass. I just did not dare to admit I needed a man for myself.

Was it so wrong, was it such a crime? In his eyes, yes, it was an outmoded way of living, and certainly not at all grown-up. My box of tricks, my false toughness, were easy to see through. I was not a good liar and I was ridiculously vulnerable. He thought me weak, and he was quite right. I had almost lost my nerve and was willing to give in to everything he asked for – because although I knew I had to change, I was petrified of what would happen to me. Women are called the loving sex, but in this respect my loving was childish. I was quite hysterical while this change was going on, not one bit equal. 'Sex is difficult,' Rilke wrote, 'but then almost everything is difficult and everything is serious.' I did not want to be the other woman in a relationship; it was destructive, no matter what anyone said. At this juncture in my life, I was not strong or convinced enough to be able to take it. Of course, I knew this story was common enough and

117

that many women would quite happily accept such a compromise. I have not seen many happy results from such unions, mind you. What finally made me end the situation I can no longer remember. A build-up of emotions, the string snapped. I have never ever doubted it was the right thing to do.

Luck seems somehow to be on my side whatever kind of misery I find myself in. Because there I was, playing a part of my own choice in London, a part that helped me work out my personal pain and dilemma. Poets and writers do it all the time; actors seldom have the chance, as they more or less have to wait for the offers to come to them, rather than instigating what feels right and important to do at the time.

Playing Nora, I realised I was speaking not only for myself, but for all the women in such a situation. This was one of the main reasons I had stuck to the theatre: it gave me the opportunity to discuss serious matters, philosophical ideas, indirectly, through a character. I had been fortunate to have acted in plays which display the universality of human emotions: Chekhov, Strindberg, Shakespeare. This fight of creation through life's hardships has strengthened me and also made me feel immensely rich. To be made to realise you are not alone, that you are sharing feelings with hordes of other people: pain, weaknesses, sentimental notions, all made clear through the poet's way of expressing it. The writer himself had lived through these ordinary pains and then made them extraordinary by the juxtaposition of words, of context, of relationships. I was a spokesman for him, communicating his feelings to the other side of the footlights, to an audience who had lived through hurts and dilemmas similar to the ones acted out on stage. I was not alone: not only was the audience there, but so were the multitudes, living and dead. And when inspiration soars, this higher state of consciousness takes over from immediate reality; you feel you are in touch with the mystical.

Whatever it is, it certainly is a high feeling. The experience leaves a sense of gratitude, courage to go on. It is the most valuable gift I can imagine. To get it, one has to crawl to the lowest abyss within one's self and not be frightened by the weightlessness and fire in the head that come with it.

It is exciting to discover not only one's self but countless layers of psyche, mysterious revelations that seem, for a moment, to make the ungraspable graspable. Hard to explain, but when it happens, it is a shock to the system and then ends as suddenly as it has come. But the effect stays in the mind for ever, and solitude becomes easier to live with ever after. I have never taken drugs, as even the mildest sedative makes me dizzy, but I can imagine, from written accounts, that the effects of mescaline or LSD are of this nature: 'light springing from darkness, things unconscious bursting into consciousness'.

The critics were divided. Perhaps I identified too much with the role of Nora, didn't have enough of the detachment which is essential to all creative efforts. But more gratifying than the reviews were the hundreds of letters I received from women who were moved by my performance. So in this at least I was right: the women's problem was far from solved.

A Man is a Man,
is a Lover, is a Husband,
is a Father, is a Man

Are you angry that others disappoint you?
Remember you cannot depend upon yourself.

Benjamin Franklin, *Poor Richard's Almanac*, 1732

Although I had broken from Herbert, I most definitely had
not solved my 'problem', which seemed now to be all about
men. So it is not perhaps too strange that I chose this
traumatic moment to decide to search for my long-lost father,
whom I had never seen. Holiday time came and I went to
Sweden to stay in a place up north with my mother and the
children for a few weeks. I have avoided writing at length
about my mother, this vitally important figure in my life.
Perhaps mothers are the most important actors of all on the
world's stage? I have no desire to seek out the traumas of my
childhood. But I do want to try to understand the reasons for
my total lack of communication with my mother, for her sake
and mine. The sad fact is that my relationship with my
mother did not improve over the years; if anything, the gap
widened.

I cannot tell when the wall between us was created. When
I began to feel something was seriously wrong, I immediately buried the thought or let it float away. I do remember
from very early on that the non-communication worried me.
For a start, mother's eyes bothered me. There was a far-away
look in them I could not comprehend. I felt imprisoned by
her eyes: when she looked at me, I felt that she hardly

120

recognised me. Yet I was her child. Or perhaps I wasn't. As I have already said, for years I had doubts about this. There was this clouded look on my mother's face that said: 'Who are you?' She would look past me, through me. It was uncanny. She would sit for hours, staring out through the double-glazed windows as if waiting for the cold and empty street to give her an answer. It was as though she had constructed a barricade, unseen by the human eye. There was no doubt in my mind that she lived *behind* something and that was why she could not see me, I argued with myself. It gave me an eerie, lonely feeling. I came to take it for granted. I moved in circles around her, trying to find a way in through that wall. Of course I could see her, but this thing that stood between us was as real as an object.

One of the thoughts that frightened me most was that her body seemed unoccupied. There was this human frame, so many kilos of flesh and bone walking about absent-mindedly. But where was *she*? I began to hate this unresponsive thing that called itself my mother. I could not understand why she cried with her eyes lost in the clouds; I did not know why she would suddenly throw crockery or cutlery to the floor in despair. She did it as if her arms were obeying some silent inner command. I did not know what she was thinking when she looked sullen and morose and the line between her eyes deepened. I did not know why things frightened her. Was it my fault? I had no idea. I crept about silently and played cruel games with my dolls, operated on them with scissors and needles, painted blood on their heads, and kept quiet. And hated. It is horrible that a child can have so much hatred stored inside. I have never had it since. In the end I could hardly sit at the same table at meal-times. I would throw my food behind the sofa because my throat refused to swallow and I felt nauseous. I couldn't know at the time that this was a fairly common sign of hysteria. I cannot remember that we ever talked – though of course we must have. But anyway, we were miserably poor in conversation in my family. Joel, my stepfather, also side-stepped my mother when he came home from work, his head almost inside the radio. His way of showing anger was

121

silence and there could be days and days, if not weeks, of silence.

Inevitably I too became silent and passive; looking past people, never at them. The only eyes I looked into were my own questioning ones, in the mirror. I got dizzy from my questioning eyes: it seemed that I too was somewhere else. I got lost in the mirror. Perhaps that's where my mother was? A strange conclusion for a child of ten, but that is what I came to believe – my mother had lost herself in the mirror that showed my reflection.

Sometimes I make up mental pictures of a situation or a *persona*, which can clarify things for me. Here, then, is a hasty list of what my mother conjures up in me: a blank wall, a foetus, darning wool, stale bread, a bleak countryside, an empty street with no trees, a cupboard, a shut door, a double lock, a mangle in the cellar, ruffled sea, thin oil, a body without arms; as for emotions: tightness of the throat, unresolved feelings, stupidity in myself, discomfort.

One of my strongest memories of her is seeing her standing knee-deep in the sea, washing herself, and a small water-snake swimming between her legs. Her silent scream, a mask of a face frozen in horror.

Mothers, daughters, echoes. Am I an echo of my mother? And is my daughter an even fainter echo of both her and my inability to give? The thought terrifies me. Perhaps to her I have the same eyes as my mother, a face with blinkers, an eyeless beast. Because we too do not recognise one another, we are also worlds apart, yet we are mother and daughter. When people admire me and say how lucky I am in life, and how successful, I would like to tell them: they don't know what a mess I have made of my family life. I have longed for a true family connection perhaps more than the average person, because of what I missed out on and my feeling of rejection. I try not to be envious or sentimental when I see the so-called Happy Family. I look for closeness outside the family because I did not find it in my own family structure. I recognise the importance of the single human being. And I realise that there is not only happiness that comes from family ties but also deep unhappiness, because it is sometimes artificial to attempt to prolong family relationships out of pure sentiment.

I feel that I have been an utter failure as a mother. I tried to appease my conscience by giving to my children all that I thought I had lost out on, materially that is. It seemed that I could not do it emotionally, that I lacked all maternal instinct.

Towards my daughter: guilt, guilt, guilt and pain, which I try to hide from myself. Her pictures – a small furry creature, the sun behind a harsh cloud, a person who leaves no footprints in the sand. She rejects me now, feeling that I rejected her when she was a child: my work, my success, my divorce, the fathers who came and went. I can never measure the sadness of not being able to help or guide her. In many ways she has become a lost person.

As for my son, Louis, how does he feel about me, who was hardly ever at home during his adolescence, just passing through like a visitor? He, like most children, wanted sameness, a proper home. I wasn't a cosy mother, I wore unusual clothes, I was in the public eye. His school-friends pestered him for my autograph. He felt neglected and missed the family togetherness, which made him resent me. He was embarrassed by my outspokenness in the media and would feel obliged to explain to his friends that I was a bit hot-headed.

Louis (a professor in ecology and sociology at Barcelona University for the last eight years) admits, however, that he has inherited some of my characteristics. We get on well nowadays and last time we met he said, 'I have a reputation at the University for being a difficult person. I stand up for my ideals; I refuse to compromise. Do you recognise that?'

I had come to Sweden to find the one who had rejected me once, the man who was responsible for my life – my real father. I felt as if I was acting out some melodrama on my own personal stage, playing the part of little orphan Mai . . . Why was it so important to find my father at this stage in my life?

We spent two long weeks in the wilderness, up north by a cool and meandering river, the children, mother and myself.

One evening, as we sat viewing the wild blueberry mountains, I brought the subject up, but I cannot have done it in a tactful way because she did not answer my question as to what his name was, only gave me a wounded look and became more remote than ever, the bitterness round her mouth more pronounced.

On the evening when she made up her mind to talk about my father, the blueberry mountains seemed even more remote, falling away on the horizon. It was a cold, stormy night. The children were asleep; although Etienne was tossing and turning and whimpering as always. What kind of pain and agony was she going through every night, while her brother slept so soundly and silently? With that painful background, mother began to talk with a somewhat similar whimper in her voice. She avoided my eyes, but she talked – about my father's fortune, his way with women, women that he loved even more than money; she said he had never bothered about or been interested in me. 'But I suppose he brags about you now that you have become famous.' That hurt and she knew it, but then she had been hurt that I wanted to find him after all these silent years. Finally it came, what I had expected all along: 'He is the only man I have ever loved.' I could have cried at that lonely statement. Instead I stared out into space, just like her. What could I say? We continued to sit there and stare, as if nothing had happened. There was emotional vibration between us, for the very first time perhaps. But we were still unable to open up to one another. The wall that had been there all those years could not be broken. Without a word she wrote down a name and address on a piece of paper and handed it to me with a sharp little 'Good-night'. She left me sitting alone with that scrap of paper and the blue hills vanishing in the night. She had moved like a sleep-walker.

The piece of paper had come from the children's sketch-pad. There were Etienne's scrawls, the usual mixture of dragons spitting and dripping blood, arrows and fishes, always fishes. And in among all the pain that Etienne's subconscious had drawn, the name and address of my father. I was disappointed by his name. What had I hoped for? My stepfather's name, which I still use today, was much more exotic. My father's last name was a common one in Sweden, Larsson, the first name David. He was the owner of a small factory in my old home town. His name was only my first disappointment.

Next day, my mother's eyes were red from crying. I felt like a traitor, as I knew that she had had a sleepless night on my account. I told myself that I was foolish and immature, that I was keeping neuroses alive by this search into my distant past. Wasn't it a bit pathetic, looking for a father figure at my age? Having just left one man, wasn't I now, childishly, looking for another, for someone who could protect and father me?

The loving world of the family was the most exotic world of all in my mind's eye. As for my father, well, I had conjured up a God-like figure, a hero to worship. Poor fellow; he was, of course, a man like any other man, full of shortcomings, and there was no way, with the best will in the world, that he could live up to being the kind of father I had imagined. What an innocent fool I still was – looking for firmer ground for myself, I still hadn't come to terms with the fact that the only firm ground is the one you stand on. My very own terra firma . . . surely that had been my quest. I didn't see that I had been waylaid by sentiment and also, I suppose, by a need that had been unfulfilled.

I caught a train to the city and took my daughter with me. I did not dare to face my father alone; also, I felt it would be good for her to be with me for a while. She was lagging behind in her development and her brother's cleverness and easy charm were hard for her to take. She needed extra warmth and comfort. To be just the two of us would be a treat. I took a small room in the Station Hotel. It turned out to be a boring place, full of drunks at night, homeless, neatly-dressed men with incredibly sad eyes. Being so near to my father, I lost my nerve completely. I wanted to go back to Stockholm and forget this ridiculous game of mine. Was all this self-inflicted agony really worth it? For two whole days I had silent arguments with myself; as for what we actually did during that time, I can't remember. Nobody recognised me or pretended not to, yet it was my old home town. I felt very lonely and decided the whole thing had been a great mistake – and what's more I made my mother suffer.

There is one thing I have not forgotten, and that is what happened to that scrap of paper with his name and address. It is as vivid as anything I have ever lived through. As I sat in my little self-made glass house, that dirty, folded, crumpled piece of paper was almost magically alive. It went through several metamorphoses. At night, it was under my pillow; my dreams became nightmares on forbidden themes. In the morning I would unfold it, smell it, stuff it into my handbag, only to take it out, put it on the window-sill in the sun, see it change colour. I would bang it with my fist, angry and impatient both with it and myself. I threw it down the loo but it would not flush away. I took it out and ironed it dry. It began to look like an ancient bit of paper, by now. I cried over it and wanted to eat it, devour it bit by bit. How could a mean little bit of paper suddenly have this weight and importance in my life? The telephone was staring at me all the time, waiting to be picked up. On the third day, exhausted by my indecision, I finally summoned up courage. I called him at his office.

His wife answered. She did not seem one bit surprised when I gave her my name, as if she had been expecting my call for years. 'Just a minute,' she said, in a cool, secretarial manner, while my heart was beating a strange rhythm. When his voice came on, it was friendly and matter of fact: 'I'll pick you up and you'll come to the house for dinner and stay the night.' It all seemed so easy.

He was short, with a certain peasant stockiness which I had inherited. He arrived laden with gifts for both of us. A large golden-haired doll for Etienne, a pearl necklace for me: 'I gave my daughter one just like that for her twenty-first birthday.' He wanted everything to be fair all of a sudden. He even insisted on paying the hotel bill. Suddenly and for the first time I had a real father who took care of such details. 'My daughter is longing to meet you; she always dreamed of having a sister. We told her all about you when she was grown-up, there was no point in hiding it from her. Any-

126

way, I am very proud of you and you are more beautiful than I expected.' When we had met, we had only shaken hands as all Swedes do. It had felt wrong to kiss him. As I had thought, the presence of Etienne helped the slightly forced situation: she filled in the spaces between the ienvitable pauses.

'You've got my nose,' he said, looking pleased, 'the typical Larsson nose.' We were driving towards his villa that lay outside the city. It was an idyllic place, nestling under some large birch trees right beside a lake. A rowing boat was tied up to a small floating jetty and the garden was stocked with fruit trees and berries of every kind. I soon found out that his was a very practical mind. I also found out that he was a bit of an inventor, and a Sunday painter who could have turned professional if he had wanted to, but he had given all that up for a secure job. His legitimate daughter was everything I was not and had desperately wanted to be. Tall and elegant, she was typical of the kind of girls I had admired from a distance as a child; wearing the right kind of subdued clothes with that one-string necklace like the one our father had just given me. She had done all the conventional things: played tennis, of course, which in Sweden was looked upon as an upper-class sport, as well as riding and sailing, at which she was also an expert, spoke perfect French and English because of her Swiss finishing-school. Of course, we did not speak the same emotional language. She was polite, with a thin note of coldness behind her smiles. She showed me snapshots of the family on holiday in Norway, where they went every year for father's fishing. We compared notes but we had nothing in common.

On the train back to Stockholm, what I remembered most vividly was a story my father had told about himself. As a young man, when he was rather wild, he admitted, he had bought a copy of a film about the life of Christ. He had travelled up and down the country showing this film in church halls and in clubs, and had made himself a small fortune. At the end of the summer, when the copy was worn out and dangerous to show – in those days film was highly inflammable – he had called a halt by one of the big lakes in southern Sweden and laid on a big party, where finally Christ went up in flames.

I came back to London just as fatherless as before. It is not possible to pick up a father in a few days.

Night Messages: Tyrone
the Magnificent

We have ample evidence of the fakery that went into
creating the stars' façades,
of the misery that went on behind these, and the tyranny of
the studio despots
who insisted on the image at the expense of the human
being underneath.
All of which inevitably raises the question
whether it is possible to be BOTH A
STAR AND A HUMAN BEING.
If it isn't, how many would have traded stardom for pale
humanity?

Molly Haskell, *From Reverence to Rape*, 1973

I was not different from other actresses in the way I would
meet a new love partner. It was usually through work on a
film or a play. Finally, I was to meet a man who had all the
angels on his side – including the fallen ones. Tyrone Power
– my one-time idol – was a man of fascinating duality, who
had a good and loving side to his nature but also a slightly
sinister one. I do not really know whether he was searching
for a balance within himself, although he was certainly
aware of the split in his personality. He was a 'catch', as they
say in the world of leading men, a celebrity and a darling to
women for the past twenty years. When we met, he was
forty-two and I was thirty-one. He was a ladies' man,
certainly, a modern Romeo, a perfect gentleman when he

129

wanted to be. But I never forgot that basically he was a dark man, with a shadowed past, as he called it. He seemed undazzled by fame. To most people he appeared uncomplicated, and he had a surface charm which was devastating.

When Tyrone first went to Hollywood at the age of twenty, he had been given test after screen test by Twentieth Century Fox Studios, before that little megalomaniac Zanuck gave the stamp of approval and a seven-year contract. Tyrone became the favourite boy in the Zanuck stable. This was the time when movie stars were rapidly taking the place of God. He had been cast from the very beginning as the romantic swash-buckling hero; he suited the part well but, if anything, he was just a little too handsome. For Zanuck, he was someone who could at last take over Valentino's mantle. Rin Tin Tin and Shirley Temple were not enough as big box-office stars: he wanted a real he-man, and in Tyrone he had found him. Being the object of hero-worship was not easy for Tyrone, who was sensitive about his good looks. After having been easy-going as a young man, he changed, privately, into a brooding, lonely person.

Zanuck wanted quick returns from his investment, so Tyrone appeared in movie after movie with sometimes no longer than a week between finishing one and starting another. And always, of course, playing the same kind of hero. 'It was like working in a factory,' he would say to me.

He was lionised and he loved it, to begin with, anyway. He was ambitious and I soon discovered why. He had a desperate need to prove that he could be a good actor, as good if not better than his Irish father and grandfather, both of whom had been well-known Shakespearean actors in Britain and the States. He felt that he had a name and reputation to uphold. Tyrone was a rare bird in Hollywood because he had good manners and was quietly spoken; his behaviour was exemplary, always nice, always polite. 'Too nice,' someone once said. 'He must be hiding something nasty. Nobody is as nice as that by nature.'

We met in England in 1956. He had made forty-two films but liked only a handful of them. He had formed a company called Copa Productions with a fellow called Ted Richmond, who would never remember my name, or rather chose not to remember it once he had found out that Tyrone and I were lovers. At best, he would call me Maya Zeiterling. He did everything he could to stop our relationship from going any further. 'Thank God I stopped him from marrying *her*,' he was later to say.

Tyrone had seen me in the production of Anouilh's play, *Point of Departure*, and had admired my work ever since, promising himself that if the opportunity arose he would work with me. He cast me opposite himself in a film called *Seven Waves Away*, made for his company in London. It was called *Abandon Ship* in the States. It was, I'm afraid, a rather tiresome story about an ocean liner which sinks in mid-ocean. There we were, twenty or so people in a tiny lifeboat, bobbing up and down uncomfortably in a large indoor tank at Shepperton Studios, wind and wave machines going full blast, a giant watershoot pouring ice-cold water over us. We could not possibly hear the director shouting his 'Action!' so a starting-pistol was used to get us going. The whole film had to be dubbed as we could hardly make ourselves heard.

Tyrone and I began to have dinner together, and I was soon falling in love with him – but I was torn between him and my loyalty to the man I was living with at the time, a young American writer who had turned out to be an extraordinary stepfather for my children. I sometimes wondered whom he loved the most – me or my children. He was trying to impose a pattern on the children's lives and make me into a better mother than I had been. Perhaps he was succeeding; perhaps we really were beginning to be a little family unit for the very first time. I knew the children loved and needed him. How could I break it up, then? I lingered, took my time. So did Tyrone. I didn't want it to be a film-set romance. But it was inevitable.

I was happy, Tyrone seemed happy, yet I wondered what would become of our love. There were too many differences in our life-styles. I knew this but did not want to admit it. Yet we worked, we travelled, we loved. We made plans for the future, we talked a great deal, we saw far too many people – at least, too many for my liking. And I, who was

131

used to sleeping with windows wide open and no curtains, who liked (and still do) to be woken by the first light of day, was quite taken aback by having to sleep in a room that was blacker than black. But here, in the blackness, we talked. For love he wanted the bright lights, the sun; for verbal communication – total blackness.

Most of those night messages took place in London or Littlehampton, where we used to take the children, his and mine together with the nanny, for week-ends. And there were a few in Hollywood and Mexico, Paris, Rome, Sicily, Stockholm – even Manchester.

One of our first disagreements was after a very well-known American columnist had visited the set at Shepperton. What had upset me was that Tyrone was as charming and seemingly open with her as with one of his best friends. He was paying lip-service; this was new to me. The columnist had a bad reputation – she fed like a parasite on people like Tyrone; perhaps he just didn't realise it . . . I had to find out. So I asked him in the darkness how he could tolerate that kind of bitch and, flippantly, he said, 'If I'm not gossiped about, I might as well be dead, so I need that bitch, I need her for my career.' What I could not bear, of course, was that the bitch thought that Tyrone liked her. When he had said, 'Perhaps I *do* like her,' it had been a strange intonation. I wasn't sure – my usual problem – if he was serious or if it was a joke. 'That chokes you, doesn't it?' he said, and continued: 'Yes, I love small, ugly, fat, Jewish women too because they want to be beautiful and loved just like everyone else. That's why it's easy to be nice to her. Sure she has become ugly and bitter and bitchy and all the rest. But I don't blame her for it.'

That was one right in the eye for me: my question about the columnist had shown up shortcomings in myself. I was always too quick in judging other people. I think I muttered something about not liking the vulture bit in that profession of hers; consuming people who were down on their luck, always using the negative aspects in her column and, what's more, making a lot of money from these ugly deeds. Tyrone answered: 'There's a lot of putrid stuff in this profession. We need people like her to pick things clean from time to time. There is always a grain of truth, my dear, in those reports. Sometimes this business is ugly, sure, but since I'm not going to be able to change it single-handedly, I might just as well turn the charm on for her. As it's part of the business, it's not worth worrying about.' But I could not accept this glib remark, so I battled on and asked him how could anyone know or trust him if he was as charming as that to someone he didn't really like? These nights almost always ended with a big teasing line he had ready-made for me: sometimes it went on for more than a minute. It would go something like this: 'Impossible, crazy, stubborn Swede, who thinks she can change the world single-handed. Little ninny, I don't know why I love such an eccentric nut, I must be crazy. You are nothing but a load of trouble, weird, difficult lady, wonderful monster, eighth wonder of the world . . .'

I have never been so looked after, spoiled even, as during those years with Tyrone. My gentleman-lover sent me huge bunches of white carnations, several times a week; he liked to wear one in his lapel, and he always wanted to share what he loved with me. He worried about my welfare in the minutest detail, liked to be able to take care of things for me: he put his secretary at my disposal, as well as his chauffeur, Arthur, who adored him (Tyrone had always loved expensive cars and his current pride and joy was a vintage Rolls-Royce). He was thoughtful in an almost fatherly fashion; he wanted to surprise and please me. I felt indeed loved in a very special way. It was as if I had found a father in the guise of Tyrone, if a rather incestuous one. He seemed to me the perfection of man in so very many ways – he was masculine and virile but he also had a gentle, feminine side that enabled me to get to know him closely.

Tyrone wanted to give me a surprise at Christmas so, with Arthur's help, he decorated my flat with mistletoe and holly berries. Underneath the Christmas tree was a sixteen-millimetre projector with one of my old films to go with it as well as one of his – a film that he had made in 1947 called *Nightmare Alley*, one of his favourites. There were also presents for the children and the rest of the household:

thoughtful, loving presents to one and all. It was a joyous Christmas and I made Tyrone's favourite food: duck à l'orange and salad of palm hearts and artichoke hearts. Then there was the vintage champagne that he had brought along, and on Christmas Day he got up early to fix Black Velvet (champagne and Guinness), as well as scrambled eggs and coffee for a feast in bed.

My present to him was a tape-recorder and on it we recorded a test tape which we called 'Christmas Night'. I have it still.

M. What happened tonight when, in the midst of all the gaiety, you cut us all off? I could almost see a shadow come over your face. Can you tell me about it, or do you prefer not to? It was strange because it was so sudden, and we had no access to you any more.

T. I'm all worn out and black inside; usually I make sure that people don't notice it. I've learnt to hide it but you have seen it and sometimes I hate you for it. There are certain things I would like to keep to myself. You must have things you don't want anyone to know too, as you are not exactly a simple lady, although you fool yourself that you are.

I tried to write a novel once about all these black things inside me but it got too damn black and it was all about *me*, so I gave it up as a bad job. Too many actors write those books anyway and I suppose I didn't want to enough and, to tell you the truth, it scared the shit out of me, that bit of writing. I became a sort of criminal in my own eyes. I started to judge myself and I hadn't liked what I saw was me. I tortured myself about certain things that I had done in my life and felt guilty. I began to see the few good things I had done as a kind of penitence. God, shit, it made me feel awful, I can tell you. I turned out to be a hypocrite and I couldn't live with that kind of image of myself, so I decided to forget all about it. It was masochistic really. It was like having a continuous nightmare. Anyway, I seem to be able to take those black thoughts a bit

better these days and I'm not ashamed any more. I
don't feel guilty right now. [He was reading Freud at
that time, quoting him now and then.]

And from my diary:
I had asked if he believed in an after-life or a god and he said it was
none of my business, telling me I was too nosy and not to ask those
impertinent questions again, as he had enough questions in his
head and didn't want to tell me everything anyway. But then he
asked *me* if I believed in God ... I could not give him a straight
answer. I had had some strange inexplicable experiences – one,
certainly, that had changed my young life – but I didn't want to talk
away those strong experiences because, every time I had tried to
explain them, they seemed to become smaller and less significant;
also, I was aware of the disbelief that I saw mirrored on people's
faces. It was all very strange. I could not say that I believed, *but I
knew.*

T. You are lucky. I'd like to be able to say that.
M. But you believe in reincarnation.
T. Sort of. Perhaps I *want* to believe in it? That is quite
    different from actually believing.

After Christmas, Tyrone and I went to Sweden to talk about
launching *Abandon Ship* in Europe, and to try to meet Ingmar
Bergman, whom Tyrone wanted to interest in making a film
for his company. He greatly admired Ingmar's work, and it
also gave me the chance to show him my country, especially
the north that I loved so much. We did the full tourist bit,
with sleigh rides in the forest by torchlight, snow falling. It
was all extremely romantic.

When Tyrone met Ingmar in Stockholm he felt that he had
something in common with him: he recognised the blackness in him, even though Ingmar laughed a lot and was his
usual charming self. Tyrone was amused to see Ingmar's
Dracula fangs and was surprised that they didn't spoil his
chances with women. In fact, he found it hard to believe that
Ingmar preferred women to men, as he felt that the women
in Ingmar's movies were bitchy and hard, castrating ladies,

and that the men were always shown in a more interesting and positive light: their suffering seemed to him more acute and sincere. It was interesting to hear that from Tyrone, as it was not the accepted view. On the contrary, it was usually held, by men and women alike, that Ingmar's films were full of compassion and understanding for women: he was the only male director who understood them completely. 'It's the women who always create the hell in his movies,' said Tyrone. 'Fascinating that he had so many affairs with those bitches in his movies and even married a few. I should have talked to him about women, I could have given him a few plots for some really black movies.'

Tyrone felt that he could have outdone Bergman as far as plots went, reckoning that what he had seen in Hollywood of family life was far worse than any Bergman movie. He said that in Hollywood, the glamour and sweet-dreamy stuff was but a façade, that it was a world of polite destruction. He also felt that Ingmar and he had this woman thing in common, and admitted to having had too many women in his life: 'Couldn't get away from them; caught, always caught.' I was horrified when he told me the sums of money he paid out regularly in alimony and he said: 'I paid gladly to get out of their grasping clutches but it still hurts my guts, when I think that I'm fucking well furnishing houses all over the world which I shall never live in, not even visit; I'm keeping their lovers as well. And I pay storage for trunks of clothes from my last wife who turned into a bitch. God damn it, I will not get caught again, never.' 'Never' became a keyword between Tyrone and myself. 'Never' in Italian – *'mai'*. It was a well-known fact that Tyrone had had more affairs than any leading man in Hollywood. He could not do without women: he wanted to be close to them all – his mother, his sister, his friends, his secretaries and his wives. 'I love you all and I hate you all. And now I'm being fooled again.'

It didn't help when I told him I wasn't out to fool him – which in his book meant getting him to the altar yet again. At that time in my life I needed as much freedom as he. He would often repeat this phrase to me: 'I love you. But don't count on me.' I didn't.

He was terrified of being caught. 'But you *wanted* to be caught as well, didn't you?' I asked.

'Sure,' he laughed, ironically. 'Sure I did. It's all bullshit, contradictions. I was lonely as hell, I thought marriage would cure that.' I wanted to know if at least he had been happy in the beginning, happy about being a father?

'It's a silly word, isn't it? Happy – what does it mean? At the moment, happiness means being with you, because of your bottom and your crazy ideas, your tits, those are the things I like about you and, for the moment, don't want to do without. But I suppose I accept the rest, like your nutty mind, your headstrong ideas. Actually, come to think of it, one would not be any good without the other and you know that only too well, stupid. I never saw anyone like you, that's for sure. You're crazy.'

I think it was while we were on holiday in Sicily that summer that I realised just how much of a star he was. The press were hiding in the bushes, behind sand-dunes, to get a compromising photo of us. In tiny forgotten villages in the mountains, people would stop and stare and follow him like the Pied Piper. They would hang around us when we sat at a bar, asking for an autograph, which he never denied anyone. 'Part of my responsibility,' he explained to me. 'They need it, and perhaps I do too. The day no one asks me any more, perhaps I shall be frightened.' I felt that autograph-hunting and picture collections of famous people were almost like cannibalism. People couldn't eat one another any more but instead they asked for those symbolic bits of the personality. It had always made me feel uncomfortable.

We went out fishing one night with a young, rough-looking fisherman, to watch him catch sardines. We had both thought it would be a lovely and romantic thing to do. The young man also tried to catch ink-fish by the light of a home-made lantern. What we had not expected was that when he managed to catch an enormous octopus, he would bite it to death, while the beast coiled its slimy arms around his head and face. Tyrone was sick. Was it the gory spectacle or the waves? I cradled him in my arms: he was shivering. 'See what a great virile man you've got,' he whispered.

'There you've got a *real* man,' – he was eyeing the fisherman – 'the kind I could never be.' He said it with both admiration and fear.

Later the same night, he said to me all of a sudden that he hated sex sometimes. I couldn't help but laugh at him, as he had just proved the contrary. No, he insisted that he meant it, that he liked to be able to do without it, not be bothered, not having to prove his damned masculinity all the time. When I said that he did not need to prove anything to me, it was his turn to laugh, calling me an impatient lady, whom he was sure would be upset if he was suddenly unable to perform. 'You who grin like anything at the mere idea, even. Ah, to be sexless – less alimony, no women, no worries, no black nights.'

I suggested that it might be a bit boring in the long run. He didn't want to agree to that; he felt sure there must be a substitute, like work, for instance. No time to think of sex. He could become a workaholic, that would suit him fine. Or go to a retreat in a cloister. But best of all would be to become a eunuch: no balls, no problems.

Back in London, rehearsing *The Devil's Disciple*, Tyrone felt lonely and frightened. He asked me to sit in the stalls during rehearsals, taking notes. Someone was acting him off the stage and he was aware of it. A couple of months later he came to sit in on my rehearsals of Anouilh's *Restless Heart*. And when I toured the provinces, he would come to visit and give me notes. We had merry dinners with Peter Bull, whom Tyrone liked because he made him laugh. But then Tyrone would suddenly hold forth with a vehemence that surprised me.

Some day I will show the motherfuckers who say I was a success just because of my pretty face. Sometimes I wish I had a really bad car accident so my face would get smashed up and I'd look like Eddie Constantine. It's so fucking tiring being everybody's darling boy at my age. They still don't take me seriously. I couldn't help I was pretty, could I? The critics thought there couldn't be any intelligence behind the façade. Shit, double-shit. But I'll make it. That film-star-hero bit hangs over me like a curse, though. Sure, I know I've been lucky, that things have gone almost *too* smoothly careerwise. What I resent about it is that it is all built on a pretty face.

Hollywood was such a crazy place, made you feel terrific at times. You felt you could achieve anything because you were treated like a god. But it sure was a bum place too. When you saw the new faces queueing up, like bloody comets, who would strike the screen and leave an old worshipped star obsolete in no time. Nobody will ever understand what this did to people, how it destroyed them, made them hollow. We *were* gods, we could do nothing wrong, we were worshipped in the most hideous way imaginable. Signing hundreds of autographs a day was enough to make anybody big-headed, full of shit about himself. Jesus Christ, I don't want to become an ageless matinée idol, having to keep up my looks, lift my chin like Marlene and never dare smile in case my face cracks.

Morelia, Mexico, during the filming of The Sun Also Rises

Zanuck, Tyrone's oldest and most ardent fan, was there producing, chain-smoking large cigars, chewing the ends. His new girlfriend, Juliette Greco, was also in the film. Ava Gardner was in the cast: a sad, lonely, lost creature. Errol Flynn was there, more or less alcoholic by now, dictating his memoirs. Tyrone and Errol had been great buddies once and had gone sailing together when they had time away from the studio lot. Flynn had a love-hate relationship with films and Hollywood; he despised being an actor: a phoney profession for queers, he would say. Tyrone was disturbed by the change in Flynn, physically. He would say to me: 'Look at him now. Jesus. I don't want to become like him. He used to be so great, healthy, full of life. Now he is just an empty shell, a wreck of a man. But he is lovely all the same – when he isn't drunk, that is – you'll see.'

Bill Gallagher was there too, Tyrone's secretary for many years; a tired, dogged-looking man. He had come to Mexico

City to meet me. Tyrone had sent me a first-class ticket from London as a birthday present. From Mexico City, we had taken a small private plane to Morelia, a pink and glowing city, lying in the heart of the country. We landed in a field full of sheep. Tyrone was there to greet me with a band of Indian Mariachas. A typical gesture, larger than life, the kind of romantic gesture that women hardly ever encounter. A summer of glowing happiness. We were in our second year together – were we moving towards the end? Bill Gallagher watched us with a somewhat cynical expression. He had been ushering Tyrone's ladies around for years, had seen them come and go at regular intervals. I think he was rather surprised that we were still together in such a happy way. Ted Richmond was more antagonistic than ever, and then there were those infuriating articles: 'Love-lorn Mai seeks Power' or 'She is determined to get him, but he has vowed never to marry again.'

The only thing that interested the press, in Denmark, Sweden, France, England, Italy and now the States, was when the great day was to be? 'Never,' Tyrone and I said in unison. One typical newspaper article ran like this:

Mai Zetterling is out to get her man. And in screenland's longest, most persistent romantic chase, the determined blonde is catching up on elusive Tyrone Power. If sheer doggedness is the way to a man's heart, she should have Ty at the altar any lap now. One of the latest landmarks in their round-the-world courtship was Morelia in Mexico. There Power was finishing his latest movie. One fine morning, Miss Zetterling appeared on the horizon. A specially chartered plane touched down from Mexico City. And out danced Mai looking for the big Hallo she's missed for so many weeks. They were constantly together when Ty wasn't in front of the cameras. When the film was finished, Ty moved to Paris. And who was waiting there? Why, little Mai. Her smile determined, her heart determined . . . to overpower Power . . . She remembered that no woman had yet been able to make him happy . . .

Tyrone was disturbed and couldn't stop talking and thinking about Errol these days, who would get up early and start the tequilas at breakfast; by eleven he would be wild-eyed. He was dictating his memoirs into a tape-recorder. A very pretty secretary would come and decipher the words, which were mumbled, as if he didn't want to share his life with the public. 'I did it for the money,' he said; he would shock the world with his escapades.

Errol saw himself as a modern Casanova and was charming to ladies in an old-fashioned way. One evening, we made a foursome down to a small Mexican taverna where the tequila was poured into great tumblers. I noticed Errol watching me to see if I could manage to drink the stuff. I don't know why, but suddenly I felt devilish and emptied the tumbler in one go, which made Errol pay me my first compliment. That, I'm afraid, started him off – he drank a tumbler and yet another and fell under the table. So I have the great honour of having drunk Errol Flynn under the table. Mind you, it wasn't hard, as he had started his drinking at eight in the morning and that had been my first and last one of the day . . .

Later, in the lush garden of the hotel, where there seemed to be crickets and nightingales under and above us, Tyrone still talked about Errol, how he had been one of those people that couldn't say no to Hollywood but that it was the broads who had really killed him; that it would have been better if he had been a queer. I must have looked a bit startled at this remark so he tried to explain to me that it was the tarty little starlets that Errol couldn't keep his hands off, especially the ones under age: 'Hollywood and the broads, it's a pretty ghastly mixture. He wasn't strong enough to take it. Perhaps I'm not either. But it's all a game, isn't it? Bullshit or no bullshit.'

Hollywood

I had just arrived after a long and sleepless flight from London. Tyrone and I had a lot to talk about, like the arrangements for the continental theatrical tour we were planning together. I had looked forward to spending the evening with him alone, but that was not to be. We had to go to a party, the silver-wedding of an old friend of his. When he saw my hesitation, he said: 'Take one of my pills. It'll wake you up.'

I had seen him take that little 'cheer-me-up' pill almost every night in order to be on form for his guests, though I knew nothing about pep-pills in those days. Anyway, we went. Someone fell into the pool almost at once; there was a lot of subdued hysterical laughter. It was a sit-down dinner for about a hundred people. I was goggle-eyed at so much fame. Irene Dunne, Loretta Young, Rosalind Russell, David Niven, Fred Astaire and the ubiquitous gossip writers, of course. One of them was on monkey-gland injections as well as pills. The speeches were nothing but insults and obscenities. The silver-wedded wife screamed at her silver-haired husband: 'You've fucked every starlet in this fucking town!' 'Fucking whore,' was his reply. When the monkey-gland dame stood up to give the main speech, it was all four-letter words. I had not known there were so many. Our hostess was violently sick on the table. By then I had stopped eating. One of the great stars, I assumed an old flame of Tyrone's, leaned over him, touched him up in a knowing way and, with a glance at me, said in a resounding theatrical whisper: 'Will she come upstairs with us?' Tyrone declined both on his own behalf and mine but I was revolted by the spectacle. I could not take it any longer, even as an onlooker. 'I just have to leave,' I told Tyrone. 'You can't go,' he said. 'You stay, I can get a taxi,' but he insisted on taking me home. His face was black and sullen. He did not talk much, until much later in the dark. He had taken that damn pep-pill so he was wide awake.

I didn't know how he managed with only three hours' sleep (he was due at the studio at seven in the morning). When I said that this was a sure way of killing himself, he had answered cynically: 'Perhaps that's what I want. What's the point of sleep? A sort of small death.'

'But you're making a film; you have to be in good shape,' I had insisted. 'And I must say that you not only look tired; to be honest, you look haggard.'

142

Tyrone shrugged it off. 'I know, I know. Perhaps I will get a face at last. Like Errol. The bastard walked away with the good single performance notices in *The Sun Also Rises* because of his boozy face and the "I don't give a shit" look. Why shouldn't I do the same?'

'Don't be desperate,' was the only thing I could find to say to this.

'I *am* desperate,' came his reply. 'I *am* desperate, although I try to cover it up. I've become so good at it that even you can't tell now.'

It was my turn to insist: 'But you have so much going for you.'

'Sure as hell I have; bills and responsibilities. Ex-wives farting around having hysterics. Yes, I have a lot going for me. What a joke! I have nothing, nothing. Not even fulfilment in my work any more – because I know now that whatever I do, the critics will not, cannot, accept that I am an actor to be taken seriously. And that kills me.'

'So you take pills?'

'Yes, my dear, I take pills, I drink, I laugh. What else can I do?'

Some years later, Tyrone started taking injections instead of pills. My doctor in London refused to give him the injections he had brought along from Hollywood. 'They'll kill you,' he said. So he went to another doctor, one who did not have so many scruples.

During my visit, Tyrone was working on *Witness for the Prosecution* with Marlene Dietrich and Charles Laughton; Billy Wilder was directing. They were all close buddies, it seemed. Dietrich was showing signs of interest in Tyrone, giving him little presents. Tyrone was both flattered and bored by her attentions. Charles Laughton followed him around with bulging, lecherous eyes. Even the cold, cynical Wilder seemed a bit infatuated with him.

I felt very strongly that I was in the way. They were all a little jealous of his interest in me. I knew Tyrone was being told by everyone, not only Ted Richmond, not to go too far this time. I had come to Hollywood in order to discuss our tour together. He was excited by the prospect of playing three great roles in repertory. His big part was to be Chekhov's Don Juan; mine, Giraudoux's Ondine.

Hollywood, Bel Air

That particular day had been a strange one. I had almost burst my insides with that coil in my womb. Then the maid who lived in, a big, black, friendly woman, saw a tarantula in the kitchen. She passed out and fell to the ground, hurting herself badly and bleeding profusely. I was mopping blood off the kitchen floor when Tyrone came home. He was perfectly calm and charming to everyone, despite the hideous mess. He was working very hard at the time and looked worn out. When we were in bed, finally, he sighed heavily again and again. Clearly something was wrong and clearly it had to do with me being there. I insisted that he tell me what the matter was. After a long pause and another sigh, finally he said: 'It's no point trying to do things, it wouldn't work.'

'What, the tour?' I asked.

'No, that probably would work, be a success even. But the rest. I want to work with you, very much, you know that. I want to be with you. You are good to be with . . . but [that heavy silence again] but what would you do if I had other affairs during the tour? I warned you. A year seems to be my maximum. Don't count on me, remember?' I remembered only too well.

Actually, we had been together for almost three years by now. I appreciated his honesty and told him so – but I also said that I did not know if I would be able to cope with such a situation if it arose, that I would like to think it over. It sounded cool but I was far from cool. I had expected something like this, sooner or later, despite all his passionate attention.

It was the end of the affair. Instead of hanging around the house being miserable and even perhaps changing my mind, I decided to leave. We would try to stay friends, if possible; we were still deeply fond of one another.

I took off with a grand old man who was a friend of some Hopi Indians near Phoenix, in Arizona. We travelled twenty-four hours non-stop, the most hair-raising trip because the old man wore Mr Magoo double glasses and the car was topless, so that in the desert the sun was almost unbearable and while driving through the mountains in a torrential storm we sat knee-deep in water. But we survived, and there followed one of the most magic weeks of my life. We slept in cobra-infested land high up on a plateau, thinking that the distant rattling was the rustle of dried seed-pods. In this dreamy landscape it was as if I came back to myself: when you have been living extremely close to someone, you lose part of your own existence.

We were guests of the chieftain and stayed in his adobe hut with his considerable family, as well as many cats and dogs and one very dead sheep which had been slaughtered for the festivities we had come to watch. What exactly happened to me in those wild hills I don't know for certain but whatever it was, it gave me the courage and inspiration to start thinking about changing my profession, seriously, for the first time. I wanted to make my own choices in a stronger and more personal way. I realised it was not possible for an actress to have that kind of control: I needed a larger canvas. Until now, I had felt like a broken mirror showing bits and pieces of a fragmented character. Now I wanted to piece the mirror together to make a single view of the world. For that, I needed to be whole; I needed a strength that I had not had before. It was as if, through the rituals of the Hopi Indians, I was lifted out of myself on to another plane, which helped me to overcome the fears that still lingered within me.

Following those rituals, which went on from daybreak to nightfall, became for me a deep, an illuminating experience. I began to change in more ways than one. I am absolutely convinced that my life would have been very different if I had not met those remarkable, sane, lovesome men up there in those remote and mysterious hills.

And now Tyrone lies in the Great Theatre of the Dead. His funeral was a farce, like so many funerals in Hollywood, where even death is turned into a kind of spectacle.

Thousands of fans waiting for the stars that have come to pay homage and for the weeping hysterical widow. Soft drinks and sandwiches, ice-cream vendors doing a roaring trade among the graves. Tyrone would have smiled a crooked smile. Music from his films was being played over the Tannoy.

When Tyrone died, I had followed him part of the way to the world beyond. At that precise moment, I had been sitting reading *Dr Zhivago* and had come to the scene of the heart attack, which takes place on a tram. I read those pages I don't know how many times. Finally I put the book away and stared into the fire in the grate, losing myself in the light of the embers until I could see nothing but colours and dots in front of my eyes. I was filled with infinite sadness and was as if in a trance. That night, watching the news on TV, I heard: 'Tyrone Power has died from a cardiac arrest in Rome while in a car on the way to hospital,' and I understood the strong emotions I had felt.

Later Arthur Ross wrote to tell me that Tyrone had visited him just before his death, the night he left for Europe. 'He felt that he had failed you, but that he could not be what you wanted him to be. That it was not possible for him to be the professional artist you believed he could be . . . He still loved you – but you could not see that.'

One of his early girlfriends, Janet Gaynor, had given Tyrone a book called *Forever*, which he had always intended to make into a film one day. She was to co-star with him. When the relationship ended, the project was put on ice. All his major subsequent loves – Judy Garland, Annabella and I – were given the book to read and offered the part. But it never got further than us reading the book. It was all about reincarnated spirits, two people who could not part, even through death. Tyrone believed in all that but he never had the courage to admit it. And he never made the film.

Night Thoughts with Jung

May 23rd, 1981

How can I possibly have any definite opinion about myself?
How can I possibly be objective, when all the things that I
remember most vividly are the emotional dramas of my life,
the passions, all the things that have disturbed me the most
and also confuse me the most?

C. G. Jung

May 24th, 1981   *Le Mazel, perched on its iron rock*
Flowers, flowers everywhere, between pink slabs of marble, on the
old kitchen range, itself covered in painted flowers on ceramic:
pansies, aquilegias, roses. By the stained-glass window with its
lilies and clematis, there is a vase of narcissi mixed with the
blue-flowering sage that runs riot by the little river. But the most
magnificent flower comes from a hill just discovered this morning
in a wild countryside. By a cascading rivulet these giant
asphodeluses grow, named after a Greek god. I am drying purple
wild thyme, which fills the house with scent. The friends who
come for the flowery birthday lunch can hardly see each other for
the bouquets on the table: cowslips and honeysuckle, wild roses,
mimosa. We even *eat* flowers for dessert: elderflower fritters, with
elderflower wine from last year and rosemary snow – whipped
white of egg and cream, rose-water and orange liqueur. We dip the

small flowering branches of rosemary in the sweet snow. My friends laugh at my flower-mania. 'But Mai, you begin at the wrong end – flowers usually come last, when the house is all finished.' So what; I get so many things wrong, I shall just continue my madness. I dream flowers, I eat flowers. Today I am drunk with flowers. Also, perhaps, I instinctively feel that the house will never be finished – so today is the day of flowers.

June 1st

What is a diary, then? A daily record, random thoughts, so as to know for myself how I have used my time, where it's all gone. Time, it's as transient as money in my hands: here today, gone tomorrow. Perhaps a diary is a kind of book-keeping? Delacroix wrote: 'All those days that are not noted down are like days which have not been.'

July 7th

I manage to work, in spite of the dust blowing in through the keyhole of my work-room. There is dust everywhere, even in bed. I sweep, work, cook, smile, sweep. We are all dusty. Glen looks like a statue at night and we go to the river every evening for a swim, no matter what the weather. We have a chemical loo that stands in a corner of the old ballroom; still no hot water. It's all right; we cope. The workmen cannot understand me, and say that their wives would never put up with this kind of mess. I'm not sure if they admire my courage or think that I am a mad woman; I suspect the latter. Sometimes I agree with that myself. I step over debris and rubbish all day and finally I cannot be in the house any more, the dust is falling everywhere. I work in the field, under a big singing chestnut tree, full of cicadas. I use stones for paper-weights to stop the sheets from flying.

What madness is all this? I live in my memories, writing about my fatherless days. I manage to put it down more or less as I lived it, or do I? Perhaps I am a rather unreliable witness to my own life. However, as I write my false or not false remembrances, hundredweights of stone and earth are shifted, back and forth, old dirty stuff is taken away and clean sifted sand brought in. My mouth is full of sand, my past an enormous sand-castle that I keep destroying and rebuilding again and again. My dreams are full of dust and pain as I remember.

July 12th
I long to find order in myself and what do I get? Bits and pieces, all mixed up.

January 1st, 1982
I've nicknamed Le Mazel 'the Ruins'. I came back here from Canada on a first-class airfare and stepped into the Middle Ages. I'm tending and feeding stoves all day, it seems. I have become a tatty Cinderella, grey from head to foot.

Still no bathroom, but hot water ... it reminds me of my childhood; Saturday night tub-baths in the kitchen. Visiting the loo that is still in the ballroom, with no window-panes, I wear my fur coat. Yes, I have definitely become an eccentric. Frosty fairy landscapes on the windows in the bedroom in the early morning, which the orange sun melts; snow on the mimosa.

The time has come to go back to the past that hurts the most, that is still too uncomfortably close. I have not yet digested its shadows and its pain. Troubled feeling, heart in my mouth.

As I feel that I am not yet at a safe distance from this section in my life, I will build myself a fortified tower, don a rhinoceros hide, protect my heart with Swedish stainless steel. I have been warding off this moment but, armed at all points, I expect to come out the other side unhurt and sane. And so I will go through with it, however bloody, in order to be able to go forward.

The Killing Game

Everything that does not kill me makes me stronger . . .

Camus

The Sad and Wonderful Story of Mai and David

The time has come for an old-fashioned romance, a true love story for the tender-hearted. It could also be called a domestic comedy, with a number of lively scenes and myself as the leading actress – or should I say clown? The story is full of sub-plots, odd details and showbiz characters. A soap opera with no moral tagged on at the end.

It is certainly a story that keeps on repeating itself all over the domesticated globe. The Great Love Affair that has its beginning, its middle and its end. Ah, the repetition of romance that seems to go on *ad nauseam*, everyone suffering from the same symptoms, sharing the same allergies which create havoc with the emotional life! But, even so, each couple have their own very personal flavour and lived-through agonies. Here it is, then: the curtain-raiser.

The setting is Mai's seven-room apartment in a large Victorian brick mansion in Kensington. It is London, 1957. 'It is a charmingly appointed place, appropriate for a busy, international star,' a journalist had written. I shall describe the décor in some detail; the lady tends to be extravagant and changes the decorations in each place she moves to according to her inner needs, also sometimes to suit the man she is living with.

There is modern furniture, black with steel frames, plants in wooden receptacles. A heavy, bold, red-and-white striped curtain covers the front door, which is Victorian and ornate and not much to Mai's taste at this stage of her life. The style she has chosen is most definitely Scandinavian – airy and chic. A long corridor leads from the main hall. The first room is her bedroom, moderately large and sparsely furnished. On her bed are two pale blue suitcases with her initials embossed in gold. Out of them spill petticoats, scarves, elaborate underwear.

She is sitting somewhat listlessly on the bed, staring into space, smoking a Gauloise. She is at home after a trip to Hollywood. She feels lonely, although the flat is full of activity and people. She has a film coming up, the money situation is reasonable, she hasn't got an overdraft. Yet she has this small ache in her heart. What a fool she's been again; she has not only thrown away love but also a fine working relationship. The planning of the world tour Tyrone and she intended to make together, and which they'd been working on for a year, had been in its final stages. And she has given all this up because she is still such a romantic fool, unable to take his vague suggestion that he might have other lovers. Was it because she could not accept other people's terms, only her own? Why did she insist on believing in the old idea of love, when deep down she did not trust it? If it did not work out for others, why should it work for her? She told herself she was too demanding, too full of self-pity, as she felt the tears rise in her eyes.

The sitting-room is as sparsely decorated as the rest, just as Scandinavian and in perfect order.

Mrs Ruddy brings tea, wants to chat about Tyrone. She worked for him when he lived in Abingdon Road; he had been so kind to her and her ailing husband. (Typical of Tyrone to put himself out for other people.) Mai avoids giving direct answers as to when Mr Power is coming and when the rehearsals start. She does not feel like chatting; she does not feel at home. Not even when confronted by the noisy reality of the children returning from school. She is relieved when they want to watch TV rather than talk to her.

151

She wanders into the children's room, which lies down the corridor. It's large and sunny. Louis's stamp collection and astronomy books, foreign coins, riding-hats and boots, cuddly toys, a globe of the world with stickers on to show where mother Mai is hiding; it's all in perfect order. In fact, everything is so well ordered that no children seem to live there.

She takes a bath for want of anything better to do. She has phoned her agent. There was no news. She has four days before leaving for Stockholm where she will star in a film called *The Doll's House*: an attack on Ibsen based on a novella by Strindberg. What to do with these days? She at once feels guilty because she knows exactly what she ought to do – spend some time with her children; take them places like proper mothers do.

She picks up her address book to see who to call. Nobody springs to her mind. She has to remind herself who her friends are. Even her children are strangers to her. She sees that they are well looked after, brings them presents from her trips, sends them funny postcards, gives them a certain amount of affection. But how much does she really care, she asks herself – and starts to feel guilty again.

Finally she rings her doctor, who is a friend. He answers in his usual manner: a formal, clipped tone he uses even for personal calls. She always feels a little taken aback.

'You must come for dinner tonight, because my other nights are fully booked, my dear. But, alas, I've already asked a young poet. I don't think I can get out of it now. How boring – I would have liked to have you all to myself. Come at eight.' He slams down the receiver. The abruptness surprises her, although she is prepared for it.

She selects a tight-fitting white dress which shows off her bronzed skin, puts on the African gold belt. Her hair newly washed, she feels she looks all right. After telling the children a story about the Hopi Indians she met in Arizona, she sets off for Pimlico in her pale blue Sunbeam Talbot sports car. Though she is not aware of it, she is behaving like a spoilt star. She lights a cigarette with the gold lighter Tyrone gave her, with the inscription 'Love forever'. Her heart gives a jolt. Oh God, will it be like that every time she uses it?

The doctor presses his pelvis hard against her, as is his habit. Strange – she has always wanted to ask him why, but never has. It is not that he is attracted to her. There are flowers everywhere, packed in vases: carnations, damn it, which makes her think of Tyrone again.

The doctor is newly showered, fresh and elegant, like his house. Soon the ice tinkles seductively in large goblets. She tells him her news about Tyrone. He is flabbergasted: 'But, my dear girl, do you really think you did the right thing?' She does not, but cannot say so. She is playing the strong and independent line now, won't own up to how miserable she is feeling.

'By the way, I tried to persuade this young person not to come.' There is a ring at the door. 'Here he is, I think. I hope he will not bother you too much. He's quite talented, I believe, and rather nice. His name's David Hughes.'

The young man enters, stooping slightly; too much poring over books in libraries, she supposes. He is thin, almost frail, looks undernourished, white-skinned with a shock of wild black hair. He is dressed totally in black and carries a stick with a gold knob; he is limping. He looks her straight in the eyes, piercingly, with a flicker of recognition. He holds his gaze in an almost rude way, without saying anything. Who is this man, so aloof and polite and off-hand?

He doesn't say much, either. Her prompt-book doesn't give any lines here. She is the one who does all the talking, the entertaining. She has a good audience in the young man and the doctor. The actress in her enjoys it all. She mesmerises them over the dinner, which is excellent as usual, cooked by the doctor's own capable hands. She is still aware of the young man's burning eyes on her. She feels suddenly elated, not knowing why. She talks far too much. Then the doctor gets an urgent call to visit a patient. She doesn't know what to say when he has left them with a pot of coffee and hopes that he'll be back in an hour or so.

There is a heavy feeling between them. They sit on the settee. She is completely tongue-tied now. Embarrassed. She

153

feels herself almost blushing, confused by that insistent stare of his, which she is beginning to find curiously attractive. He is scrutinising her and doesn't seem to worry about the silence. She wants to leave but is unable to do so. The silence becomes almost unbearable to her; she would like to break it but can't find anything to say. Then she feels his hand on hers. There is a burning sensation, an electric current between them. She knows nothing whatever about him, guesses his age to be about twenty-seven (he is twenty-eight), can't remember anything he's said during the evening. He takes her in his arms and kisses her. They still don't speak to each other. All she wants to do is touch, swallow his breath. An hour later, foolishly perhaps, she breaks the silence. Perhaps it would have been better to part without words. And what she says is so tame that it's an insult to what has happened to them: 'Why don't you come to my place and have a cup of tea?' So very English and yet so improper at the same time.

She scribbles on a copy of the magazine *Encounter*: 'Encounter you another time, dear Dr.' David laughs at this, a small ironic laugh. When he has fastened his bike to a railing, she watches him getting into her car. He makes her feel maternal: he is so obviously underfed, does not see enough of the sun. In his long black overcoat and with the gold-knobbed stick he looks positively Byronic. The car doesn't suit him one bit. She feels all wrong now, a bit of a show-off for owning such a vehicle.

That first kiss lasts all night. They cannot manage anything but the kiss, as if there isn't room for anything else. As dawn starts casting sidelong glances through the windows, making blotches on the wall, he seems to wake up from some kind of a spell. He looks at her in a different way now, slightly askew. The burning eyes have become shifty and full of questions.

He leaves before the children wake, walking across the park to Paddington Station, she discovers later, to have a cup of tea from one of the tea trolleys. This is a habit of his: he is an incurable romantic about stations, trains, books, poetry, possibly also love.

154

They have made a date for the following day. He arrives: cold, detached, full of ironic asides, kissing her cheek in a guarded way, looking around the flat as if to find clues to her personality. He speaks Oxford English. He makes her feel timid, ill at ease now. She becomes ashamed of her material goods, sees that he disapproves of her home and everything in it; when his eyes rest on an oil portrait of her from some movie, her embarrassment is acute. She has meant to get rid of it for years. What has become of their night together? Was it all a hallucination?

David was a budding young writer who had just finished his first novel. His flat was very different from hers, with many dead flowers and dusty first editions of Priestley and H.G. Wells amid bundles of the *London Magazine*, for which he was working part-time. In this basement flat, the bedroom walls were damp, the bath-tub was in the kitchen, under a plank of wood. As for the loo, the doctor had once remarked, coming out of it: 'My dear boy, that place is perfectly hygienic – no germ could ever survive there.' At this time of her life, being still a very hygienic Swede, she found his living habits somewhat disturbing.

They had only two days before she left for Stockholm and they didn't make much headway with one another. David left for Spain with an old girlfriend on a long-since-arranged holiday. Mai was so confused that she leapt into the arms of a former lover in Paris which, of course, was a mistake.

So there she was in Sweden, alone, and preparing for work in her make-believe world once again, a kind of work that did not satisfy her any longer, biding her time, waiting for that big change in her life. They exchanged a few letters: his that seemed written for posterity, hers full of spelling mistakes and concealed longings. Would he laugh that special ironical laugh when he read them? She wrote about her sense of being in a foreign country, there in the midst of her countrymen. She was no longer a part of it; communication was difficult in that northern climate. So she explored new ways for herself, going on a weekend cruise where, to everyone's embarrassment, she was the only woman present. She sensed the fishermen's curses behind her back but ignored them. They tried to freeze her out but she persisted. It was not a great success, even when they grudgingly admitted she had as much right as they to do the trip. They changed tactics and tried to get her to join in the heavy drinking and the equally heavy language, or to tell her their sob stories. Selfishly, she made herself deaf to them and their problems: she had come for the trip, the air, to get away from the city and the unreal world of the cinema, to concentrate on herself and the watery world.

But let us return to the Penny Dreadful, for now it begins in earnest. David arrived in a snowclad Stockholm, and they were both full of apprehension, remembering that first magic meeting. In London, they had been unable to recapture it, but here, in this cold birthplace of hers, in the city without faces, here they recaptured all that had been lost.

All the usual love symptoms were there, only she felt they were hitting her stronger than ever before. Those bitter-sweet feelings that upset the stomach and the digestion, like adrenalin that stimulates the heart's action and raises the blood pressure, producing a sense of excitement. The tingling sensations, the pain in the pit of the stomach, the rise in body temperature that made her face glow. She felt as if it were high summer, although it was chilly autumn.

The acting area now changed to the north of Sweden. Surrounded by a sullen ice-bound river and seemingly endless pine forests, with billions of prickly dark pine needles that can cast black shadows in a man's soul. A Nordic pastoral, covered in hoar-frost.

The house was a timber log-cabin in the midst of the forest. For water they melted snow in great pans in the big fireplace. They spent their time in bed, under bearskins, by the fire.

Elk and deer peered in at the windows from time to time. It was the wildest place David had ever seen. His face had taken on a bewildered look. He stopped working on his manuscript. He hated to admit he was frightened to go to the loo, which lay in the darkest part of the forest domain. He stared at her in an uncomprehending way while she learned to laugh at his English jokes.

No word-by-word account here about their doings but, to put it simply: they were the first lovers in the world. Love was a word that belonged to them only. Nobody had loved like this before, surely. Here the paper should turn rosy pink and the text be etched in ruby red.

She was never quite sure of what was going on in his mind. He was such a secretive person, even to himself. Not wanting to confront things, playing a hide-and-seek game, frightened of emotions, although a romantic at heart.

But their sensuality brought them together and in those moments she felt she knew him truly. Afterwards, no. It was as if he was frightened of having given too much of himself. He would shut off and become a person apart. The impossibility of the male-female connection even in that great love; the need for total commitment always so much greater for the woman. He was totally supportive of the changes she made, which all happened at tremendous speed after they met. Perhaps at last she had found a man who could accept her life as she wanted to live it, with all the contradictions she needed so much. Was that possible? She had botched up so many relationships in the past; she desperately wanted it to work this time.

The next romantic setting for this springtide romance was Christmas Common in Oxfordshire. A small workman's cottage was their abode now. He was to finish his book on J.B. Priestley, she to appear in a comedy at the Oxford Playhouse, a translation from Rousseau called *Darling*. He had rented the crumbling place for one pound a week.

An article appeared in a Sunday paper:

MAI HIDES IN A LABOURER'S COTTAGE

In Oxford, I asked about England's favourite Swedish actress, who has just made a very big personal success in a new play there. 'You'll probably find her at Christmas Common.' We gradually nailed our quarry down. At dusk, we were confronted by a row of rough, countryman's cottages. I knocked at No. 3. A dark young man, stooping and slightly sinister in the half-light, opened the door a few inches. The whole thing was sheer Ibsen.

IN BOOTS

After a whispered conference, I was ushered in and, true enough, there she was, an elfin, blonde, slip-of-a-child thing in Russian peasant skirt, Russian boots, and with the most delicate hands in the world. The only furniture in the tiny, primitive room was a table with papers and manuscripts on it, and a clutch of candles in wine bottles. A mattress stood against the wall, up-ended. It was one of those moments when you don't quite know what to say because I could see that she was disturbed at being run to earth.

SADNESS

Defiantly, I decided to throw out the most direct question I could think of at her: 'How's TYRONE POWER?' I said, 'You've been travelling all over the world with him for the last two years or so, haven't you?'

It was partially dark now but I could see the bleak sadness in her eyes and she lowered them from my question and said: 'I couldn't tell you. I haven't seen him lately. He's in America I believe.'

She looked so defenceless and so child-like, sitting there. I felt as I would if I had struck my daughter across the face.

SO SAD

As we said a sad good-bye, she said, with a wisp of a wintry Scandinavian smile: 'Leave me my Christmas island.'

Footnote for the curious: Why is Mai living like this and who are her companions? It's top secret, apparently. Only Mai knows, and she won't tell. (I wasn't even introduced to the dark young man who opened the door for me.)

Second Chapter of the True Romance

Lying close to David, whose head was deep in a bank of primroses, Mai asked: 'Why not get married?' (She, who had shot off her mouth so many times in the press, saying things like 'Marriage is an idiotic contract, one that rarely works', 'a process of inevitable, mutual destruction', etc.) David looked at her with dancing eyes and said: 'Why not?' in a very matter-of-fact voice. 'I can't think of anything better to do right now.'

Funny, really, she had never been asked the Big Question; it was always she who had taken the step. She wondered if it was so in most cases; whether women still needed marriage vows more than men. She was, after all, just the same as everyone else, with her need for extra security, the urge to tell the world that she belonged to one man only. Not only did she play comedy on stage but in real life too.

They would get married in Oxford. She liked the idea because it was a contrast to her own background, a good joke, but also quite fitting and proper for him. It was April 1958. No fuss, no wedding cars, no wedding cake: definitely informal. They had intended to keep it a secret, but David's publisher of the time thought that the publicity would promote his new book, so they were greeted by a barrage of reporters and a crowd of two hundred or more.

'No presents?' one reporter asked. David smiled. 'We have just exchanged the most enormous present in the world.'

She wed, to the surprise of everyone, a cautious young Londoner, with a bookish, boyish air about him. What is it about this pale, book-writing six-footer that persuaded her to haul down her anti-marriage banner in his favour?

I think I can see why Mai Zetterling's resistance to wedding bells has been effectively vanquished by David Hughes. He is everything that most film stars and actors are not. He is tweedy rather than trim; the sort of man whose collars turn up by mid-afternoon. He has none of the professional actor's glamour, conceit or *'side'*; replacing those qualities with a modest and reflective calm, with just a touch of male helplessness, which always helps.

The happy couple were now to be found in Wales, mainly because of David's family ties there. The only reading matter they'd brought was the *Good Food Guide*. He was a sensualist *par excellence*, she was to find out. It was not just a matter of pot luck for refreshments; they had to go to places with many knives and forks and palate-tickling dishes, had to check out the specialities of each region. But in Wales the restaurants were few and far between and as the weather was black and windy, their car nearly toppling into the Devil's Punchbowl, they finally decided to head south. They started looking for a house within a fifty-mile radius of London, while continuing their epicurean journey.

The third house they looked at was Berry Grove, in the heart of Hampshire, and this was where they were to live for almost fifteen years (a record for her). She would never forget that first visit. It was a grey and windy day. The place was smothered with creepers, the three acres choked by weeds; it was hemmed in by a graveyard, the tumulus of a Danish chieftain, and an avenue of huge chestnut trees. Spine-chilling decay everywhere ... and who had placed the black-witchy objects so carefully around the house? A dead snake on the north side, a frog by the wall facing east, and a big black branch in the shape of a cross facing south. The back door bell-string kept on being pulled, although there was no one there. It had an eerie feel and yet the house managed to convey a sense of welcome, as though people had lived happily there, and ghosts too. (Of course, our couple didn't know about the phantom gardener yet, nor about the kindly ghost which haunted one of the bedrooms, putting in an occasional appearance to overnight guests.) It was a large, rambling place, which had once been the vicarage of the adjoining thirteenth-century church. Since it was full of woodworm, cracks and damp, they bought it for a song: it had been on the market for two years, but no one had seen its potential until David and Mai came along.

They moved into their new-found paradise within six months, with a large Regency four-poster bed. She started to hunt for objects that some people would call rubbish but, in her eyes, were quaint and fitted the house. They also happened to be cheap, bought in the back streets of Portsmouth and Southampton. She had changed her style completely. Gone was the Scandinavian chic. Now it was bric-à-brac, antimacassars and horsehair sofas, a glorious and happy mess. She had it all her own way as David had no interest in furnishings. For the first time she felt she was putting down roots in this fair country of England, instead of being a visitor; and now the musical score had changed from Schubert, Bach, Mozart and Brahms to Elgar, Vaughan Williams and Benjamin Britten.

We are now in a straight domestic play which seems to be a smash hit. The hero and heroine have a free-flowing dialogue. The script keeps good pace with plenty of exciting interludes to keep everyone interested. It is a success.

The actress was still pursuing her profession both on stage and screen, but with less and less enthusiasm. As a result of her work at the Oxford Playhouse, there came a query as to whether Miss Zetterling would agree to do a test with Peter Sellers for a part in his new film *Only Two Can Play*. Never having been tested since *Frieda*, she was somewhat taken aback, but accepted: it might be a good chance to prove that she could be wicked and reveal a sense of humour, for a change.

In Swansea with Peter Sellers and Kingsley Amis, who had written the book on which the film was based, she became tongue-tied once more, as the two of them tried to outwit each other with reminiscences and dirty jokes, Kingsley punctuating his with resounding farts, to everyone's embarrassment. David was the leading man in Mai's life, despite Peter Sellers' ardour. She was very much the married woman; there were to be no stand-ins for either of them for years and years to come. Berry Grove became a heaven. The children were happier than ever before and so was she. A proper family at last. But money had to be earned, alas, so in 1959, she accepted a part in a film with Pat Boone that she decided would most definitely be her last one as an actress. *The Main Attraction* didn't do very much for her or for anyone else.

She underwent what can only be described as a gradual disillusionment with acting, which so far had been her only channel of expression. There were too many limitations, not enough creativity. She had come to realise that she was not a bit passive; that she was a doer, a fixer of things, with many ideas of her own which she wanted to explore and communicate to others.

To break with the past had always been her way in life, so why not now?

As for the cinema, she could not see herself as an ageing vamp on the silver screen. She decided she wanted a hell of a lot more out of life and that she didn't have the time or the patience to hang around waiting for yet another lousy part to come her way. That was when she decided to make a five-year plan. Start small, with documentaries on matters that she cared about. Try to learn the ABC of film technique. If she had not managed to make a feature film within five years, she promised herself she would give it up and become an actress again.

David had been asked if he would write about his actress wife for a women's magazine and as they were invariably short of money, he accepted. Here is one of the first extracts from those articles.

FORGED IN FIRE

When we married we bought an old four-poster bed for next-to-nothing in Peckham and Mai was sitting in this bed one morning, eating a piece of my soggy toast, when she suddenly said: 'We're going to Lapland to make a film.' We had been married almost two years, and I was accustomed to surprises, even during breakfast. But this was a stunner.

Still more stunning was the fact that within three weeks we were in Lapland, making a film and eating smoked reindeer for breakfast. Reading between the lines of this small incident, you learn a lot about Mai. You discover that she is unpredictable, even when you live with her; she is apt to take things into her own hands. Once she gets an idea, she is quite single-minded, and wears away the opposition by ignoring it. People who try to fight her – me sometimes, too – feel strangely in the wrong, as well as

162

knocked sideways. Her ideas come, without warning, as violent as bombs.

That is why I soon stopped having breakfast with her; it was hard on one's nerves. Nowadays, I get up a couple of hours before her to fortify myself with bacon and strong tea, to stand up to her instinctive ideas with a bit of masculine common sense. The trouble is that her instinct invariably wins, because it is right. My cooler view prevails only, thank goodness, on the much smaller issues.

For instance, I did manage to persuade her one morning that buying me an owl as a work companion was a somewhat fifth-rate idea, since one had to wrap all the food in fur before the bird would touch it. She agreed at the time. One day, however, I know I shall find an owl on my desk, looking hungry.

I was not against the Lapland idea, but everything was. We had no experience in making films of our own, and we had no spare money. We would have to leave our home and the children. Mai's agent laughed raucously when she told him about it, decided she was crazy and did nothing.

It was Mai who rang the BBC, Mai who dug out the right man to talk to, Mai who cut through all the bureaucratic delays, Mai who hired Swedish technicians and Mai who left behind her a trail of slightly dazed and anxious men, all wondering if they would lose their jobs. None did. For this was no sudden whim, it was part of a plan. If I say that she was forcing life to do what she wanted and believed in, does that sound forbidding? It shouldn't. Mai sets about everything – from arranging flowers to spending too much money – with innocence, humour and concentration. I have not been cross with her except over spending too much money. Certainly not over the plan. This plan led us, during the next few years, into panic, disasters and unspeakable delights.

At a single stroke our whole life changed. I was no longer the novelist sitting quietly in a Hampshire farmhouse doing nobody any harm, but an insane pioneer tottering on skis in thirty degrees of frost, with tape-recording equipment slung around my neck. Mai had icicles hanging from her fringe, and was loping through the snow like some eager and amiable bear. She looked less like a glamorous actress than anyone I had ever seen. And she was probably happier than ever before.

Trial and Error

Life is either a daring adventure or nothing.

Helen Keller

I was in my element at last. I was not only exploring a new medium but also exploring the world, as I had always wanted to do. 'If I can't be a sailor, then I will be an explorer,' had been my words. I felt a little bit like it, working in the Arctic . . . which was both a revelation and a shock, as the Lapps and the Swedes are worlds apart, and I found I was much closer to them than to my own kin. We most certainly spoke the same language, a mind language. Here were people who believed in the supernatural, took it for granted, and lived on many levels, instead of being trapped in the present. They seemed to have unlimited horizons; they communicated with the stars and plants and animals, and by keeping themselves on a certain primitive level, they had retained their belief in magic.

One of the very first scenes we filmed was of an old and bent little Lapp who had been in the mountains alone with his reindeer for three months. Now he was being fetched by helicopter. The contrast between his traditional Lapp costume (vivid blue with borders of daffodil yellow and tomato red) and the gleaming helicopter from which he emerged was striking. Despite the largest of pompoms on his peaked blue cap, he barely reached my shoulder. His eyes were full of tears as they skimmed the horizon. It was the first time we

165

had met. He wasn't startled, he just followed his own thoughts and told me solemnly: 'They have all left.' I wondered who had left. He replied 'The little ones.' And when he saw my consternation, he added: 'The fairy folk – they have all gone, every one of them.' I decided to be as matter of fact as he was and asked if he had any idea where they could have gone. 'Oh, up to the Russians or the Finns, I suppose. And they are right – too many people, too many machines for them here. No, they don't like it here any more so they've gone.'

These things I learned about the making of a film almost from the word go: the need for organisation, patience, tenacity; to be tolerant yet demanding; to take total responsibility; to be resolute and calm whatever the worry and pressure; to repeat to myself again and again, 'Everything is possible,' when things appeared totally impossible; to be indefatigable; to spur others on with my enthusiasm and action; to have eyes at the back of my head; never ever to be satisfied with what I had in the can; to leave no stone unturned; to demand too much of myself.

The Polite Invasion was shot in a landscape which was totally winter-bound and frozen. Not only was it December but the place, a village called Jook-Mook, was situated smack on the Arctic Circle in Swedish Lapland. The frozen smile I wear through this tough little half-hour black-and-white movie is funny to watch but it was no laughing matter then. We filmed the separation of the reindeers during violent snowstorms, and the horrifying sight of blood and entrails on pure white snow made me retch in between takes. Wrapped up in double overcoats, I still felt the chill to my bones.

We lived in a hotel run by a couple of gay twins who were great film fans and had insisted that we have a one-day film festival. It wasn't too much of a success as people kept falling under the restaurant tables dead drunk. Jook-Mook was definitely not a happy place. Everything seemed to be happening under cover of the dark: drunks thrown out of hotels or cafés for disorderly behaviour would fall asleep in snowdrifts on their way home and freeze to death.

It was also an uneasy place, because of the strained relationship between Lapps and Swedes. At that time – 1960 – even the young people of the village seemed to be at odds with themselves. Bored by the long black winter nights, with nothing to do, they resorted to strange games. A small gang of girls had the quaint hobby of spying on adulterous affairs; they would telephone the unsuspecting wife and tell her the news.

Meanwhile at the hotel, we had to pry open the windows of our rooms with a crowbar. The hotel was heated like a sauna and we suffered from nose-bleeds right away, having been out in temperatures below thirty degrees all day.

It certainly was a tough assignment but nothing could spoil my excitement. I was making my very first film, God damn it, and Lapland and Jook-Mook had been my own choice. In no time, I became a little bully, so I was told. I didn't care; I was doing a job that I felt was worth doing. I did a hell of a lot of pushing and forcing to get what I wanted and thought nothing of persuading people to do things they had never done before. I even dragged David out on skis: I took it for granted that he would be able to master this Scandinavian habit.

This first film of mine got some hot comments in Sweden, because I had dared to criticise the delicate but very evident problem of the Lapps versus the Swedes. What I wanted to show was that the old nomadic Lapp way of life was in danger of disappearing and that the Lapps, who had not caught up with the rest of Sweden, seemed to get the worst of what our welfare state had to offer. With the advent of power stations and railways, the grazing grounds were diminishing, so the reindeer were in retreat. No longer able to follow the same paths, they would get crushed to death on the railroads or be drowned in the new dams. It was an insidious incursion into the Laplanders' way of life.

During the editing, I discovered my many shortcomings as a director: for example, the shots I had missed, in spite of having a professional cameraman. I decided to spend all my time in the cutting-room, even though the editors were bored to see me hanging around them, night and day. But I was learning, and I tried to ignore their irritation. Finally the film was accepted by the BBC and was even shown at a festival or two.

I had spent about six months all in all on this first effort and I was out of pocket, because of my lousy budgeting, which I was to find was not one of my strong points. It is a very expert job. The film was to cost two thousand pounds, which, even for that time, was an extremely small budget, but I was eight hundred pounds short. I became worried about money matters. I passionately wanted to continue with my five-year plan but we had to eat, as well as pay the mortgage and school fees. Then came an offer of a play in New York, a role that I had always been interested in and had never acted: Hedda Gabler. I broke my promise to myself and accepted.

The whole venture got off to a bad start with the boat-trip from Southampton. I had been booked to travel first-class and I had enjoyed the thought of this sea voyage, with time for reading and for myself. But this was not to be. I had been invited – no, put – at the captain's table, which turned out to be a small disaster and spoiled my trip. The captain was a food freak. He ordered, for the first lunch, Russian caviare rolled up in smoked salmon, followed by the tiniest of fillet steaks stuffed with oysters – horrendous! I was the only one to complain, saying that my stomach wasn't strong enough to take such things. When I heard him ordering the second meal – lobsters with crayfish and asparagus – I said that I would prefer to have my meal in my cabin. From then on, it was open war between the captain and myself. Finally he shouted at me: 'Doesn't your husband spank you for being so obstinate?' It was going to get even worse in New York.

At first I was lucky. I didn't have to stay in a hotel: through friends I had arranged to stay with some people in an old house in Brooklyn. That is how I came to meet my now closest friend, Sheila La Farge. Sheila took me under her wing and introduced me to places like the Russian Tea Room and the Palm Court in the Plaza Hotel, complete with orchestra. This time I didn't cry but listened to Sheila, who has a way of speaking that is very special. She has a deep knowledge of many things: animals, botany, astrology, Buddhism, cooking. At first, I was overwhelmed by her but she made me laugh at things, even at myself. After a while, I moved to her place. We struggled in a heavy snowstorm through a paralysed New York, with my two suitcases that seemed to be filled with lead – mainly books and records.

Despite Sheila's company and friendship, I was unhappy because I missed David and I felt lost in New York. I slept badly; I felt that I could hear the monster city breathing with a kind of nervous excitement. But it wasn't only the city that worried me. The set-up at the theatre, the 4th Street Theatre, was amateurish to a degree that I had not imagined possible. The director spent most of his time picking his nose and eating bagels and shouting at everyone to be sexy, because didn't we realise that Ibsen was a real sexy guy of a writer.

In the past, I had never had any problems in learning lines, but all of a sudden I couldn't. I just didn't want to learn them because I didn't want to be Hedda any longer, certainly not under such circumstances. I stopped eating; my healthy peasant body packed up almost completely. They sent me to a doctor, who at once wrote out a prescription for sleeping pills. Since I respond badly to drugs and hardly ever take an aspirin, I asked him how I would be able to function the next morning, whereupon he wrote out another prescription for a waking-up pill. But what if that one over-excited me? There was a third one to be taken then, a slowing-down pill. It was normal; he had used this three-pill routine for the last ten years himself and he was still alive, wasn't he? I looked at him carefully for the first time. Not only did he look like a wreck but he also twitched and sighed heavily, and his hands were constantly moving over his face, tweaking his ears, pulling his nose. He was just like one of those night bats – twitching, neurotic little beasts. I left without the pills.

Sheila did everything possible to cheer me up: helped me to learn my lines, made exquisite little meals. I learned the subtlety of cooking not only for taste but also with colours, and to make the preparation of food a feast for the eye.

In the theatre, things went from bad to worse. I had no

respect for the director and hardly any for the actors either. They were a very mixed bag, working against each other and with totally different techniques. From mumbling, hair-twisting, humming and hawing to the complete opposite – heavy dramatic gestures and pauses. I was in the midst of all this and didn't know what to do with myself. Michael Meyer, the translator of the play and also a friend of some years' standing, came over from England and was shocked, not only by the production but also at my performance, which did not yet exist, although we were only a few days away from the first preview. I rang David in despair, but he could not possibly understand, and refused to take it seriously. Everyone was so sure that I would be able to manage. I was the only one who knew how bad it really was, but I did not have courage to say so or to walk out. Everything went wrong at the first preview: no props, not even a gun with which to shoot myself. I had to hang myself in the drapes. After all, the woman had to die at the end of the play.

Just before the previews, I had to move from Sheila's place. Another friend lent me her flat as she was out of town for a week. It was in a new skyscraper block. The walls were paper thin; I would run to answer the telephone when it rang in the next flat and I would hear the most intimate conversations from the one above. The couple upstairs would have rows that lasted all night, no matter what I screamed at them or how hard I banged the broom on my ceiling.

That night at the theatre the chaos was, if anything, worse. Still no props; and now we could also hear the Tannoy giving cues to the electricians and to the dressing-rooms. I did the unforgivable thing that no actor should even think of doing: I faked a fainting fit. I had always been told at the National Theatre that whatever happens, the show must go on. Your mother might be dying but you must nevertheless go on stage and give a performance; no one should be able to see your private grief.

After I had been carried to my dressing-room, a doctor was sent for. When I told him the truth and my feelings of despair he said: 'My dear, you have just saved yourself from a nervous breakdown.'

I felt awful. I was suffused with dreadful feelings of guilt and nervous about what I had done – but I *had* saved myself, and I made a vow never to act on stage again. I wanted to continue my five-year plan, even if I wasn't sure that I had enough talent to be a film director.

I managed to persuade the BBC to give me another chance. It was a similar contract to the one I had for *The Polite Invasion*: a flat fee of two thousands pounds, me narrating and appearing for no extra money. My theme was still nomads.

The plight of the gipsy was the same as that of nomadic peoples all over the world. Society was moving in, trying to integrate and standardise them. The difference between us and them was that with us, the process had taken place gradually, over a long period of time. With the nomads it all happened too fast.

Lords of Little Egypt was made in 1961 in the Camargue, in a small town called Sainte-Marie-de-la-Mère, where thousands of gipsies congregate in the month of May for a very special religious festival. We lived in a camp with six thousand gipsies from all over Europe. Like them, we stayed in a trailer. Juanita, an English gipsy friend who spoke the Romany language, had come along to help and translate. Otherwise, there were just three of us – David doing the sound, one cameraman, and me doing the rest. Again, it was tough. This time the main problems were the mosquitoes, the heat, and the strange, childlike temperament of the gipsies.

One evening they would share our meal over the camp-fire and we would sing and dance, play music half the night. The next day was a different story altogether; then they wanted to throw all our equipment into the sea. On one of these occasions, not knowing what to do, I started to snap pictures with my Polaroid and handed the results out like sweets: that stopped the threats. I had been in a panic – I wasn't used to such volatile temperaments. There were many misunderstandings. For instance, we persuaded a splendid

171

gipsy lady to appear in the film for a small fee (her smile had been truly dazzling in the sun because she had a set of all-gold dentures). After the scene had been duly shot and we were about to pay her, the whole of her family turned up and demanded to be paid as well. We could not possibly afford to do this so we invited them to dinner instead – but it took hours to sort out, amid heated arguments.

One of the most exciting things about making a documentary is the research. In the Camargue I investigated first by Land Rover, then, when the roads became impossible even for that tough vehicle, on horseback. I took it for granted that everyone else should have the same enthusiasm that I did. I hadn't been riding for years, but my excitement made me able to sit in the saddle for a whole day without being bothered by it. However, with David it was a different matter. He refused to get off his horse at lunchtime because, he said, 'If I get off this damn thing here in the wilderness, I shan't be able to get back up on it again.' He was in real pain and suffered for days afterwards. I didn't feel guilty about this but teased him mercilessly instead.

I continued with my research, sneaking in and out of tents and trailers, making friends with the most outlandish characters who, in normal life, would have scared me stiff. It was exhilarating to meet people in this intimate and unusual way. I felt I was discovering new worlds. I cared deeply about their fight and about their right to keep their independent way of life.

I met the poorest of gipsies and the richest. I learned about their hierarchy, which is complex. One day I would be sharing grilled snails on the beach with a down-and-out, the next I would be dining sumptuously with a Russian family in their big tent, covered in rich wall-hangings and with two samovars. On one occasion I was offered a week-end trip by the king of the gipsies in his grand limousine – just him and me. When I tried to explain, in my poor French, that not only was I working but I was also married and had two children, he laughed and said that he was married as well but he had twelve children, and didn't I want a third anyway?

And while the pretty gipsy girls were floating on the sea

like so many exotic flowers because they did not take their skirts off when bathing, Juanita received a proposition from a twelve-year-old boy. The idea was to meet him and his father and brothers on the beach at night. Father would be first, then the eldest brother, then the next eldest and so forth, until finally it would be his turn.

Sometimes we would spend an evening with Lawrence Durrell – he lived near by – and with his great friend Henry Miller, who was paying him a visit. They seemed like a pair of giants, larger than life. They were so full of questions, ideas and laughter that they baffled me no end. They also intimidated me. I wasn't up to their kind of structured arguments, their battles with words. At times, they seemed simple to get along with but they also seemed remote, taken up with their own crazy ideas. They lived in a world to which I had no access, a fact which I accepted. I was the fascinated onlooker who kept her mouth firmly shut. I probably looked very stern and remote in a Swedish kind of way. David and the cameraman, however, would be happily joining in the discussions about politics, metaphysics, the afterlife. I now realise what a fine pair of misogynists Larry and Henry were – women were barred from conversation with them – but it seemed not to matter at the time.

There was a rather funny end to one of these slightly drunken evenings. We were taking Henry and his girlfriend back to the hotel in the Land Rover and he was sitting in front with David and me. Henry kept casting worried glances towards the back of the car, where our cameraman was having a petting session with Henry's girlfriend. For some reason we had a goat-bell hanging by the side of the car, next to where Henry was sitting, and at every twist and turn of the road it would ring out loudly. Henry seemed to think that we were taking the mickey out of him, that it was a big joke being played at his expense: he, supposedly the sex maniac of all time, the author of *Sexus*, being cuckolded in his own presence.

I was excited by this new world of the cinema and the life it was bringing me. I had thrown myself in at the deep end, not knowing a great deal; standing in front of the camera all those years had not taught me much about how a film is actually made. The books that I had read had given me some theories and hints, no more. I know now that the way I had gone about learning the rudimentaries was the right way for me. I was such an unacademic person that I would not have fitted into any kind of school system; it would only have intimidated me, made me feel more insecure. It was a hard way to learn but a stimulating one.

I must admit that life at home in Berry Grove seemed a bit dull in comparison. Routine has never been my forte. The children now went to local schools but didn't much like them, and Etienne refused to eat school food, claiming that she had once found maggots in her dessert. It was a very English kind of girls' school, with neat uniforms and hats and two roly-poly headmistresses of a refined sort. When their beloved dog died, they had a shawl made up from its fur and wore it on alternate days.

I went to a couple of school plays, opened a school bazaar and a few others in the village, became president of the film society of the Cheshire Homes and opened their garden fête. I quarrelled with the local vicar after having been a guest of honour at a Saturday night get-together at his church: I felt that he was playing up to the rich people in the community.

Those periods at home between films were, I suppose, the nearest I came to being a proper mother, but perhaps they were never long enough to give the children any real sense of home life and security. For me, they were in-between times: I just couldn't wait to get my teeth into another film. But I couldn't yet stand on my own two feet; I needed David's help in structuring the films and I needed him with me. I was still to be unsure of myself for quite some time to come. David was willing to work with me, although he was half-hearted about the actual filming process: he was more interested in travelling and seeing new places. He didn't much like to push himself on to people in the way that you have to sometimes, especially when you are making a documentary. He was happier when I started to work with actors.

Of course I tried to fit in with David's world, but with no

great success. We would spend lazy week-ends in country houses, reading the Sunday papers and watching cricket, which David was inordinately fond of but was like Chinese to me. After his first boss, John Lehmann, had spent a week-end at Berry Grove, rumours filtered back that he had no sooner drunk his first glass of sherry than I had started to say rude things about his godmother (in fact she was a genuine eccentric whom I had liked very much but had had great difficulty in understanding because of her pronounced upper-class accent). I was more fortunate when we went to stay with J.B. Priestley, while David was writing his critical biography of the author and playwright. In his great mansion on the Isle of Wight, a near-Victorian breakfast was served every morning: a feast of kippers, porridge, prunes, bacon and eggs and a great ham on the sidetable.

One morning I was asked, as the only driver in the party, if I could take them down to the beach. Priestley wanted to do a bit of gouache work and his wife, Jacquetta Hawkes, wanted to look for mushrooms on the downs. The car was a large black old-fashioned monster; my nose hardly reached over the wheel and David had to help me to change the gears, which were stiff with disuse. On the twisting narrow road between the downs that led to the beach I was very scared indeed, while everyone else was enjoying themselves hugely. Priestley did a lot of sketches at great speed and afterwards he and Jacquetta ran hand in hand, like children, picking mushrooms. After my chauffeuring experience, I enjoyed my stay a lot more and felt almost relaxed with my host. The evenings would invariably end up with him at the pianola, tramping away at an old tune and sucking his pipe.

Another place where I was accepted with open arms was Jersey Zoo, by Gerald and Jackie Durrell; I became godmother to the first baby gorilla to be born there.

The films were still losing money. We took out loans that were crippling and David did some freelance journalism, which he hated because it gave him less time for his own writing. We went my way, not his. I had given myself five years to make it and I felt I was of an age when it was now or never. My terrible will-power that allows nothing to stand in its way. I moved on that straight line towards my goal and I moved David with me.

When I was asked to make a third short documentary for the BBC, David got a commission to write a travel book about Sweden so that he could come with me. This film, *The Prosperity Race* – an objective look at middle-class life in Stockholm – got me into serious trouble. When it was shown in England, there were savage screams from my country: I was a traitor, I was just like the rest, just like the foreign journalists who came to Sweden to learn about the welfare state. Sweden had a tremendous reputation in those days, and rightly so, for being advanced in many ways. But when all these journalists came to write their comments, they were not always in favour of what they saw. I, on the other hand, was Swedish. How dare I betray my country? Yes, how dare I? For the first and last time, I wrote a letter to the press, in an attempt to justify my approach:

I don't believe my film is perfect. Far from it. But I did honestly try to explore our aims and the way we live in Sweden. First then, I want to make absolutely clear that I am proud of my country in more ways than one, proud of my city. In less than a hundred years, Sweden was transformed into a modern industrial state. Such rapid economic development has naturally brought about radical structural changes in Swedish society. This country has been regarded by the world as a model, socially and culturally. Today it has the highest living standard of any country in Europe. Yet I think it important to remember that, as recently as the mid-nineteenth century, Sweden was one of the poorest and most under-developed countries in Europe. Were we perhaps advancing too fast, had we become too pleased with ourselves?

As people from all over the world looked to us as an example, had I not the right to query this state of affairs? And if we, on the way to trying to make a perfect community, had made some mistakes, could we not admit them, in order that others could learn from our mistakes?

Witches who have read the lines in my hand, astrologers who have written up my birth-chart, have all been unanimous about one thing: that I absolutely must live in the south. They didn't tell me why, but it was something I instinctively knew already. I have always been drawn towards high blue skies where cicadas chirruped and where I could grow fields of sunflowers. I knew that, sooner or later, I would end up in a southern climate, but in the meantime I was also drawn to the far north. And there was one place that haunted me and still does, despite its cold and frozen name: Iceland.

Sheila, the friend I had met in New York, had said that if we did another documentary, she would like to join as a voluntary worker in order to learn something about filmmaking. I sent her a telegram:

WE ARE GOING TO ICELAND SEPTEMBER 15TH STOP BRING BATH-
ING SUIT AND GARLIC STOP

Sheila and I spent a hilarious month together in Iceland before David and the crew arrived. As usual, there weren't many unexplored corners of that island left by the time the film was finished. I wangled free tickets on aeroplanes that usually only had sheep as passengers, begged and borrowed cars and horses, brass bands, trawlers. The Icelandic Tourist Office didn't know what had hit them, but obligingly sent us someone to help out with the fieldwork. She turned out to be a charming and bright lady called Vigdis Finnbogadottir, who is now the country's president.

We criss-crossed Iceland in every possible way. We flew to Grinzig on the Arctic Circle: a tiny, greener-than-green island with one of the strangest graveyards I have ever seen – all the graves are surrounded by what look like children's iron cots.

In the greyest imaginable landscape, by an equally grey lake where the black lava beach was strewn with the bones of sheep long dead, we stayed in the Co-op Hotel. We soon found out that the village was a giant slaughterhouse and that sheep from the neighbouring villages were brought there to be killed. All day long we heard the cries and echoes of the beasts. It was an eerie place, surrounded by dark mountains with not a tree in sight. Children with ashen faces played in doorways; some grey-clad grown-ups stared at us as if we had come from another planet.

The evening meal served at the hotel was one of the most horrendous I have ever faced. As a first course, a greasy soup of sheep bones with some of the unfortunate animals' hairs floating on top. Then lambs' livers, with little yellow waxy potatoes, all swamped in a thick lumpy gravy. At a long table sat the crew of butchers with bloodstains still on their leather aprons. They were a noisy and tough-looking lot, eating heartily what they had killed. Then the door suddenly opened to a sight so unexpected that it took our breath away. Into this grey environment stepped a woman dressed entirely in red from top to toe: her shoes and bag were of a red shiny plastic, her red nylon suit was clinging, with a slit in the skirt, her golden hair was tinged with orange and, to crown it all, she wore a red beret with a pompom. She looked more like a plastic sunset than a woman. She sat herself down at the long table where the butchers were and started to flick through some magazines that she had brought with her. She never once looked at the men, who had stopped talking. She ate her meal heartily, no, lustily is the right word, dipping the coarse bread in the thick gravy. Sheila and I had also stopped talking, fascinated by this red creature. When she left, we followed, feeling like spies in a bad movie. Who on earth was this woman who dared to be so different? The grey village made a spectacular setting for her as she swung her red plastic handbag like a professional. She was heading towards the church. An old ramshackle bus was parked outside and she went into it for a moment, then came out swigging a can of beer before entering the church. We followed her.

The scene that greeted us was startling: lines of rope were hanging over the pew and the altar, between crucifixes and fastened to the benches, and hanging from the ropes were stockings, corsets, aprons, hats, long woollen underwear, all fastened with gaily coloured clothes-pegs.

Later on, we learned that our Red Lady was a travelling saleswoman – she was using the church to display her wares – who went all over Iceland in that old beaten-up bus outside. This was remarkable because the centre of Iceland has no roads at all; you drive through this wild country with a compass and hope for the best. The rivers are treacherous because they gather quicksand. (A bus with German tourists had sunk without trace just a week earlier.) To say that we were impressed by her is an understatement.

We went on a trip into the interior on one of these non-existent roads between two glaciers, the pass being open only for a few weeks every year. We travelled with two young, eccentric Icelanders who had forgotten to bring a spare tyre, and in one of those treacherous rivers we had a puncture. The night was not far off and it was getting chilly. Sheila and I, being of a practical turn of mind, gathered reindeer moss and dried sheep's droppings for a fire that would have worked a treat, although it might have been rather smelly. As it was, we didn't need to use it because the boys fixed the tyre and eventually we found the tourist hut where we were to spend the night. The setting was spectacular: a wild, wild place, an ice world, but full of hot geysers of the most intricate shapes and sizes, spitting and hissing, sending up sudden spurts of boiling water several metres into the air. A small frail building standing over a boiling river intrigued us: we found it to be the loo, a most comfortable place as by now it was freezing cold. It also had the most astonishing view over the long glacier, which was sparkling in the setting sun. The boys had brought along typical Icelandic food and invited us to share the blackened sheep's head with them. It looked positively cannibalistic to us to see them carve out the tongue and eat it. As for the eyes, they gouged them out and sucked them like sweets. Perhaps it was a fitting way to eat in the wilderness but we couldn't do it.

I hired a small neat house in the suburbs of Reykjavik for the crew and ourselves. Sheila was to be in charge of the meals. This was no mean task in Iceland at that time as there were hardly any vegetables: everything was frozen, even the fish. The only thing we thought quite superb was the black lava bread, baked in the hot earth of the sulphur springs. What we hated most of all was the sulphur-tasting coffee. Sheila worked wonders with the available foodstuff, and the garlic string that she had brought certainly livened things up. Sometimes she had to make meals for a hundred people. One night she made soup for that number and the next day she drove a borrowed Coca Cola van through the mountains to our location, where I had assembled a group of Icelandic wrestlers. They were dressed in nothing but the briefest of shorts while the snow lay thick on the ground. I managed to make them excited enough about the film to wrestle in the snow, for the first (and probably the last) time in their lives.

Madness sets in when you start making a movie. The most dangerous enterprise of that film was when I made a group of men haul down a flock of sheep from rocks into little boats that were rocking on a violent sea beneath. It was a giant undertaking which, thank God, I only realised after the scene was in the can. It had taken me about three days of talking, begging, insisting, to convince the people in the Westman Islands, where the scene was shot, that it was necessary for them to do this in order to show off the character of Iceland and the crazy things they had to do to survive. By now I was slightly mad myself. I had become more and more stubborn, more insistent on having it all my own way. Was I, I began to wonder, becoming more and more my true self? Had I simply been repressing my need to be in charge, and now, finally, it was all coming out?

In Iceland, I have climbed smoking volcanoes which emerge from a boiling sea; I have even spent my birthday on one of them, drinking champagne. I have pony-trekked across its barren interior, skiing behind a snow-tractor across huge glaciers. I have been on trawlers on a rough sea, fishing for cod. I have flown over spouting geysers and swum in rivers that were hot and bubbling although they lay between snow-covered mountains. And I have fished in a river where you can catch your trout at the cold, deep end, lower it gently into the boiling holes without unhooking it and, voilà, it is cooked.

Iceland is a place where the occult still flourishes; where, until recently, soothsayers were listed in the telephone book. An Icelandic friend told me this story:

Some years back, a new road from Keflavik airport to the main city, Reykjavik, was to be constructed. There was just one snag: about halfway through the mossy, ancient lava fields lay a hill of a rather curious shape. It was a boring obstacle and the road architect wanted to go right through it. That was impossible, said the workmen. The villagers and even the townsfolk of the big city said the same. Nevertheless, the plans for demolishing the hill went ahead. The architect would not listen to rumours about the fairy folk who lived there.

The big machine arrived, the noise echoed across the wasteland. Then the nightmares began. The workmen broke their legs, had minor but nasty accidents. Everyone who worked on the hill was afflicted in one way or another. The hill stands there today, untouched, with the road twisting and turning below it. The fairy folk had their way.

We called the film *The Do-It-Yourself Democracy*. It was shown by the BBC in 1963. I was as perplexed as the critics were by my choice of subject-matter. I had certainly come a long way from Kenneth Tynan's description of me as 'the sexual "enfant terrible" of the 1950s'.

My five-year plan involved making a short feature before embarking on a full-length film. I wanted to find a story with something to say, but that would, at the same time, be entertaining. I was keen to make it in thirty-five millimetre this time. I put up most of the money myself, and my parents-in-law and a friend also each put in a couple of hundred pounds. The theme was to be one that I kept repeating in all my movies in one way or another, sometimes as a sub-plot: war, or rather anti-war. The work was also to be a condemnation of the stupidity which can lead to war.

Two boys, playing on a building site, become more and

more engrossed in their game, until things begin to get nasty. We called it *The War Game*. When we ran out of money, the British Film Finance Corporation helped out and in the end it won first prize for a short feature – the Golden Lion – at the Venice Film Festival. Alas, I was not there to receive it: we were stupidly poor at that time, living on an overdraft and spending all our money on film and cameras. I heard the news on television at home. In Venice, there was confusion as to who had actually made the film; they thought it was my husband, a Dr Max Zetterling. Never mind, it won the prize, and was later distributed by British Lion.

The War Game was the last step towards preparing for a feature film. Now I felt I had the confidence to tackle one. One day, strolling around in the library at Berry Grove, my eyes fell on the books of Agnes von Krusenstjerna. A Swedish Proust, she had been called. Her eight-volume family drama, which had been an eye-opener for me in Sweden as a teenager – was this to be the big film? But no; surely it was too enormous an undertaking. The saga was called *Loving Couples*: it was a severe, funny, often moving critique of family life and hypocrisy in human relationships. It was very Swedish, but had a universal theme.

While I was contemplating all this, I received a call from an agency in Sweden: not asking me to direct a picture but to appear in a Lux advertisement – the 'one out of every ten stars uses' slogan. They were mighty surprised when they got a prompt yes, even before I knew what the fee was. Out of the blue, here was my chance to go to Sweden, all expenses paid!

Here I will admit to a certain amount of luck in my life. When things are seemingly impossible, something will often appear on the horizon that solves the problem. But I am also a firm believer in the will that comes from a hidden place deep within, in the creation of my own personal energy. If I visualise my desires in my imagination, making them first of all totally real to myself, I can often convince others.

It was a somewhat embarrassed lady doing the commercial but a persuasive and excited one talking about *Loving*

20 *Above left*, David and I in the garden at Berry Grove

21 *Above right*, at home with David and the children

22 *Below*, with David in the kitchen at Berry Grove

ÄLSKANDE PA

en film av Mai Zetterling med Harriet Andersson Gunnel Lindblom
Gunnar Björnstrand Jan Malmsjö Anita Björk Eva Dahlbeck m.fl.   S.

23 *Above left*, on location in
Copenhagen, directing
Doktor Glas

24 *Above right*, the *Loving
Couples* poster which was
banned by the Italian
authorities

25 *Right*, directing *Night
Games*, which was filmed
at Penningby Castle near
Stockholm

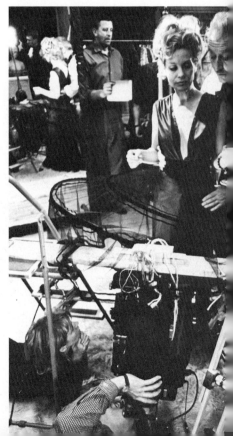

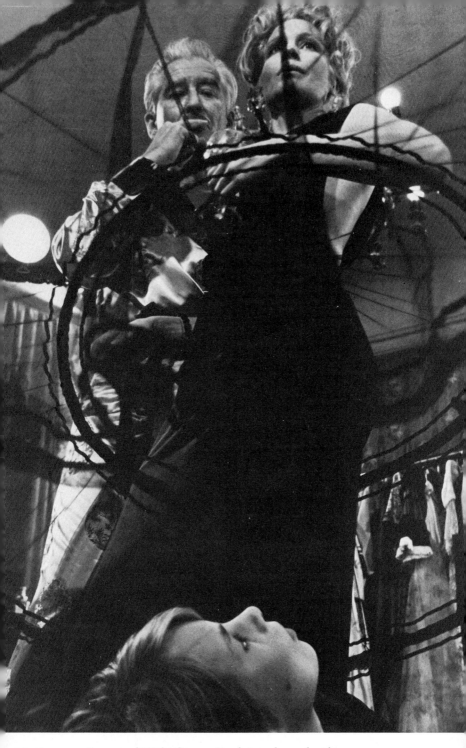

26 *Above*, on the set of *Night Games*. I'm lying down by the
camera.

27 *Above*, scene from *Loving Couples*
28 *Below,* from *Doktor Glas*

Couples with the producers – who, to my great astonishment, said yes, they would back me. And what also made me dance with joy was that it would all happen well within the time-scale of my five-year plan.

Loving Couples was a film about women and their deeper attitudes to the fundamentals of life: birth and marriage, sexual relations, human feelings, freedom. It explored the differences between their attitudes and those of men. The tragedy of women, Agnes von Krusenstjerna believed, was their natural loneliness, which only a child can fully assuage; a man is not enough. Women are imprisoned in a world that doesn't belong to them, whose language they don't speak. And yet, a woman's world without the rough texture of men is unhealthy.

I knew that it would be tough to make a big feature film, but if I had known how tough, I wonder if I would have tackled it? The trouble was that it was not just an ordinary little film; it was one of the biggest and most costly Swedish productions that had ever been undertaken, with a huge cast. I did my best to ignore the sheer size of the operation, but I was scared to death many, many times: only those nearest to me knew of my fears and rages when I felt that people were working against me.

I asked Sheila if she would like to come and help me out yet again. At that time, she was writing hard and wasn't keen to take on a full-time job, but she did want to go to Sweden and decided to come. So did Paul Davies, the English editor who had worked on *The War Game*.

There were moments when I feared that I just wouldn't make it, that I would collapse with fatigue and nervous exhaustion. For the first time, I was working with profes-sional actors, and I hadn't understood how much game-playing, cajoling and diplomacy would be needed in order to get the best out of them. I also had to cope with producers and technicians which, again, was entirely new to me, and while all this was going on I had to make everyone enthu-siastic about their work. To be totally in charge, I realised that I would have to be superhuman, cast off my little feminine tricks of being helpless, intimidated. I was there to command, to organise; it needed a fantastic amount of will-power and belief in myself.

Had I taken on too much, I wondered? I hadn't learnt the art of delegating – I still haven't – I didn't trust anybody. 'She even chooses the actors' shoelaces,' they said. Perhaps I was over-zealous and worked everyone too hard. But making great demands on myself I also, of course, made great demands on others. I got myself some good and long-lasting enemies in that first film.

It didn't help that, when we were in the middle of shooting and just about to begin the big scenes with hundreds of extras, I was struck down with appendicitis. Once the operation was over, I lay in my hospital bed for two days, planning all my shots on a little model stage. By the third day, I was on the set again in a wheel-chair which Sheila pushed; I only managed to stay in it for a day. But there were other problems brewing: the crew and the actors had become divided in their loyalties towards me because of one enemy I had made in the first few weeks of shooting. It is perhaps one of the worst things that can happen when making a film and it was particularly painful for me because I had, in my innocence, hoped to avoid all the usual bitchiness: I had wanted the whole thing to be a living experience, not only for myself but for the actors and the crew as well: a family as well as a film unit. Perhaps it was ingenuous of me.

We did have one piece of good fortune, and that was the house we found to stay in: a magnificent old wooden fairy castle, lying all alone on a peninsula just outside Stockholm, with a fine view of the water. It was all towers and balconies and tall ornate fire-places, and it had a huge picture window with paintings of fairies and flowers – a truly extraordinary house. It had been empty for many years, and it contained no furniture, but the studio soon put that right – and what furniture! The frilly lampshades had been made by Greta Garbo's milliner for a silent movie; they were rather moth-eaten and fraying at the edges, but they were spectacularly theatrical. The embroidered sheets for our beds came from Bergman's *The Devil's Eye*; the big dining-table, complete with ornate candelabras, with seating for twenty-four, from his first great success, *The Seventh Seal*; the iron bed from *The Silence*; and the bulk of the furniture – baroque and cumbersome – from *Smiles of a Summer Night*.

The prop room in the studio must have been quite empty, as every bit of furniture, not to mention pin-cushions and grandfather clocks, had come from it. When Nora Sayer, my friend who was an avid film fan and was later to become the film critic of the *New York Times*, came to visit, she could not believe her eyes when she walked into the house and recognised almost every one of Bergman's films, which we were so casually living in.

A large number of friends came and went, and every other week-end we would have a grand feast, inviting all the actors and staff. The student brass band in the movie, all forty of them, would come and play. One night, when there were still about four more weeks of shooting to accomplish and I was dog-tired, there was a violent thunderstorm directly over our fairy castle. It raged overhead, passing only to return again. That childhood fear of thunder and lightning was still with me and I could not sleep. Finally, unable to stay in bed any longer, I decided to get up and work. I went to the little tower in the bedroom, where my desk was, and started to sharpen my pencil with a knife. At that very moment, the lightning struck the conductor that was wired to the house and was only a metre away from where I was standing. I had not known that it was there, nor could I have known that there was a crack in it so that when the lightning struck, a small amount of electricity sparked out on me. The noise was tremendous and David, who was always a sound sleeper, woke with a start: 'What happened?' I stood like a statue with my hair on end, unable to answer him. When I was finally able to speak, I told him that I had been struck by lightning; he didn't believe it until I showed him the long burn on the arm that had been holding the pencil.

I had always wanted to confront my fear of thunder but, so far, had been unable to do so. Perhaps I thought a touch of lightning might add more fire to my personality. Whatever the truth of the matter, there was general agreement that I seemed to have more energy after this little accident. Will-power, if that is what it was, certainly cured me of my fear of lightning, and gave more power to my elbow at the same time.

The *Loving Couples* poster won first prize at a film week in Vienna, but it was banned in Cannes. *Variety* decided they could not afford to publish it, because it might lead to problems with the post office and the whole issue might be confiscated. Of course, I had something to do with the poster: the idea was mine. The image: black silhouettes of a row of intertwining people. The mayor of Cannes had it painted over, and a priest declared that the whole Swedish nation should be censored. It was a farce.

Of the film itself, Kenneth Tynan said: 'No doubt it will be called typically Swedish. I wish more people would realise that, so far as the middle-to-upper classes are concerned, it is also typically British. It is full of corrective truth . . . In sheer narrative technique, *Loving Couples* is one of the most ambitious débuts since *Citizen Kane*.' Others were less enamoured: 'Une chronique scandaleuse,' thundered *Le Monde*. And I was called all kinds of names: 'Swedish and shocking', 'The tough Mai Zetterling who directs like a man'. It occurred to me that the world had not moved on very far since *Loving Couples* was first published.

A film can drain a director completely. There must be a time for rest, for renewal. I have never been able to under-stand how some directors can go from job to job without a break. Perhaps it is the woman in me that must settle down, scrub a few floors, bake some loaves of bread. A total change from the neurotic, hectic scene of film-making where every-one is on one's back. Also, at this point I needed to assuage my feelings of guilt about being away from home too much. I was not available when dramas occurred in my children's lives and they were teenagers by now – that terrible no-man's-land time. I was worried about David too. Was I uprooting him? He denied it then, though now I see that I should have been more persistent in my questioning. At the time, we both avoided the issue; playing gentle games with one another because we were in love. Life seemed glorious then. Of course, I was more in the limelight, because I was the director who had made it after being a mere actress. In those days, David got only the overflow of my fame. Yet he seemed so very happy about it and proud of me. Then one day I overheard a remark that chilled my bones. 'Mai and David are a tragic couple.' I would never forget those sinister words. They etched themselves into my brain, and they hurt. They were spoken by an extremely perceptive and intelligent friend of ours, so they were bound to have an effect. Did I expect to live happily ever after? Yes, I did. But a perfect life, full of never-ending happiness – would that not be asking too much?

At the Burial Grave, as David used to call Berry Grove, I was knee-deep in my beds of flowers, in my cook-books, and in David. We were supposed to be having a break . . . But then an idea came into my head, a strange idea from nowhere. I started to write in my attic room, secretly.

I was amazed to find myself writing something all by myself; the pen would hardly stop, for hours at a time. Sometimes I didn't know where the ideas came from; it was almost like being dictated to, and I surprised myself a great deal when reading over the material the next day. I was very excited by the progress. First it was just a short story, but it grew and grew. Perhaps it could even grow into a book? It did – and what's more, it grew into a film too. I called it *Night Games*.

David had been intrigued by what I was doing up in the attic. I spent almost every morning and afternoon up there, scribbling away. Finally, I showed it to him, of course, and he suggested typing it out for me in his spare time: he thought it was worth it. But I felt quite strongly that it would be wrong to get it published because it was David who was the writer in the family, not me. I was supposed to be a film director. So I went to see producers in Sweden, armed with a synopsis. It was accepted.

Sometimes I feel embarrassed when I think about the actual shooting of *Night Games* at Penningsby Castle, our location spot, some eight Swedish miles from Stockholm. I'll try to explain why I was called 'the little tyrant', 'a second Mr Bergman', or 'the demon director in female form'.

We were stuck in an isolated place for weeks on end in a rather dreary little hotel in an equally dreary small-time town. So it was understandable enough that some of our crew drank too much and got depressed. I thought I had had a brilliant idea when I called a meeting and suggested we do something with our free time. Why not get a sixteen-millimetre projector from the company and, following Bergman's example, show a movie once or twice a week? This suggestion was greeted with what I thought I recognised as enthusiasm. What else? 'Learn French,' was our cameraman Rune's idea. Two or three people suggested underwater diving in the local baths; I said I would give a dinner once a week. We did all this while making the film and, what's more, had a couple of unforgettable evenings in the fairy castle when a famous string quartet came and played in the great hall, although I could see a few odd bodies crawl away after the first movement of Bartók.

The film was accepted for the Venice Film Festival and this is what I wrote in the programme:

> I tried to film a story of modern Europe. I try to be honest, so it shows signs of decadence. Perverted sex is one of those signs, perhaps the most dramatically obvious, and I use it because I believe you can only come to a positive view of things by passing through innumerable negative views.
>
> I tried, too, to be positive. Not for nothing did I choose some words of Leonardo da Vinci as the epigraph for *Night Games* – 'The thoughts turn towards hope.'

From my journalist friend Marianne Hook in Stockholm came a letter:

> They have written a silly article again about the dear lady, headlined 'Her David'; by the way, give him a kiss on the forehead. To think that there exists a man on this earth who does not get hysterics when his wife does things . . .

he ought to have a medal. Also, I must tell you that Ingmar
said nice things about *Night Games*, which he saw, by his
usual request, alone at Sandrews; he couldn't wait (the
snake) for the film to have a première, he wanted to be the
first to know if you had managed it. But he said: 'Isn't it
gruesome that she, a woman, has used the boy the way
she has?' I could not help but laugh a bit, and reminded
him how he himself used women in films, like Ingrid
Thulin in *The Silence*. 'Oh that was something else,' he
said. 'The boy was in his early teens, he could be hurt.'
Well, there he identified . . . isn't it fantastically funny,
really, that Ingmar said a thing like that. The old moralist.

By the way, the papers are beginning to scream. Now
you are becoming the great pervert, before it was Ingmar.
But it is worse, of course, because you happen to be a
woman, and women, as you well know, are not supposed
to know about certain things – and if they do, to keep
quiet about it. Oh, it must be boring for you when they
keep on nagging on the same theme all the time, to be
showered with idiot-indignation, as though you were
something wild in the zoo.

In Venice, it all started with the bloody poster and, once
again, I was involved. From the Queen's collection at Wind-
sor, I had selected a Leonardo da Vinci print of an anatomical
drawing which seemed to me to express a lot of things that
were relevant to my film. Amazingly, the Venice Film
Festival committee banned it; they banned their own
Leonardo da Vinci. Black paper covered my beautiful poster
and nine hundred copies of the programme.

The festival carnival was even worse than Cannes. The
committee decided that they would show the film only to the
critics and when I arrived I was met by a horde of over-
excited journalists and photographers, not to mention about
two hundred policemen. The whole thing was a nightmare.
What surprised me was that it had been selected in the first
place; the Italians must have known it would create trouble.
The merits of the film were of no importance to them: it was
only the sexual aspect that caused the stir. I was stunned by

the hullabaloo, and retreated to my hotel room.

I began to prepare myself for the bombardment which I now realised would come at the press conference. One journalist wrote: 'Mai Zetterling obviously intends to raise all kinds of hell on the other side of the cameras.' Was I aware of this while I was making the picture, I asked myself: had I set out to make a sensational movie? I almost began to believe all the reports that came through the letter-box of the hotel. For all the wrong reasons, I was at the centre of that festival – had I gone too far? As for only allowing the jury and the press at the première, I said, 'I'm still not sure whether this means that the press are incorruptible or that they are already totally corrupted.'

An Italian headline screamed: 'The shamelessness of middle-aged women.' *The Times* was (I like to think) more discerning: 'Surely as a lure to prurient and sensation seekers, it has no peer, but since it is also a film of quality and of taste, wider box-office horizons may be open to the picture than the mere exploitation belt which girds the globe.'

In San Francisco, my former idol Shirley Temple had this to say: 'I, like many women, am round not square. But I am squarely against pornography for profit.' She resigned as a director of the San Francisco International Film Festival, in protest against the showing of *Night Games*. A graffiti was born: 'Shirley Temple Still Plays Night Games.'

The Gastronomical
Years

Then love was the pearl of his oyster,
And Venus rose red out of wine

A.C. Swinburne

During the years with David, I began to take a serious
interest in cookery-books, because of his passion for the
foods and wines of the world. I had never met anyone with
quite such an appetite for taste and flavour. At every meal
the next day's feast would be discussed and glutted over. We
seemed to go from one celebration to another, forever
discussing how mussels and little fishes could be prepared,
or which kind of sauce to have with which kind of dish.
Even tea-time became a treat, delicate paper-thin brown
bread with cucumber and watercress, special varieties of tea
to go with it. No restaurant of great repute was too far away,
as long as the menu was intriguing enough: even my
children became gourmets. My library of cookery-books
grew rapidly from a mere dozen to three hundred. This was a
time of bumper suppers and lavish entertainments, no cost
spared. Pink champagne for Christmas, that created equally
pink hangovers. Sparkling red Lambrusco with Parma ham,
melons and fresh figs, wild rice from Canada, omelette
soufflé with Grand Marnier. (The list is long and almost
embarrassing. In my saner moments I felt guilty about all
this gluttonising while more than half the world was starving.) Food and wine became a drug, almost a way of life, that
I had not known before.

These were succulent, strawberry days. The money came and went, faster than it was earned sometimes. Life was just one sensual delight after another, a body trip. David would collect guides to the best restaurants and vineyards in Europe, get hold of the train time-tables so that we could plan our gastronomic excursions. How could I ever forget the greatest ever pepper steaks in the square in Bruges, the gold medal mussels in Brussels, the bouillabaisse in Nice, the tapas and dry sherry in Spain? Specialities from Bergen to San Francisco. It was as if we were worshipping some personal belly-god. It was a world of menus and first-class tickets to all corners of the world, of endless invitations to film festivals.

Once, we went to Los Angeles to do some research for a film that never came off. Arthur and Gail Ross, my old friends in Hollywood, welcomed David with open arms: they came to love him almost as much as I did. David and I slept in their daughter's bedroom, pink, full of teddy bears and Barbie dolls. I saw Hollywood with different eyes this time, became a tourist almost. I took David to the Back Lot at Universal Studios, where as many as fifty thousand people a week would throng during the summer months, mainly star-struck kids hoping to catch a glimpse of someone famous. It wouldn't necessarily be in the form of a human, but something like Lassie or one of the pensioned-off chimpanzees from a Tarzan movie.

On those four hundred acres lies a glorious conglomeration of Hollywood movies, both good and bad. We view this papier mâché world from a small brightly-coloured electric train called City Studio Tours. And we visit the Chinese Theater, where a girl is trying desperately to fit into Shirley Temple's feet. I see Tyrone's name; beside his firm footsteps and his generous hands is the inscription 'I am walking in my father's footsteps.'

We go to Forest Lawn, Disney Land, Marine Land; we travel through Pacific Palisades into Henry Miller country. Henry lives in suburbia, in a double-fronted house with bay windows. It is so unexpected, so unlikely, that it is funny. Henry wears 'pepper and salt' trousers and talks in a very slow and deliberate voice. The house has two well-stocked bars and everyone has a glass in their hand when we arrive. A ping-pong table stands in the middle of a large room with chairs placed around it, as if it were the centre-piece of the house. We discover that it is: Henry is mad about table tennis, and good at it too. In the swimming-pool a large inflated rubber swan is floating about serenely. Among the guests is a tough Hollywood stunt man, naïve and knotted. A secretary and her husband busy themselves in the background. David loses 5–21 to the master, who flirts with a tall, elaborately-dressed dark girl. There is also a Japanese girl, Henry's wife: she and her sister are chatting away in their language like small birds. Henry says later that he has been fooled by the myths about the Japanese. It is all hokum, he says. He married one in order to have his domestic life well organised: then, when his wife brought her sister along, he was pleased, expecting the housework to be diminished for his spouse. Not a bit of it. His wife and her sister were so busy chatting all and every day that nothing was ever done; never any food in the house, so they had to resort to restaurants all the time. Typical.

Henry showed me that holiest of holies, his work-room, with its very special wallpaper; that is, intricate charts written in different coloured crayons: work schedules which covered a whole wall. He had also penned down his favourite places in the world. One of them was Uzès, where David and I were later to live; then there was Pont du Gard, Chartres, Bruges, and many more. Favourite men were on another part of the wall: Hermann Hesse, Lawrence Durrell, Rabelais, Rimbaud. Next to *Tao Che Chin*, written in large blue letters, was:

> There once was a fellow called Dave
> Who had a dead whore in a cave

and Thomas Aquinas' dying words: 'All that I have written seems so much straw now.'

'Book', said Henry, 'is my favourite four-letter word.'

One reason why I felt so intrigued by Henry Miller was

that he was the only person I have ever met who could match my mania for pinning aphoristica all over his walls. In his hide-out in California, they were everywhere: in the loo, on the panels of the door to the living-room, surrounding his bed like a canopy. His work-room was a splendid wall mosaic of green and red and black, with drawings from the master himself, as if to emphasise their special meaning. I got quite lost in it while the others were playing table tennis. When drinks and dinner were called, I was found in a corner in a contorted position trying to decipher a sentence scribbled rather hastily, it seemed, at a very awkward angle and very low down.

I was excited by that work-room wall and later imitated it, on a somewhat smaller scale, in my own. And as the years passed, or rather galloped away, David was forever making writing charts in all colours of the rainbow, as he sweated over deadlines for journalistic pieces, tweaking his ears, waiting for an inspirational thought, sucking his knuckles in such desperation that he developed rheumatism in them, while I worked on new film ideas and trying to be a good wife.

I suppose I had to follow my roaming instinct and obey the gipsies who had read my hand and told me that I would live in a hotter climate than England could provide. Also, I was longing to grow my own grapes and live in a wilderness far from crowds and the conventional life.

I had wanted to find a small hide-out, the kind of barn that all my friends said was possible to obtain for a couple of hundred pounds. We went to Greece to look for one but we found that altogether too remote, so we went back to England via the wild west of France, which we both had a great fondness for ever since we had made the gipsy film there. My aching desire for the south made me persuade David that we should look for a small place then and there. At Lawrence Durrell's house, we met a formidable but likeable lady by the name of Daphne Fielding. We had an immediate rapport, exchanging the fossils and stones that we both somehow had in our pockets. This splendid lady, who had once been the Marchioness of Bath, wrote books about other, equally splendid and eccentric ladies of the past. And it was she who put me on to 'the Ranch of the Living Waters'.

A broken-down farm, lying in the midst of an impressive landscape. I loved it so much, as soon as I clapped eyes on it, that money was immediately borrowed from the Swedish film company which I was working for at the time. Then, it contained only one habitable room and a dirt floor, and the land was as full of living water as the name promised. I signed the contract on a filthy, stormy night in the house of the estate agent and just at that moment the lights went out. Was it an omen? That same night, David and I drove back to England in our van, through the storm. I was shocked at having bought the house just like that. What a terrible responsibility: did I know what I was doing? David, I knew, felt the same fear, and we were both speechless with apprehension at what we had done.

Back home at Berry Grove, David was eager-faced, and would spend the days in his writing hut behind the Viking's Tumulus. I spent the afternoons in my attic, working out an idea for a film to be based on Aristophanes' *Lysistrata*, which had created such a furore when it had first been played in Greece. Here were all the ingredients that I was so fond of: humour, sensuality, even downright bawdiness. Yet it was at the same time a critical look at the state of things in society. It was most certainly anti-war and its heroines were strong, thoughtful and plucky.

I must have persuaded David that it was a good idea, as he was willing to give up half his working day for us to get going on the synopsis. It turned out to be one of the most exciting of our collaborations – me up in the attic, sending down papers to him, which we would then discuss at great length in the library at night. Next day was David's turn, then back to me again at about tea-time the day after, in order to be torn apart that evening at dinner; and so on. We seemed to re-energise each other, and it was a fruitful period for us both.

The film was to be set in Sweden. On tour with the play *Lysistrata*, three actresses, whose own lives are in a mess,

195

begin to realise that the play is a tragedy after all, and become totally involved with the light-hearted way in which Aristophanes treats serious matters – so much so that their own destinies are affected. The synopsis was accepted and we started work on the screenplay.

In the meantime, I received a proposal for another venture, this time via Twentieth Century Fox and a company in Denmark. They wanted me to make a film of a novel written by a Swede called Hjalmar Söderberg. The subject appealed to me strongly. *Doktor Glas* was the story of one man's battle with himself, the battle of a weak, passive man who is longing to take life into his own hands. Söderberg won me over when he wrote: 'Why does one hate another human being? People who hate each other usually believe there are such big differences between them. But this isn't so at all. Rather the opposite – they are so very much alike, always wanting the same thing. A bull hates another bull. He never hates a cockerel.'

The story was gripping, the cast small. The chances for experiment, both with actors and with cinema techniques, offered a genuine challenge. Although the action was set in 1905, the idea was to present it in such a way that the audience would feel it was happening in the present; the special use of music and lighting effects and camera stock would create a fusion of fantasy and reality. But how, was the big question, would I be able to fit it all in? I decided to do the impossible, to make both films, one after the other, with hardly any break. Shoot *Lysistrata* first – which I had now named *The Girls* – but not edit it. Go direct to *Doktor Glas*, finish it completely and then return to the editing of *The Girls*. It would mean almost four years' non-stop work. I didn't want to admit the sheer size of the undertaking.

While *Doktor Glas* was a kind of chamber music, *The Girls* was a symphony with all stops out. It was full of ironic twists and turns and from the start I had great difficulty in explaining these to my actresses. I began to think that after living in England for so long and with an Englishman who relished just this quality, I had perhaps become more English than Swedish. But otherwise, it was a jolly unit. I had begun to find my own team now, after two films. My cameraman, Rune Ericson, completely unlike me and therefore extremely valuable, is also a brilliant technician. There were still many gaps in my knowledge: the laboratory, for instance, was a mystery which he helped to reveal to me. I felt more and more the need to master the technical side of film-making in order to achieve the results I wanted and in order to have more freedom.

The Girls was the happiest picture that any of us had worked on. It was just amazing: no big upsets, only mini-dramatics that were always good-humoured. As usual everything was shot on location – I have always hated the sterile atmosphere of a studio. In many ways this makes things harder, especially for the sound man, in this case, Bob Allen, a man passionate about sound, with whom I had worked on *The War Game*. Without being aware of it, I seemed to have been inspired by Ingmar Bergman's habit of working with the same crew and, up to a point, with the same actors, making the unit almost like a family.

For *Doktor Glas*, we rented a large country house outside Copenhagen. Normally David and I slept in our bus in the garden but sometimes I would insist on sleeping in the room used as the bedroom of Doktor Glas, in the hope of finding new inspiration and ideas. I had become a maniac about my work; I lived it, ate it and dreamt it. I was as if possessed. I would get up in the middle of the night in a trance, insisting that a scene had to be shot there and then; I would cling on to the bed or the cushion, whatever was to hand, using it as a camera, until finally David would have to put the light on, and gently wake me.

The actual filming of *Doktor Glas* was a joy and I loved working in Copenhagen; such a jolly city in comparison with Stockholm.

I rushed back to Sweden to edit *The Girls* and David left for England to arrange for the sale of dear old Berry Grove. We had come to realise that we could not afford to have two houses, also that a double life was far too complicated to deal with. I wanted to start a smallholding and become self-sufficient. In England, between films, I had squeezed in a

197

week of bio-dynamic farming, and had been very taken with it. We would grow our own vines and fruit; I would have a large herb-garden so that I could distil medicines and make potions. Herbal medicine became more and more attractive to me the more I studied it; it was my only bedside reading in those days. As for David, he was fed up with the commuter belt and the two-hour trip into town bored him. It seemed the right decision at the time.

Then I discovered that I was pregnant. This time, I wasn't so sure I didn't want it. Perhaps it was our last opportunity to have a child together. Until this happened, we had been very much against having children, thinking it would split us up. But now I felt that it was important for David to know what being a father meant. And also, for the first time in my life, I was ready to accept the idea with some excitement. I was slightly worried about my age – I was forty-two – but the doctors told me it would be possible to go ahead if I wanted to, provided I took certain tests to make sure that the child would be normal. However, the foetus was not in the right position and I was not sure of myself. David and I talked at great length on the phone and by letter. He wrote:

I am not at all anxious about children; we do not need them, we would not be able to give them what they need because all our urgent concerns lie away from their care, they would be a stumbling block to the crucial things that we unquestionably *have* to do and it would be sentimental to allow ourselves to be seduced by the idea of them.

Was I being a sentimentalist all of a sudden? Or was I frightened of missing out on this motherhood bit, because I had never fully appreciated it? Or was it simply that I feared losing David one day, if he ever decided he wanted a child after all and I was too old to bear him one? And, I asked myself, how would I be able to cope with a child, now that I was at the peak of my creative strength and always so careful to retain as much of my vitality and time as possible for work? Freud wrote: 'Children are completely egotistic and

29-30 *Above and below,* stills from *Doktor Glas*

31 *Above*, Le Mazel, my home in the Ardèche

32 *Below*, with Keeper the wolfhound and Lucius the donkey

33 *Above left*, with Glen and Keeper

34 *Above right*, filming *Loving Couples* with Sven Nykvist, Ingmar Bergman's cameraman

35 *Below,* on location at Penningby Castle, filming *Night Games*

36 Scene from *Scrubbers*

they will strive relentlessly to satisfy their intensely felt needs.' Wasn't I doing the same thing myself? Had I decided to stay a child all my life?

In my pain and confusion, I forced myself to look back over my previous pregnancies, all of them unhappy memories. I could by now have been the mother of twelve children: at one stage of my life, I had so many abortions that I felt like a slaughterhouse on legs.

When I was pregnant with Etienne, more than twenty years ago, I was working at the National Theatre in Stockholm, in Paul Vincent Carroll's *Shadow and Substance*. I played a simple country girl who is an archdeacon's maid. The girl has visions, is shot at with arrows and is finally stoned to death, after which she is declared a saint. So complete was my identification with the part that it took me a good hour to come back to a more or less normal life after the performance. My pulse rate would be lower, breathing would be difficult and I could hardly use my legs. I was totally immersed in my part for those three hours. I lived an exalted existence, full of emotion and awareness that made real life seem dull and meaningless. I became ever more distant from reality. During the day, I would just be waiting for the time to prepare to go to the theatre and start living again.

I suffered a lot from morning sickness – only mine went on all day, except for those few hours when I was performing. Finally, when the child began to deform my body, I hid myself from everyone, including Tutte's family, who always wanted to discuss the event. Why could I not be happy? Why could I not be ecstatic about it like some of my actress friends who were also pregnant? I was a silent, angry mother-to-be, hating every single moment of my pregnancy. I began to sit by windows, feeling a bit like my mother, like her, staring into nothing and day-dreaming. I felt that something important had been taken away from me, just at the moment when my own personality had begun to develop, giving me my first bit of happiness and fulfilment. I never, for a moment, believed that the child could supply me with any of these things.

199

Sophie Tolstoy, who was the mother of twelve children, said this about pregnancy:

> Those nine months were the most terrible in my life, the less said about them the better ... I am nothing but a useless creature with morning sickness and a big belly and a bad temper, a battered sense of dignity and a love which nobody wants, which nearly drives me mad.

Of the ordeal of Etienne's delivery, all I can remember is a confusion of pain and relief. She cried a lot and I wanted to join in the crying. I wonder now if many of the problems, not only mine but also Etienne's, would have been averted if I had been able to talk to someone at the time about my depression and my feelings for the child. I realised that I was behaving somewhat abnormally and the guilt that I felt weighed heavily on my chest.

At home, I made a half-hearted job of being mother and wife but a long tradition made me organise the household so that it functioned quite well. Tutte, pleased at first to play the role of father, took it less seriously. For him Etienne was a temporary play-thing that he could easily forget. I was the one who hired nurses and maids, paid the bills, shopped for food, arranged for the child to be taken to the theatre and fed her during rehearsals and in the wings during the performance.

We began to worry about Etienne's progress; she was what is called a slow developer. Later, our worries grew more intense when she started to draw pictures. Her drawings were blood-curdling – hands with blood dripping from them, arrows hitting people and drawing blood. They were horrendous paintings for a small child and all the more sinister for being so well executed; her colour sense was vivid. I was suddenly reminded of the play in which I had been acting when I was pregnant with her, and in particular of the scene in which I had been stoned to death, shot with arrows and carried on to the stage a bleeding mass. Was there a connection? Tutte laughed and scorned the idea, so did the doctor, and as a result, I kept this anxious thought to

200

myself. It was only some years later in London, when she was still having problems, that I managed to get a sympathetic hearing from a psychiatrist.

I worried about her in secret, so it's no wonder that I was haunted by her in my dreams. In Hollywood, in Berlin, on tour in grim northern cities, I was plagued by nightmares about her, all rooted in worry and guilt. When I leaf through my dream-books, she seems to be one of its stars:

Hollywood

Small children, one of them Etienne, turning into wolves, suffering from isolation and hunger, want to eat the world.

Berlin

I am being called by telephone, I must come and see Etienne at once. I answer that I cannot, I am too busy. Later I do go and see her in Stockholm. She lives in a very high building, like a skyscraper. I start climbing the stairs with some other people. The steps twist in a strange way and I get vertigo when I look down. The last step before her front door is very high. I need help to get over it. Then, in front of her door, I see a small white animal that I must kill. I crush it with my foot, it turns out to look rather human. Inside the room, Etienne is sitting looking depressed. All the blinds are drawn. I am horrified to see the state she is in and the way she looks. I release all the blinds, one by one until the room is flooded with light. Etienne can't bear it, she wants darkness.

On my wanderings around the globe, I never remember having pictures of the children with me. Other parents or grandparents proudly handed round snapshots of babies, but they all looked much the same to me. I had nothing to show except some faded pictures of my garden, of which I truly was proud, as it was all my own work. Later on, I had pictures of cats and dogs, the goats, the donkey and, of course, the house, in my wallet, but none of the children. Nor did I save their first little booties for sentimental reasons. I cared about them and loved them, but I resented the demands they made on me. It was not simply that I had a full-time job; I have known other single mothers with an equally heavy burden who have found their children stimulating and their main purpose in life.

Pondering all this, I began to feel that it would be irresponsible to continue with my pregnancy after all. I knew, deep down, that I would resent that child; it would hamper me, make me feel as if I had had my wings clipped. I had to face the indecent fact that in *my* life, the family would always take second place. I was, I had to admit, the ego-tripping mother; motherhood was not on my chart; I was a bloody no-good mother.

Since David was reluctant too, we decided jointly that I would have to have an abortion. But despite all the reasoning, there were many ambivalent feelings. Society's indoctrination is not easy to get out of one's system.

> It is not of vast importance that I make a career or achieve great things for myself. What is important and meaningful to my life is that I shall live as fully as possible to fulfil the divine will within me.
>
> Carl Jung

At the final party for *The Girls*, which we held on a boat in Stockholm, I was so exhausted that I had difficulty in focusing. The very next day, we were to make our final move to France, packing our belongings in the big bus that I was to drive, while David took the wheel of the Land Rover we had just bought. The trip was a nightmare, in heavy rain and wind; the bus was a difficult vehicle to manoeuvre and I often had to stop for little naps.

When we got to Beaune, we decided to give ourselves a real treat – best hotel, best meal, best wine. I was still extremely tired, and perhaps that explains the strange thing that happened to me there. Certain kinds of phenomena can occur when the body is starved or over-fatigued.

What happened was that I was awakened in the middle of the night by the sweetest imaginable scent. It surrounded me, it was almost overwhelming in its strength and, what's more, it made me feel blissfully happy. I didn't think I could contain it in my body, it was so powerful. I didn't understand it.

I began to wonder where the scent was coming from. It was just another hotel room, without much character. I looked out of the window but there was no evidence of anything strange going on. Back in bed, I sank once more into a state of euphoria. I tried to define the scent; lilies at first, sweet perfumed old-fashioned roses, then Parma violets. No scent-bottle in the world could have competed with this aroma, which so sweetened my mind and all my senses. What was it all about?

My down-to-earth brain wanted an answer, but as I found out later, there was none. Finally I woke David and asked if he could smell the perfume which was making me feel so happy. He could not. Together we investigated the corridor, the steps, the room itself, but there were no clues. And all the time, I was glowing with happiness. But it saddened me that I could not share this happiness which had come so powerfully out of nowhere.

As we went about our business, testing and buying wine, the scent was still with me, until later that day when I realised that my tiredness had disappeared; I was as new again. The aroma gradually faded and by late afternoon it had gone. I still have no rational explanation for this experience. I am a person who likes to know the whys and wherefores. I like logic and hence I am puzzled by some things in my life that I can't find any explanation for. I would like to be able to remember these occasions as if they were dreams. It would make things simpler, but they are real enough, and what's more, the reality of them seems to be more real than reality itself; they are heightened moments, such as you experience when you are desperately in love, or in a state of fever. The only coherence I can find in it is that each time I have had a visitation of this kind of goodness (because that's what it seems to be) it has come before a particularly tough period in my life. It has certainly always signalled change.

At Living Waters we picked our cherries – three thousand

kilos of red, ripe cherries celebrated my birthday and I bottled, canned and preserved them: everything you could possibly think of doing to a cherry was done, with love and devotion. When I flew to England I would be laden like a peasant going to market, with big baskets full of strings of garlic, herbs and brown speckled eggs from our chickens, our wine and, of course, cherries. The stewardesses had never seen such a passenger, but they laughed with me. I was becoming more and more myself, and didn't care any longer what people thought and said about me. I was living the strong and salty life that I had chosen, I was loving my new-found profession, and I had complete support from David. Without it, I would have flagged many a time. I had come to take my good luck for granted: perhaps I felt I had a right to it after my somewhat pathetic past.

My happiness was complete when news came that *Doktor Glas* had been selected for Cannes – but it was 1968 and the French student revolt stopped the Festival. It was shown in New York during a sultry summer and didn't survive many weeks despite a favourable notice in the *New York Times*. In Denmark, one critic suggested that I had been influenced both by Buñuel and Fellini, which I took as a great compliment since they are my two favourite directors. In Sweden, however, they didn't much care for *Doktor Glas*. And there was worse to come.

When *The Girls* opened in Stockholm in 1968, it was a resounding flop. Swedish audiences seemed unable to grasp the ironical nature of the film, and at the time, we could hardly take comfort from the fact that when it was shown again, some six years later, audiences all over the world were to shout and applaud throughout. In Paris, Simone de Beauvoir was so impressed that she asked me to make a film of her novel *The Second Sex*. She wrote in *Le Monde*:

All the images have multiple dimensions, the theatrical scenes reflect real life . . . Ironic and comic, this film moves us by the beauty of its landscapes, its poetry and above all its subtle tenderness.

But there was more to come. The initially hostile reception to the film was a disaster for me at that stage in my career. David and I were preparing another film for the same company – a totally different film, full of young, revolutionary ideas and concepts. We were suddenly told it had been cancelled. There followed an extremely tough year, with no job offers from Sweden. We spent part of the time researching and writing a script about meths drinkers in the East End of London, which from the human point of view I will never regret. But the film was never made, and I became restless, dissatisfied at not having a big project to put my energy into.

I started to write again, or should I say to have ideas. I didn't know anything about the structure or the art of writing: I just let go and told myself to be patient, to see what would happen. After the first hazy scribbles, shapes began to emerge. The outcome was four short stories, the theme, incest. I called the volume *Shadow of the Sun*. David was finding it less easy to work away from London. He was often miserable in his work-room tower at Living Waters, staring at blank pages, and I could sense his depression mounting. One of his main problems – and one familiar to all writers at some time in their lives – was that he believed that he had nothing to write about, nothing that he cared deeply enough about in the world. Whereas I had envied his serene childhood and education, he told me that he envied my early struggles and hardships, as it meant that I had so much to draw from.

In the hot Midi, where everyone wore shorts or bikinis, David would don a typical Englishman's outfit, complete with tie. He looked a fine portrait of a gentleman, as he lolled around, glass in hand. Later, I understood that it was his way of protesting against this foreign place. Never giving his body a chance to be hit by the sun's rays, his body became whiter than white – except for his face, which was a handsome colour, so that the contrast was somewhat startling. He missed *The Times*, the City, his friends, his club, the language, the London Library; dry sherry, smoked salmon, English cheese, even the colourless bread he'd been used to

205

since childhood. He refused to eat an English breakfast because he claimed that tea was undrinkable in France. Instead, he would climb the great cherry tree, clutching a bottle of bubbly, breakfasting on cherries, like some strange, dressed-up bird.

Despite all our travelling, he felt distinctly uneasy about living permanently in Frogland, so full of foreigners. He loved London, with all its musty smells, the rain, the wind, all the colours that go with that climate. His sky was always at most a mackerel sky, while mine was a mistral blue. To relieve his boredom he would tease the cats and dogs mercilessly, swat flies and bury his dirty socks in the garden instead of washing them (one of the very few stipulations I made when we got married was that I would never have to do those most boring of all chores: washing socks, ironing shirts).

I suggested that he ought perhaps to go away for a year, take an unliterary job somewhere. David agreed, but I suppose my suggestion must have been somewhat half-hearted because nothing came of it. I racked my brain for ways of helping him. Should I give up this nonsense of trying to write? It didn't seem fair that I was penning as much as ten to twenty pages a day, while he was wasting his time and talent in despairing thoughts. The shock of *The Girls* had not left me yet and I didn't feel in any fit state to go job-hunting. For the first time since I had started in the theatre and cinema, I felt like a complete failure; perhaps, I asked myself, it was time that I experienced that emotion to the hilt? So I continued to write – and finally, at the end of that year, the pages became four interconnected short stories. David helped out as usual by typing them out for me and acting as an editor and critic all along. When *Shadow of the Sun* was accepted for publication I was ecstatic. I think David was somewhat surprised but he seemed happy for me as well.

That book meant a lot to me, and in the main story I drew on my childhood experiences, hiding behind fictional characters. But somehow I had to get back to movies. I had no offers whatsoever in those days, so finally I said, 'To hell with it, let's make a movie of our own.' That's how I came to produce and direct a one-hour TV film about Vincent Van Gogh, for the BBC and educational television in the States. I was deeply moved by the letters of Van Gogh to his brother. I read them as I walked the goats in the hills that summer in the Midi, the same kind of landscape as the one in which he went mad. 'The only time I feel alive is when I work'; 'I will never become important.' Sentiments like these made my heart contract.

I visited his little cell in the asylum at St Rémy de Provence, where he painted his painful images; the place was as if still alive with his spirit. I was immensely moved.

For five months we worked, David, myself and John Bulmer, the cameraman. It was Bulmer's first film, but I trusted him implicitly because of his extraordinary sense of colour. I needed someone sensitive to light who could also understand Van Gogh. I had chosen the right man. I had also been lucky in my choice of Michael Gough as the leading actor. This time I went even further than before in *living* a film. They all stayed at Living Waters, which was still extremely primitive, and we tried to duplicate Van Gogh's style of living as faithfully as possible. We lived as roughly as we could manage, denied ourselves all but the barest essentials. It had an extraordinary effect on all of us and we got very close during those months. The film itself was not, perhaps, so much about Van Gogh as about the act of creation. 'When I read that I was becoming rather a success,' he wrote, 'I got frightened. I was sure I was going to get punished. Success is the worst thing that can happen to an artist.'

We worked in the early mornings in order to catch that very special light, took four hours off for lunch, and then worked again in the late afternoons, making use of the sunset hour. That four-hour break was no rest for me: I was busy preparing lunch, cleaning the house, washing smalls, preparing the next day's work and, to my horror, trying to keep a book of our budget. I would record every single item in a school exercise book: four buns for breakfast, chewing-gum, hire of cameras, four ice-creams, safety pins, etc. The book soon burst at its seams. By the end of the filming it was much thumbed, a bulging ledger, shabby, covered in oil and wine stains, held together by a rubber band. When I handed it over to my accountant, proudly thinking it was a masterpiece, he took one look at it and threw it away. All the agony as well as the ecstasy of our film was contained in that small book.

Vincent the Dutchman, as we called the film finally, received several awards and was sold all over the world, but I still was a ninny when it came to finances and had an overdraft on account of it for five years. I decided that I was a bad businesswoman and that I should stick to directing. More importantly, this film marked a turning-point in many of my most valued friendships – and the beginning of the end as far as David and I were concerned.

Then, out of the blue, came an offer from the States to be involved in a feature film about the Munich Olympics. I was an odd choice because I had never had any interest in sports whatsoever and I especially disliked competitive sport. I remembered reading Orwell a long time ago and being struck by his assertion that sport had nothing to do with camaraderie and fair play, but that it was bound up with all kinds of jealousies about money, status, politics and hatred; that in a sense it was very close to warfare, except that there was no shooting involved.

The film was to be called *Visions of Eight*, because of the structure, which consisted of eight different directors representing eight different countries. I turned it down twice before finally accepting, when, then, being greedy for work, I thought, 'Why not? I will learn a lot: perhaps I can even contribute something.'

To everyone's surprise, I chose to make my contribution with a study of the weight-lifters. I had in fact been offered the segment on women in the Games, but I turned it down because I felt it to be too obvious a choice. I wanted to do the most 'un-obvious', as far as possible from what I am and what I know about. I also felt it was a strange kind of sport; it's not popular, it's lost somewhere in the shadows, even at the Olympics, and it's obsessive to a degree. It seemed so far-out that it intrigued me. At the first press conference in Munich, I said: 'I'm not interested in sports, but I am interested in obsessions.' After some preparatory work, I had two headings in my notes: 'Isolation' and 'Obsession'.

But first of all, I started to read about the Olympics. I found out why the Romans had stopped the Games. It had been the issue of 'Professionalism of the Romans' that had caused the discord, scandal and free-for-all fighting, which had made the ancient Olympics a public nuisance and resulted in their suspension. And also the decadence which went with the Games; they were no longer the idealistic uniting of body and spirit. Then I read about the Mexico City Olympics in 1968, where three hundred students were clobbered by the police because they protested with the words: 'Why spend money on fun and games when people are starving?'

In Munich, security was extremely tight. Forty thousand military personnel were involved, as well as the police. Despite that, and the customary ten thousand white peace doves released over the stadium on the first day, there were fifteen men dead by the end of the Games. I realised that I had entered a mad world where there was not much room for the great brotherhood of sport. The point of the film was not to criticise, but to be a more or less passive onlooker. So I did my filming, listened and looked, and made notes for a future date.

When I returned to Living Waters, it was clear that decisions had to be made. The home truth that a man can never be in the shadow of a woman was one of the contributing factors, without a doubt. The man-eating woman, the vampire lady, the castrating bitch, all in the shape of a loving wife – was this what I had become? David was likeable, full of charm, tolerant, with his sly witticisms, making no demands, while I was domineering, heavy-handed, a disciplinarian, stubborn. Had he become too relaxed, perhaps, too indulgent about the life of the senses? Had I over-pampered his sybaritic tendencies? The round of pleasures was beginning to take a toll. A certain heaviness and fatigue on his part, soft edges around the sentences, and finally a kind of despair and fear of the years that had crept

209

up on tiptoe behind him. Our life was still full of love and easy-going living. I was beginning to long for austerity all of a sudden – for spartan, wholesome food, for the waters of Vichy rather than the bubbly.

Did I unwittingly do a bit of upstaging? Did I take the centre stage with its brilliant and directed spotlight, while David was left out in the wings, or even, at times, in the audience?

Was it true that I left my men weaker, emasculated and, in the end, uncreative? David's English heritage had been full of people who were avoiding the truth, whereas with me he was suddenly confronted with danger, because I was always in search of the unpredictable. David wanted my strength, my virility, my hunger for truth, while I needed his gentleness, his intellectualism, his cool-headedness, his ironic wit.

By now I had realised that we were approaching the end, but that didn't make parting any easier. We had come to rely on each other and there was still a deep fund of love between us. I decided not to do anything but I had a strong sense of confusion and loss long before anything had happened. If we had to part, I wanted it to be David who took the first step. I felt, with childish *naïveté*, that if it happened like that, all would be well.

David's mind was to be made up for him sooner than I thought. His mother and father came on a surprise visit. They had, it transpired, been worrying about him for a long time. It was a summer when the flies were particularly bad and the heat was unbearable. David's father was swatting flies with the same violence as David, and he seemed moody. He was a man for big cities, cafés where he could chat to people and extract their life stories. He was an extrovert: at Living Waters, with just us and a few goats and chickens and a crazy donkey, he was lost and bored, as well as worried about his son.

It was David's father who took the decision that David must leave now and go back with them. They would pay for his ticket, pay for a psychiatrist in London, get him a flat. His father, all of a sudden, came to life, helping David finish the chicken-house that had been half-done for months, putting locks on all the doors, selling the donkey. He worked as if in anger, even forgetting to swat the flies. He certainly helped David in his inertia: he was a great mover, a tyrant of sorts who had always lovingly dominated both his son and his wife. A man with a lot of pent-up anger and power, a man who hadn't made it in the eyes of the world but who was convinced that his son would make up for it . . . It was father, as much as David, who felt that I took up too much space. David was thus ruled by two tyrants, me and his father. Yes, it was escape with the help of father. Also, both father and mother wanted David to see sense and get married to a young girl and have babies . . . He has now done just that.

How difficult it was for David to leave I shall never know. It was all so damned English, stiff-upper-lip and all that: detachment, no emotion shown and promises, of course, that all would soon be well. He must have known he was lying then but didn't dare to face it. Sometimes I hated that detachment, that civilised analytical intelligence, that non-involvement – and yet these were all things that I had admired once upon a time and had wished for myself, thinking that I was too emotional, too unbalanced. I had wanted his kind of composure, his ease in life. A clean break would have been best for both of us. What we did was to live in lingering hope.

There I was in my self-sought isolation, feeling like a wreck. I was close to breaking apart but I was playing the stoic. I didn't tell many of my plight or my raw emotions. When people came to visit, that sultry August, I let them take over the house; I would sleep out on the terrace, not wanting to stay in our bedroom. I would ring up David in sudden panic and cry out for help. I feared that I would come to nothing without him. I needed him more than I had thought. Was love the great moving factor, then, in my life? Was I just like most women, driven by love, motivated by love? I had not believed so but, at this particular juncture of my life, I felt some sympathy for those women who feel that their lives would be meaningless without it.

I was finishing off a novel, called *Bird of Passage*: I put a lot of my emotions about David into it.

Crawl Away

We are never so defenceless against suffering as
when we love, never so helplessly unhappy as when
we have lost our loved object or its love.

S. Freud

A heroine in a romantic novel would have a nervous
breakdown at this point, be rolled off in an ambulance, given
sedatives. This was not my way. The cure for me, I realised,
if there was a cure, was work. Physical work that would
occupy both body and mind. But that, too, was a quiet form
of madness. 'Nobody is safe from unhappiness,' I tried to
remind myself: to reject the pain of separation would be to
reject life. I could not run away. Where was there to run to?
To death, possibly, but that solution was not acceptable to
me: I had far too much respect for life.

I could no longer stay in our house; it was full of ghosts.
Some years previously, we had given our doctor friend a
piece of land near by, in the village. He had built a little
stone house on it and I went there to stay for a few months to
find my bearings.

I have lost my nerve all over again. Being on my own in the dark in
this wilderness, I see bogey-men everywhere. All my newly-found
courage has flown out of the window. I am lost. The electric lights
are on all night; I hardly sleep. I keep my fingers busy and my head
empty – as far as I can.

212

I had bought forty thousand lavender plants which had to be planted, but before that they needed topping and tailing.

I'm doing all-nighters for at least a fortnight; sitting on the floor, clipping, snipping, until I get calluses on my hands. I keep the music high, drink too much coffee and refuse to have anything to do with my thoughts, which are unruly and full of self-pity. I refuse them – I keep busy. I plant the lavender in neat, long rows, in a blustery mistral. When I catch a glimpse of my image in a mirror, it seems like a frozen frame in a movie. In order to avoid myself, I hang drapes on the mirrors.

Then there was this thing called sex. Having been happy sexually for so long, suddenly there was nothing: I did not want to have anything whatsoever to do with men; even the thought of contact was repulsive. This was an entirely new and surprising emotion for me. David and I had been totally faithful to each other for fourteen years, something our closest friends had had difficulty understanding.

I can feel my own deterioration. I knew that this moment would come. But I managed to fool myself that it could never happen to me. We all come across a personal crisis at some time in our life; so here then is mine. Why should I expect to be singled out for a charmed life?

I force myself to sleep by counting sheep, backwards. I lie there frozen in that hysterical present, not daring to think, just count. I put my arms round myself. A silly consolation; they feel like broken wings. Trying to forget that I was once unique and wonderful, I feel that I have become a prisoner, a squatter. Death seems so close, because once upon a time there was you and me. My whole being is locked up in that far-away time. Enormous dreams, waking and sleeping, fill my head. I count objects in the room, like pots, grains in the wood, windows, my fingers and toes, to see what number it will add up to. What madness . . .

The whitewashed room feels like a pothole: and to believe that we and other people, friends, were happy there, that we laughed. It feels like winter outside, yet it is not. I feel as if I had spent thousands of white, harsh days with myself.

I had no idea how long it would take to get back to normality again – didn't dare think of it. The child in me, the one that would never give up said, 'Things will, must, change. At least it can't get worse.' But it did.

I remembered someone saying: 'Can't she pull herself together?' An angry horse reared inside me. I had flung bottles against a wall – wine, blood had mingled – 'pull myself together'?

When I begin to dare let thoughts linger in my head again, I realise how cliché-ridden I have been; so deeply ingrained is the idea of romantic love, that I have become a victim of it.

I don't know how many days and nights I've spent hanging as if on a crooked arm over a cliff. I'm not at all sure whether I'm going to make it or not.

Then suddenly one day, the sun felt warm again. I didn't understand why; it was as if I had been released, just like that.

I've lost weight, my hair's turned a little white, but I have *won*, that's what I feel. And now I still believe in love, and when I see a star fall across the sky . . . Well, it can never be quite the same but I'm willing to give it a try. I don't mind the silence any more. I can take the darkness and the lonely house, dare to listen to my own thoughts again. I have survived the ordeal, though scarred.

I tell you that the past is a bucket of ashes . . . but ash – wood, that is – is good for the soil: feeds it, makes it fertile again, for growing things in, and that's what I hope I did to that dark past of mine.

Healing Time

He that fears every bush must never go bird-hunting.
He that fears every grass must not piss in the meadow.
He that is afraid of wounds must not come nigh a battle.

Proverb

March 10*th* 1981   *Le Mazel, my home: a ramshackle*
                                       castle, perched on an iron rock

I took my self-protective rhino hide off this morning. Here in my
iron fortress I am above the fog which lies thick and blue down in
the valley; it is whirling in spirals as in a Van Gogh painting. I
know it is only vapour suspended in the air, as any dictionary will
tell me, but for a dreamer it is something more. When the cold red
sun peeps over the edge, the blur miraculously changes to cycla-
men pink. Bits of it decide to part from the main fog-bank and
encircle the little hill in front, like an opaque Saturn ring. Magic
mountains begin to appear, one after another, in the whirling fog,
which has now turned greyish, only then to become milk-like and
still. The black silhouettes of the mountains seem like floating
islands; the fog turns into sea foam.

A lonely woodpecker is drumming up his breakfast in the big
chestnut tree. Squeaks and twitters come from the dense budding
tapestry on the hill opposite, and I hear, distinctly, one bird calling
out again and again, 'Stupid, stupid, stupid.' The wool-pack of the
fog has dispersed; the mountains are all gone once more and the
fog is spreading itself into the wood. Twilight all of a sudden. The
sun has made streaky patterns everywhere. Soon the fog will whirl

215

itself up the little hill and envelop me, and I shall become a ghost figure on my terrace.

A large pink camellia is in flower in a bright terracotta pot; the red of the sun makes the petals shiver. The first swallows have arrived and whizz past me with excited shrieks. I join them in their excitement and shout to the sky: 'I have survived, survived, survived.'

I was back at Living Waters again and although I had recovered up to a point, I felt listless; I didn't know what I wanted to do with my life, or where I wanted to be. I felt spent – no future, no ideas. I still slept outside on the terrace with the stars for company. And then yet again came the helping hand. I wasn't looking for mystical solutions, or praying to any god. But I would wake up suddenly in the middle of the night in total ecstasy, my heart warm and full of love. I would lie there for hours in a state of total bliss. Happiness in the midst of deep unhappiness – I had never experienced this before, and with such regularity. In my diary for January, 1977, I wrote:

January 1st
Nature seems to be totally alive, stronger than ever, the sky touchable and today it seemed full of cobwebs, floating in the wind. It is as if I can see through and beyond the sky.

January 19th
The heart *shakra* so strong at night I don't know what to do. Hardly sleeping; great excitement; a flow of warmth and love, whole body throbbing – feeds me and makes me feel incredibly strong.

Sometimes it even came during the day, in the midst of being very busy on the farm – and sometimes the perfumes too, though not with the same intensity as in Beaune. Friends around me saw the ecstasy on my face, but I could not talk about it; it seemed so outlandish, so unreal. I had died my little death and now I was being coaxed back into life again, in this almost brutal love that flooded over me. Most of all I felt astonishment at what was happening, then gratitude: I was no longer alone.

The unhappiness I felt was very physical. But I still couldn't think of going out into the world again. I was milking my goats and making herbal medicines, yet I knew I would have to face the world sooner or later, and money was running out. I needed the soil more than ever, and my garden was running riot. It was truly a healing time.

Friends came to visit. Good friends from Sweden – Brita, my personal assistant from *The Girls* and her friend Tina, who was hairdresser and make-up artist on the same film as well as *Night Games*.

I had met Brita years earlier, when she was a young teenager and I was with Tyrone; we had been friends ever since. She has a devastating sense of humour which was a tonic for me. Both Tina and Brita pushed and prodded me. 'You just have to work, Mai,' they said. 'If only for the money that you'll soon need.' And they were right.

Finally they got me going. Perhaps I could write a very personal story for the Women's Year that was coming up. After all, I had had an experience which I knew countless women shared with me – that of being left after a long and happy marriage – but I was fortunate enough to be able to fall back on my work. What about the others, those who had nothing but the home and their grown-up children, no chance of a job because they were middle-aged and un-wanted? Yes, why not write a simple story that all women could identify with and understand – even some men, perhaps?

It was Brita who fixed up meetings with the producers for Swedish television. They wanted me to play the lead part as well as everything else, and though it was a hard thing to do, it worked, because I was able to direct myself through video. *We Have Many Names* was yet another film in which I drew on my own experience: in it I used all the pain and misery of the break-up of my marriage. It was a bitter medicine.

Then women's film festivals started to pop up all over the

world in the most unlikely places and I was invited to many of them. It was now that *The Girls*, which had been so rudely received by the Swedes, suddenly found favour, which took me to Paris, Lisbon, Copenhagen, Rome, Australia, Africa, even Stockholm. It was a joy to be appreciated after all the rejections I had had and it was also important to meet other women who were trying to direct films. It went to our heads; we were elated at our new-found communication with each other.

Most of the time we liked each other a lot but some of these women were tougher than any man I had ever known. Perhaps it was sometimes a put-on toughness but it was there nevertheless, and I didn't find it very attractive. I had always liked women with guts but I didn't like to see them behave like steam-rollers, without the slightest trace of humour.

Sometimes the atmosphere could be ghetto-like, which I didn't much care for either – but being so close to women in friendship and work was new and important at the time. We were all interested in each other's work and cared enough to listen to one another, unlike the men I met, who were frightened and intimidated by our new strength. At first, I was horribly surprised at the effect I had on men in those days: instead of falling in love with me, they ran away as fast as their legs could carry them. It was girls who found me attractive now, weren't scared of me and even fell in love with me. It was like having a girl in every harbour when I arrived at those film festivals. Perhaps it led to some self-indulgent flirtation but it was also restful not to have to put on a front, to be able to be totally one's self. We had a tremendous lot of fun and did a lot of work together, forming film workshops throughout the world in order to help young women to make films. It was all positive and therefore joyous.

Healing time continued but I was still not completely myself. I began to jump continents, to accept job offers all over the world. I took them all because I could not afford, either financially or emotionally, to say no: I had to get back to work. Montreal, Toronto, Stockholm, Manchester, Vienna;

documentaries, a play, a children's film. It was not easy because I had always relied heavily upon David's skills and I lacked confidence without him. But little by little things began to fall into place and I met a person who was to mean a lot to me – Glen.

There is a deep need in me to test myself with new surroundings and tough living. Is it the element of danger, the unknown? Or has it to do with my childish but real desire to become a sailor, an explorer? Wally Herbert, the Arctic explorer, was doing a round-Greenland trip for the BBC that would take him two years, and I was asked to go for a few weeks every six months, to cover four very different aspects of Greenland and even do a polar-bear hunt. I was astonished to get the job but was later told that a woman can bear those tough, raw conditions a lot better than a male director.

My first trip was just to meet the Eskimos, see the country and get to know Wally: there was no filming to be done. I went to the northern-most tip of Greenland, in winter, when not the faintest ray of light penetrates the darkness; even so, we went on a fourteen-hour trip by dog-sledge, and one night I fell in love with the icebergs. They seemed like crystal castles which the winds had polished. I strained my eyes in the moonlight in order to see as much as possible; I felt that I would never see such sights again. It was that same night that I fell in love with Greenland, having met my first Eskimos, on an island that lay frozen in a great river. Alas, the project had to be cancelled; because of the exceptionally bad winter, it was impossible for Wally to continue his trip. It was almost as much of a disappointment for me as it was for Wally. I knew I had to return to Greenland somehow, and during my trip back through Copenhagen I managed to talk the Greenland Trade Department into making a film on Eskimo seal hunters. Seal hunting was a dying trade and a most difficult profession in that tough climate.

I came back the following year, in the month of May – a blinding contrast, when a mad sunlight kept me awake day and night – with a mini-crew: myself and Rune Ericson, who had done the photography for *Night Games*, *The Girls* and

Doktor Glas. He took his own cameras and sound equipment and worked for free, as did I. We had only food and lodging as our payment, but the film would be ours to sell to television. Glen came as camera assistant and second camera and he also took over David's old job doing the sound. I found in Glen a versatile and exciting partner, who didn't mind sharing the discomforts and who had the same taste for adventure as I did.

We travelled through all kinds of ice: rubber ice, the kind that bends when you walk on it; rocking pancake ice; sludge water which lay on dark blue ice; fresh water ice that was silver-grey and had a hollow sound. And snow, snow as far as the eye could see, with mountain ranges covered, some of the snow blown off the peaks, here and there, making the combination look like chocolate and cream. Magic country. I had always wanted to make a film about Eskimos, they had haunted my imagination as much as the Hopi Indians, the Lapps, the gipsies. Were the days of the Eskimos as hunters numbered? It would seem so. This proud group is no longer needed in their society as it was in the olden days and their shamanistic qualities, which make them wise and humble, are now ridiculed. No wonder they shoot each other in despair on those frozen tundras, or become alcoholics or drug addicts. I called this film *Of Seals and Man*. It was 1978.

I finally had an offer to make a feature film in England – my first in the British Isles. Called *Scrubbers*, it dealt with young female offenders who were sent to Borstal. The judicial way of dealing with female delinquency was in a pitiful state, and magistrates were full of moral judgments against these sad and disturbed girls whose main problems were dealing with parents, school, work and their own sexuality. Tragically, these poor girls who needed love and understanding were locked up in institutions which were originally designed to have as many locks, bolts and bars as a prison. Small wonder that so many of them became true delinquents after their term there. Somebody had called Borstals 'penal dustbins'. I felt it to be a worthwhile cause to fight for and an excellent subject for a film. The more I saw and read and heard, the more I realised that it was an outmoded way of punishing and dealing with difficult girls. One lady warder frowned when I politely called it a training centre; she looked me hard in the eye and said, 'You mean prison, don't you? We lock them up in here.'

I soon felt very strongly and passionately about the making of *Scrubbers*. My own headline for the movie was one word . . . COMPASSION. It took me months to do the fieldwork in order to get the documentation that I wanted, the knowledge and hundreds of girls passed in front of my video camera before I found my loyal group of thirty unknowns. We had a week of rehearsals in a Victorian mental hospital in Virginia Water, where we also filmed: no studios for me. The walls had their lived-in pain and the corridors were long and aching. The rehearsals were a must, in my opinion, in order to bring the girls together so that they would act as a group. And we had to get to know each other intimately. This was also a time for finding each of the characters through dancing, mime and talking and doing improvisations . . . By the end of that one week, the group was firm as a sailor's knot. Now we could start the work, which sometimes was hell on roller-skates, as I could be doing up to twenty-five set-ups in one day, the crew running after me. Painters were forever decorating large areas of walls white, and the paint just had time to dry before we took over.

I went back to France exhausted, but deeply satisfied, at least with 'my girls', who were wonderful, totally loyal to the film and to me. There had been fun as well, because I had found that the girls out there, in the real prisons, had a tough, earthy humour that pleased me and that I could use in the film. Without their black, ironic way of looking at the world, they would never have been able to stand it inside.

Catching Up
on Myself

I speak truth not so much as I would, but as much as I dare.
And I dare a little the more as I grow older.

Montaigne

December 7th, 1982   *Le Mazel*
Clouds clearing this morning, clouds heaving and pushing, and
swirling, which makes for that sea effect down in the valley. I am
very careful that no one steps over my dreams in the morning, so I
sneak up early and make coffee and a blazing fire and sit there
dreamy-eyed. The room seems full of dream-dust.

January 3rd, 1983
I have been doing everything to music these days: that is,
scrubbing and polishing the big room to Vivaldi's Gloria, sewing
up the hem of the curtains to Bach's Cantatas, played by Glen
Gould, washing up to Beethoven's Sonatas, staining the panels for
the bedroom to Stravinsky, crying a bit listening to the Christmas
Carols sung by the King's College Choir (nostalgia for the past),
making food to Indian Ragas.

January 9th
I feel lazy and sluggish, which is unusual for me, and of course I
think that I will never ever work again. The kitchen stove is now on
twenty-four hours a day. I make nourishing soups and stews;

222

mushrooms are drying, chanterelles and trumpets of death hang in pretty garlands in the fireplace and give out a smell of wood and moss; and there are flowers, of course – amaryllis, hyacinths and a Christmas cactus just coming into bloom, which reminds me of grandmother. *Scrubbers* is doing well and has been sold to fourteen countries; I am invited to two film festivals in Sweden.

January 11*th*
I am finally catching up with myself. I work long hours again; mad and splendid long hours deep into the night. Energy comes back and I realise I needed that 'nothing time'. I had been starved of 'present, everyday kind of life' and I know now that I need it like I need air. And as I work, new ideas start springing up, ideas that I have carried with me for years without realising it . . .

February 12*th*, 1984
I am making notes for the feature film which is to be my next big project. It has been accepted by the Swedish Filminstitute and Sandrews. It is based on the life of Agnes von Krusenstjerna, whose family saga I filmed as *Loving Couples*. Why have I come back to this author? She wrote about men and women in conflict with one another. She wrote about love, to be sure, and the pain of love. She also wrote about family ties and tragedies: marriage, children, madness. She wrote lyrically, sometimes sentimentally, religious documents, fairy stories for grown-ups that often turned into horror stories. She wrote honestly about the dilemmas that women face. And because she lived her own truth so severely, she broke within. I am in total sympathy with this woman called Agnes. It is probably the most exciting project that I have ever had.

I make up new headlines for myself:

Sleep less, dream more.
Be less of a slave.
Be more in touch with secret dimensions.
Accept my failures. Accept that I am not and never will be good
    enough, just less inadequate, and let that suffice.
Accept the total insecurity of my life.

223

Never let myself be caught in eyes that mirror scepticism.
Make a habit of thinking about Death in a positive way.
And forget the private me, think of the universe.
AND STOP FEELING GUILTY.

March 15th

Turgenev wrote: 'Do you know the worst of all vices? . . . It is being
over fifty-five.' I don't agree – I realise that I'm beginning to know
myself just a little. It has taken me a long time to grow up but that
doesn't depress me any longer. Nor am I now depressed at having
to wash dishes . . . Why? A year ago I fell from a hot air balloon and
broke my leg. Today I stand on two sturdy legs and therefore I am
glad to be able to wash dishes, however badly.

One of the biggest changes is, I suppose, that I now call myself
lucky – yes, lucky. It doesn't matter if I seem to be on the wrong
side of the ladder. I'm lucky to have been born, lucky to be alive,
lucky to be me.

I also feel lucky to have had my cradle up near the Northern
Lights. That bit of Viking blood has nourished me.

Perhaps I am just a Mad Hatter Swede, who got lost in the world.
A person with too many windmills in her head and as crooked as
the letter z of her name. Sometimes I feel very far from the norm of
just about everything. But 'on, on' is the cry, and 'courage': courage
to dare to believe in one's self. I agree with Camus: 'I live with the
idea that work has not even begun.'

March 20th

I carry on cleaning, sweeping, cooking. I feed the fires in the
bedroom, the work-room, no longer with the stuff that looked like
plastic fur balls, but with shiny pieces which are like black jewels
from the earth. I like handling them – they make a lovely, brittle
sound. Three cats keep me company; I play Beethoven Sonatas on
the stereo. I do the weather report in my diary each day, fill in my
dream-book. Glen goes on a hunt and comes back with a story
which even he finds horrifying. In the café there is a diseased
rabbit in a cage, whimpering. One of the hunters grabs it, takes an
axe, cuts the rabbit in five pieces and throws it to the dogs.

Suddenly there is no more suffering rabbit; but it is a brutal and shocking act.

This new village of mine is perhaps even more strange than the one I have left. Today I heard a story: a tramp turns up in the village one day. He is American, shabby, smelly, unkempt. He is sweet-natured though, makes friends in the village and wants to stay. He decides that, after all, he wants some kind of family life. He is rejected by many people before someone finally takes pity on him. He says he can pay for himself and that helps, to be sure. The man who takes him in is almost a tramp himself. The accommodation is cramped, the living is primitive. One fine day the wife of his 'landlord' discovers to her amazement and horror that the American wipes his ass with dollar bills. She promptly recovers them, cleans and irons them into shape again. After a while she is doing quite well out of this. She begins to feed him better with the prospect of more dollar bills. When he finally dies he leaves the couple a fortune. Today they are the most prosperous people in the village.

I am called the 'Wife of the Hunter', although I am neither. I am certainly not a legitimate wife, and as for Glen, he just pretends to hunt, gun carelessly slung over his shoulder. He is more interested in the fast-flying clouds and the smell of grass and earth, and Achilles, the hunting dog who accompanies him, is more interested in the bitches he meets on their wanderings than in rabbit or wild boar.

Round the corner a stonemason's wife is busy designing and making frilly, naughty knickers for the sex shop in the big town while the husband carves stone phalluses in all sizes and shapes – a cosy family scene.

I am living in this house as a squatter almost, but day-dream about making this place into a creative beehive for friends and fellow travellers . . . If I can't achieve my community dream I will change my plans.

Wander off to another corner of the globe, and start all over again.

Index

226

Index

Index